American Literature
and the Dream

Frederic I. Carpenter

American Literature
and the Dream

PHILOSOPHICAL LIBRARY, INC.

NEW YORK

COPYRIGHT, 1955, BY PHILOSOPHICAL LIBRARY, INC.
15 EAST 40TH STREET, NEW YORK 16, N.Y.

PRINTED IN THE UNITED STATES OF AMERICA

CONTENTS

PART I

1. Introduction   3
2. The American Dream   5

PART II

3. The Transcendental Dream   11
4. Emerson   19
5. Bronson Alcott: Genteel Transcendentalist   30
6. Walt Whitman's Eidolon   40

PART III

7. The Genteel Tradition: A Re-interpretation   51
8. Scarlet A Minus   63
9. Melville and the Men-of-War   73

PART IV

10. The Pragmatic Realization   83
11. C. S. Peirce: Pragmatic Transcendentalist   94
12. William James and Emerson   105
13. Sinclair Lewis and the Fortress of Reality   116

PART V

14. The Romantic Confusion: The Devil in America   126
15. The Romantic Tragedy of Eugene O'Neill   133
16. Death Comes for Robinson Jeffers   144

PART VI

17. Thomas Wolfe: The Autobiography of an Idea 155
18. John Steinbeck: The Philosophical Joads 167
19. The Time of William Saroyan's Life 176
20. Hemingway Achieves the Fifth Dimension 185

PART VII

21. The Good and the Bad 194
22. The Logic of American Literature 199

Notes 208
Index 216

ACKNOWLEDGMENTS

Seven of the following chapters, including all in the introductory and concluding sections, are here printed for the first time. Fourteen chapters were first published, in whole or in part, in the following magazines: *The New England Quarterly, The Pacific Spectator, College English, American Literature, The University of Kansas City Review* and *PMLA*. I am indebted to the editors of these magazines for permission to reprint. The chapter on Emerson is rewritten from the author's Introduction to the Emerson volume of the American Writers Series. I am indebted to The American Book Co. for permission to use this material.

I acknowledge my debt to the many writers who have contributed to the interpretations of this book, but for the most part I have indicated this debt in the text and notes. I would thank especially Professor C. C. Walcutt of Queens College, Professor Henry A. Myers of Cornell University, and Professors Henry Nash Smith and James D. Hart of the University of California for their advice in the preparation of the book.

F.I.C.

Berkeley, California

American Literature and the Dream

PART I

---

1. INTRODUCTION

"The American Dream" has never been defined exactly, and probably never can be. It is both too various and too vague: many men have meant many different things by it. I shall therefore follow popular practice and use the phrase inclusively.

But "American Literature" has been defined more exactly, and has been outlined in courses and embodied in anthologies. Most men agree that it is something very different from English literature, and many have sought to describe the difference. This book began as a series of essays in interpretation of the major American authors. But in the process of writing, an idea crystallized: American literature has differed from English because of the constant and omnipresent influence of the American dream upon it.

But this influence has usually been indirect and unconscious, because the dream has remained vague and undefined. Few Americans have said: "Go to— I will imagine the perfect democracy." Even the phrase "American Dream" is of recent origin. But the vague idea has influenced the plotting of our fiction and the imagining of our poetry. Almost by inadvertence our literature has accomplished a symbolic and experimental projection of it.

Traditionally, American literature has been described under such categories as "romantic" and "realistic," "transcendental" and "genteel." But considered in relation to the dream, it falls into new patterns: the old words persist, but in new relations. Using the old words, I shall describe the Transcendentalists as the philosophers of the dream, the Genteel Traditionalists as its opponents; the Romantics as the emotional enthusiasts of the dream, and the Realists as its sympathetic critics. This interpretation will emphasize neither the technical forms of literature, nor the historical patterns, but the ideal attitudes of American writers toward the dream.

Before considering American literature in general and its authors in particular, I shall partially define the American dream by recalling some of its most famous and explicit expressions in history, and examining the ideas which these have held in common. However abstract, the words "freedom," "progress," and "democracy" recur,

3

and have meaning. Then I shall reconsider briefly the traditional categories of American literature, and suggest new definitions. Finally, the main part of this book will re-interpret the major American writers individually, emphasizing their attitudes toward the dream.

2. THE AMERICAN DREAM

In 1654 "a new heaven and a new earth" in the new world was announced to the common man:

> Oh yes! oh yes! oh yes! All you the people of Christ that are here Op-
> pressed, Imprisoned and scurrilously derided, gather yourselves together,
> your Wifes and little ones, and answer to your several Names as you shall
> be shipped for His service, in the Westerne World, and more especially for
> planting the united Colonies of new England . . . Know this is the place
> where the Lord will create a new Heaven, and a new Earth in new Churches,
> and a new Commonwealth together.[1]

And for the next three hundred years the millennial hope of an ideal
new world was constantly repeated in different forms. It inspired the
Declaration of Independence and the Bill of Rights, Emerson's address to "The American Scholar" and Whitman's *Leaves of Grass,*
the wisdom of Lincoln and the idealism of Woodrow Wilson. But
not till 1931 was it described specifically as "the American Dream"
—"that dream of a better, richer, and happier life for all our citizens
of every rank which is the greatest contribution we have as yet made
to the thought and welfare of the world."[2]

This dream, always vaguely present but never clearly defined, has
been one of the motivating forces of American civilization. But because of its vagueness, its central importance has often been overlooked. Whether Americans have believed that their new world would
progressively achieve a more perfect democracy, or whether they
have attacked this dream as delusion, it has determined the patterns
of our thinking. Even when denied—and perhaps most clearly when
denied most completely—the dream has been our distinction.

This dream has been our distinction, but not our salvation. In the
twentieth century "the modern temper" has become increasingly
antagonistic to it, for in an age of recurrent world wars, a perfect
democracy has seemed increasingly impossible. Yet even today it
distinguishes American writing, if only by the intensity of its disillusion, and only a generation ago most Americans believed it wholeheartedly. Earlier, in the nineteenth century, it was almost universal:
in that era of confidence the vision of an ideal democracy caused a
renaissance in American writing. Therefore this book will focus on

5

that century. But the lines of force lead backward into the colonial past, and forward into the contemporary present. The dream has always been a fact of American history, and even if a delusion, it remains a motivating force.

Across the centuries the earliest proclamation of "Sion's Saviour" and the latest celebration of "The Epic of America" have emphasized certain constant ideas. Both have looked to the achievement of a new and better way of life in the new world, and both have declared the democratic basis of this new way. In America "the Lord will create a new Heaven and a new Earth," or (according to the modern version) "a better, richer and happier life." And in America He will create "a new Commonwealth together for all the people of Christ," or (according to the modern version) "for all our citizens of every rank." These two ideas, of progress ("a new and better life"), and of democracy ("a new Commonwealth together") have remained constant; and always they have been projected upon the new world ("this is the place").

Of these three ideas underlying the dream, only that of place has been wholly "American," for essentially the dream is as old as the mind of man. Earlier versions had placed it in Eden or in Heaven, in Atlantis or in Utopia; but always in some country of the imagination. Then the discovery of the new world gave substance to the old myth, and suggested the realization of it on actual earth. America became "the place" where the religious prophecies of Isaiah and the Republican ideals of Plato might be realized.

But the localization of the old dream of a better life in the new world did more than merely focus it—it changed it radically. The philosophic Republic of Plato and the religious kingdom of heaven became secularized. And the myth of a timeless perfection in Utopia or heaven became projected upon the temporal future of America.

In this process of localization, the old Christian ideal of heavenly perfection became one of progressive realization. "A new heaven and a new earth" became "a new heaven on this new earth." Perfection was projected not upon another world, but upon America—it might not be achieved at once (except by certain souls elected by the grace of God), but it would be achieved gradually by all. Progress toward the better life, and freedom for the pursuit of it, became the modified, secularized ideals of the American dream.

Yet "the dream" remained a dream. The choice of this word to name the old millennial hope as projected upon the new American world implied a certain ambivalence. For a "dream" suggests an unconscious contradiction, or unreality. Either the word must be redefined as an ideal more conscious and pragmatic than common, or "the American Dream" can scarcely be called a great "contribution to the thought and welfare of the world." The local and temporal application of an essentially universal and eternal ideal has raised problems.

Is the dream of a perfect democracy realizable? And is genuine progress toward it possible? Is the dream good, because it gives a goal and sense of direction? Or is it bad, because it is unrealizable, and deluded? These questions, though seldom simply stated, have occupied Americans since the beginning of their history. And the attempted answers, whether symbolic or specific, have given form and significance to our literature and philosophy.

Logically, four answers to the problem of this dream are possible. First, a perfect democracy is realizable, and the dream is good. Second, a perfect democracy is not realizable, and the dream is bad. Third, a perfect democracy is partly realizable, but the dream is bad; because a "dream" creates an image of perfection which can only be achieved gradually and pragmatically. Fourth, a perfect democracy is not realizable, but the dream is good; because a dream is more beautiful than reality, and the tragic attempt to realize it gives nobility to man.

These four attitudes toward the dream have existed throughout recorded history. The idea of the millennial fulfilment of prophecy in history is older than Christianity, and has been constantly repeated through the centuries.[3] The idea of progress—so essential a part of the American dream—has even been compared to one of the early Christian heresies.[4] And as the old ideas of "Millennium and Utopia" have been applied and illustrated in American experience the old attitudes have found new expression in the successive periods of American history.

Historically, the dream of realizing a heavenly commonwealth had early been projected upon America, but the old habits of thought and the old ways of life usually dominated the early colonies. Although the Puritan theocracy had rebelled against the English church, in America Puritanism became largely "orthodox," again. *The New England Mind*[5] had its moments of dreamy enthusiasm, and even Jonathan Edwards hoped, and worked, for the establishment of the "kingdom of God" in the new West. The eighteenth century revivalists found a quick response to their gospel on the American frontiers. But for the most part colonial Americans followed the old traditions, and even when they indulged in dreams of a new world felt them to be doubtful, and perhaps heretical.

The American Revolution, however, broke with the past, and officially affirmed the new dream. The Declaration of Independence assumed certain "truths" to be "self-evident." And its quasi-religious assumptions of freedom, equality and the inalienable rights of all individuals, became the basis of the democratic ideal. Although the Declaration was often discounted in its own time, it leavened the thought of later generations, and inspired the great literature of "the American Renaissance." When Emerson pronounced "America's declaration of intellectual independence" in 1837, he merely expanded and applied the transcendental assumptions of Jefferson's earlier Declaration of political Independence.

In the nineteenth century, the American transcendentalists celebrated this dream of a new America, freed from the courtly traditions of Europe. In their new world, the values of the human individual were declared all-important, and his potentialities infinite. The new society of free and self-reliant individuals was to become the perfect democracy. And to "this new hope," Emerson and his fellow transcendentalists gave (as they freely admitted) "a greater trust than the laws or the popular opinions will well allow." Optimistically they affirmed that the dream was both realizable, and good.

In the nineteenth century, the Transcendental Dream leavened the imaginations of all American writers and thinkers. But many distrusted it then, just as during the Revolution many had distrusted the democratic idealism of Jefferson. Conservatives were disturbed by Emerson's attack upon the traditions of the past. And aristocrats opposed the rough "democracy" of Whitman which seemed to deny all the culture of Europe. Against "The Transcendental Dream" of a brave new world, these reasserted "The Genteel Tradition" of the old.

But in preferring the old tradition, the great American conservatives of the nineteenth century effectively criticized the new dream, and indeed, often chose it for their ideal subject. So Hawthorne described the transcendental freedom of Hester Prynne as heroic, but as leading to moral anarchy. And Melville achieved his masterpiece by describing Ahab's fanatic dream in such terms as to suggest both its heroism and its tragic delusion. To the traditionalists, individual freedom seemed to lead to anarchy, and ideal democracy to despair. Therefore they declared the dream unrealizable, and its effects evil. But they sympathized deeply with it even while they emphasized its delusions and denied its possible realization.

Thus the great writers of the American Renaissance carried on a kind of imaginary debate—Emerson, Thoreau and Whitman affirming the beauty of the dream, while Hawthorne and Melville denounced its falsity. But the Civil War seemed to establish the final victory of the ideals of democracy and freedom, and to end the matter. And for the next generation American writers took their idealism for granted. Only the rise of realism in literature and of pragmatism in philosophy emphasized that the problem still existed, and suggested new answers to the questions.

The philosopher Charles Sanders Peirce first introduced pragmatism as a theory of "How to Make Our Ideas Clear" by relating them to their consequences in action. William James shifted the emphasis to the problem of how to make ideas effective in action. And John Dewey declared the "instrumental" value of ideas to be paramount. But all these emphasized the value of ideas, and (as a corollary) the need for describing them effectively. What the philosophers of pragmatism and the novelists of realism both attacked was not the old American idealism, but the vagueness of its ideas.

But the immediate popular effect of pragmatism and realism was to discredit the earlier idealism, and to criticize the abstractions of the transcendental dreamers. The dream was bad, they implied, because it described the perfect democracy so vaguely that Americans could neither conceive it clearly, nor plan effectively the means of realizing it. They attacked the dream, that is, for being a dream. But at the same time they emphasized that the earlier ideals might be realized to the extent that they could be defined pragmatically. "The dream" was bad, but progressive efforts to realize some of its ideals were good.

From the turn of the century through the first world war, a pragmatic realism dominated American literature and philosophy. But William James' emphasis on the "cash value" of ideals seemed to deny all aesthetic values, and the realists' emphasis on the ugliness of reality seemed to deny all beauty. By reaction, a group of aesthetic idealists attacked the materialism of the "Philistines," and celebrated the beauty of those dreams which could never be realized. And after the war, the "disenchanted" or "lost" generation decided that although the American dream could never be realized, it should be celebrated for its beauty.

Having lost faith in the dream, the modern romantics nevertheless have praised all those dreamers who revolt against or escape from the ugliness of reality. Eugene O'Neill's dramas described the tragic beauty of a romantic escape "Beyond the Horizon," or of a romantic quest for "The Fountain" of youth—all the more beautiful for being impossible. Robinson Jeffers' narrative poems celebrated the "flaming" of the human spirit in its deluded quest for what can never be realized. And more realistically, Scott Fitzgerald emphasized the nobility of *The Great Gatsby,* who dreamed greatly even if falsely. While making clear that American dreamers have been "enchanted," many moderns have preferred the romantic quest for the unattainable to the dull acceptance of the actual.

Historically, these different attitudes toward the dream have dominated different periods of American literature. But just as the dream itself has found expression from the earliest proclamation of the "Wonder-working Providence," to the latest "Epic of America," so the different attitudes toward it have been repeated throughout American history. If the enthusiastic acceptance of the dream found fullest expression in nineteenth century Transcendentalism, it has recurred in such modern novelists as Thomas Wolfe and John Steinbeck. If the traditional rejection of the dream found classic expression in the novels of Melville and Hawthorne, it has been repeated by the "new" critics and the modern poets. If the pragmatic realism, which criticized the dream but embodied many of its ideals, dominated the early 1900's, it had earlier characterized the autobiography of Benjamin Franklin, and continues "from here to eternity." And if the romantic but hopeless celebration of the dream gives tragic beauty to the modern dramas of O'Neill, it was, after all, typical of the historic "romanticism" of Poe too.

The American dream, and the patterns of thinking and feeling which it has inspired, has given form and significance to American literature.

PART II

3. THE TRANSCENDENTAL DREAM

" 'Transcendentalism,' said the accomplished Mrs. B—, with a wave of her hand, 'means *a little beyond.*' "[1] And Mrs. B— was exactly right. Transcendentalism meant "beyond," in the sense of direction, or progress. But it asked only "a little" progress at a time. Thus defined, it was no borrowed philosophy or alien religion. It expressed an attitude of mind and quality of spirit typically American. It described the philosophy of the American dream.

The transcendental dream had flourished in the puritan past. "Transcendentalism," said Parrington, was a "curious throwback to earlier times," a "flaring up of old fires of idealism, before the scientific and materialistic reactions destroyed its romantic dreams."[2] It renewed the mystic faith of Jonathan Edwards, according to its first historian: "Indeed, whenever orthodoxy spread its wings and rose into the region of faith,"[3] it became transcendental. And the latest interpreter of *The New England Mind*[4] has traced the developing logic of the old religion from the first puritans to Emerson. Although later Transcendentalism sometimes seemed to deny the earlier Puritanism, it rejected only part of the old religion. It relegated puritan morality to the realm of the individual conscience, but it developed puritan faith into a philosophy of secular idealism.

The transcendental dream found clearest expression in the romantic nineteenth century; but it was not romantic. It specifically opposed the Rousseauistic philosophy of emotional escape. Emerson rejected the "antique and future worlds" of romanticism and utopianism in favor of the world of "today." American transcendentalists dreamed only of making this new world better, by following "the discipline of nature" rather than the traditions of man. Indeed, these dreamers spoke so much about "discipline" and "the moral law" that Santayana (among others) thought them merely "genteel." Certainly they were not "romantic" in the usual sense of the word.

By contrast, the transcendental dream was realistic and modern. It sought to use the real opportunities of the new world, and the real changes which science was bringing about, to make the American world more free and more democratic. In philosophy, it prepared the way for pragmatism, and suggested the ideas which the later philosophy was to "make clear" through experimental action. And in literature, it inspired many of the major writers of modern America from Walt Whitman to Thomas Wolfe and John Steinbeck. Like much contemporary idealism, it went a little beyond the immediate realities of its time to imagine an "economy of plenty": with a "society full of industry and abundance, . . . with unity among all, with freedom for each . . . and no restrictive policy to hinder the welfare of mankind."[5] Because this ideal was not entirely impossible, "the scientific and materialistic reactions" of modern times have failed to destroy it.

The transcendental dream fulfilled rather than denied the idealism of puritan New England. It opposed the irresponsible romanticism of its own time. It was realistic in its attitudes toward science and democracy. In all respects it was typically American. To contrast it with the ideas of puritanism, romanticism, and pragmatism is to realize its central importance in the history of American thought.

I

First, the transcendental dream was not a philosophy borrowed from Germany, but a faith inherited from the puritan past. Its original inspiration was the inspiration of all protestant Christianity. It carried the old religious protest against the injustices of this world to its logical conclusion, and actually applied the religious idea of freedom to the worldly affairs of men.

It is true that the philosophy of Immanuel Kant gave it a name, a method, and an air of authority; but none of the major American writers knew the German well, and most other Americans not at all. Emerson did appeal to "the great idealist" who had "replied to the skeptical philosophy of Locke" by defining the transcendental "intuitions of the mind itself"; and later scholars did fasten on Kant's name and words to describe their faith. But if American idealists denounced skepticism in the name of Kant and praised the intuitions of the mind itself, they inherited their faith from their own past and proclaimed their own intuitions. They translated the German imperatives of "God, freedom, and immortality" very freely into the American principles of natural law, liberty, and the infinite potentiality of the individual.

Rather than Kantian philosophy, the American dreamers remembered the Christian doctrine that "the kingdom of God is within you," and the later Augustinian formulation of an ideal "city of

God." But this ideal implied a condemnation of "the kingdoms of this world," and of "the city of Rome." It therefore led naturally to an actual "protestant" revolt against all worldly tyrannies. Where Augustine had argued that the authority of the Catholic Church was absolute, because it was the perfect embodiment of the kingdom of God, protestantism argued that the Catholic Church had suffered the corruption of all worldly institutions. And where the early puritans had sought to "purify" the Church of its worldliness, the transcendental dreamers argued that all institutions were inevitably corrupt. Therefore they appealed anew to the kingdom of God within the individual self.

In historic Puritanism the protestant religious ideal was applied most clearly and forcefully to the reformation of worldly institutions. In England the puritans sought to purify both the Church of England and the kingdom of the Stuarts. In America they sought to found a new purified church and state. But on both continents they struggled to embody the ideal authority of God in new institutions and new rulers. Therefore they retained the "catholic" ideal of institutional authority, even while appealing to the "protestant" ideal of individual freedom.

Thus Puritanism, like all protestant Christianity, faced a dilemma: if worldly institutions are subject to corruption, and if the Catholic Church itself has failed to avoid this corruption, how can any church hope to remain "pure"? Or, stated differently: if the kingdom of God is within, how can it ever be translated into external institutions? Puritanism sought to answer these two questions in two ways. The Church may remain pure by interpreting strictly the moral revelation of the Bible. And the kingdom of God within may be translated externally by God's grace, working through the medium of chosen individuals. But in time these two answers turned out to be contradictory: the first merely altered the catholic principle by locating worldly authority in the theological interpreters of the Bible, rather than in the hierarchy of the Church; while the second pointed toward the transcendental, or democratic idea that the grace of God is present in every individual.

Puritan theology found itself impaled upon the horns of this dilemma. One school of Puritanism emphasized the immutability of "the moral law" defined in the Bible. The other emphasized the mystery of God's grace, which appeared to certain "pious" individuals. The first school became known as "moralism," and the second as "pietism."[6] In the seventeenth century this conflict was glossed over by formal logic and by theocratic authority. But in the eighteenth century "the moral livers" and "the gracious Christians" had become separate groups. While the churches moved toward a moralistic conservatism, Jonathan Edwards and the later evangelical preachers strove to intensify the piety of the "gracious Christians."

In the nineteenth century, the transcendental dreamers merely carried the logic of puritan "piety" to its inevitable conclusion. Opposing the genteel traditionalists, who developed the logic of puritan "moralism," the transcendentalists preached that "the kingdom of God" exists within every self, and that through "self-reliance" it may be realized on earth. They "protested" not only against the actual authority of the Catholic Church and of the English King, but also against the catholic or authoritarian principle itself. In the name of individualistic puritan "piety," they revolted against formal puritan "moralism."

The trouble was that in protesting against the moralistic puritanism of the past and the genteel tradition of the present, the transcendental dreamers often fell into the same error that they were fighting against. They often exalted one half of religion at the expense of the other half. They renewed the old faith and re-interpreted the old dream, but they rejected the old forms and revolted against the old traditions.

Even so, this transcendental half of puritan Christianity proved more valuable to America, and therefore more "American," than the traditional half. Its protest against traditional abuses continued the logic of all protestantism. Its revolutionary "piety" found realization in the actual American Revolution. And its dream of a new world corresponded to the actual newness of the American world. Even at its worst—even when transcendentalism denied the formal or institutional part of its puritan heritage—it made articulate both the historic realities and the historic dreams of America.

II

Even when the transcendental dreamers opposed the moralism of the puritan past, they did not espouse the emotionalism of their romantic contemporaries. If they rejected one half of their heritage, they did not blindly exalt the other half. Rather they re-interpreted the old "moral law" as "the discipline of nature," and converted the old religious "piety" into a new, practical idealism. Opposing the romantic escapes of time and fantasy, they preached a new religion of the here and now.

The European romantics of the nineteenth century usually exalted the antique and the remote. They revelled in medieval myths and feudal legends. In fiction they celebrated the old heroes of chivalry and the victims of Gothic dungeons. But the American transcendentalists used "the strong present tense" and discarded the traditions of the past. Even when they praised "the primitive" and "the wild" they spoke in terms of living red men and the actual wilderness of their new world.

In space, as in time, the European romantics exalted the remote. They sang of Mazeppa's ride and the wars of Saracen chiefs. They imagined the castles of Xanadu and the walls of Timbuktu. Even when they spoke in the present tense, they described the treasure islands of the South Seas. But the transcendentalists exalted America because America was the land of "the near and the common." When Emerson attacked "the courtly muses of Europe" he appealed to American actuality. Thoreau, remarking that he had "traveled a good deal in Concord," implied his scorn of all romantic wandering.

American transcendentalists became "romantic" only in their dream of the future. Like their European contemporaries, they went "beyond" what was customary and practical to imagine a new way of life. Like them, they protested against traditional injustices, revolted against oppressive governments, and cut through logical arguments with appeals to "the immediate intuitions of the mind." Envisioning a better society, they paid scant heed to the conservative customs and practices of their fellow men. Gazing into the future, they sometimes neglected the present.

This was their greatest fault. Like the romantics, the transcendental dreamers underestimated the inertia of the actual world. Like all idealists they overestimated the power of "spirit" to mould "matter." But when they planned realistically to improve the present world, they avoided the blight of romanticism. And even at their worst, they never exalted their "intuitions" into a rigid system of absolute idealism.

The American transcendentalists claimed only personal authority for their ideas. The individual must rely upon himself for guidance, but he must recognize the equal authority of other selves, and must not set up a tyranny of his own intuitions. The basis of self-reliance was this democratic tolerance of others. And this tolerance distinguished American transcendentalism from its German cousin, which exalted the intuitions into "categorical imperatives," and ended by idealizing an absolute, ideal ruler. American dreamers erred, not in the direction of romantic absolutism, but of individualism.

And they avoided the dangers of individual "relativism" by their appeal to common experience. "Only so much do I know as I have lived," said Emerson. Their intuitions were suggested by experience and were later tested in action. If they exalted the ideal above the material, they derived it from and referred it to the actual world. Unlike the romantic dreamers of a perfect age to come, these American idealists sought to project the opportunities of the present into the future, and to realize them through individual thought and effort.

In methods as in ends, they disagreed with their more romantic contemporaries. Both imagined a new world, but Americans wished to build it gradually, in their new land, whereas Europeans preached sudden revolution. The American Revolution itself had only asserted the right of native forces to develop without alien interference. The gradual "method of nature" was American. Therefore Thoreau, affirming his ideal of freedom, asked not for his ideal at once, but "*at once,* a better government." Through personal revolutions ("civil disobedience") and gradual changes ("So hot, my little sir?" Emerson had mocked), Americans hoped to make their world better.

Because they could hope for improvement by gradual means, the transcendental dreamers did not idealize violence, as did the European romantics. When revolution is the only alternative to despair, men are almost forced to glorify it. And then Satan, the eternal rebel, may take the place of God, the tyrant. But where gradual change is possible, Satan becomes merely an agent of potential progress. So Emerson could welcome "the good, old devil," and Whitman could even add him to the trinity. But the transcendentalists never made Satan supreme. Diabolism and the "flowers of evil" were outgrowths of the romantic ideal. Against both absolute rebellion and absolute despair, the American dreamers stood firm.

Therefore the charge of romanticism, moral confusion, and philosophic "relativism" does not apply to the transcendental dreamers of America. Latter-day puritans and "the new humanists" have accused them falsely.[7] Between the conservative moralism of the right and the romantic emotionalism of the left, these transcendental dreamers stood with their "feet tenoned and mortised in the granite" of the American present, while they gazed—perhaps over-optimistically— into the American future.

III

In opposing the puritanical moralism of the past and the romantic emotionalism of the nineteenth century, the transcendental dreamers prepared the way for the realism of modern America. On the one hand they suggested the pragmatic realism of philosophers such as C. S. Peirce, William James and John Dewey. On the other, they suggested the fictional realism of novelists such as Thomas Wolfe, John Steinbeck and William Saroyan. Later chapters on "The Pragmatic Realization" describe the development of transcendental ideas by the pragmatic philosophers. This development is historically clear. But many realistic novelists also have translated the transcendental dream into modern terms. This "translation" can only be suggested.

Just as Walt Whitman celebrated an "eidolon," or ideal picture of himself in his nineteenth century poetry, so Thomas Wolfe did in his twentieth century fiction. Both men celebrated not merely "myself," but an ideal, democratic, American "self." But Wolfe went beyond Whitman to narrate in concrete detail the autobiographical realization of this ideal self. Where Emerson had described it abstractly, and Whitman had imagined it poetically, Wolfe embodied it realistically. But the pattern was the same: first the rejection of conventional "society" (*Look Homeward, Angel*); then the quest for an ideal American life; and finally the partial realization of that ideal (*You Can't Go Home Again*). Thomas Wolfe not only realized the democratic ideal in his fiction, but in his own person, as well.

Where Wolfe described the personal realization of this dream, John Steinbeck imagined its social realization. Wolfe—like Emerson and Thoreau—sought to reform himself before reforming society, but Steinbeck's characters struggle to achieve a new life by social means. Yet most of his heroes are dreamers before they are men of action, and in *The Grapes of Wrath,* the dreams of Casey, the preacher, motivate the actions of the Joad family, and these actions illustrate a philosophy which combines the old transcendental idealism with a modern realism.

Finally, the novels of William Saroyan have developed other aspects of the old idealism. Less realistic, perhaps, than *The Grapes of Wrath, The Human Comedy* localizes the idea more completely, and suggests that it is not merely historical, but recurrent in American life, because it is appropriate to the recurrent pattern of the development of a new, young country. Because the American West of the 1940's repeated much the same conditions of the New England of the 1840's, a kind of new Transcendentalism has developed there. Meanwhile, the modern philosophy of Pragmatism, and the literary practice of realism have done much to modify—and also make real —the dreams of the old Transcendentalism.

IV

To summarize: American Transcendentalism was not a revolt against puritanism, but a development of the old puritan faith, divorced from the old puritan formalism. It was not a romantic philosophy of emotional escape, but a philosophy of "the near and the common," which sought gradually to improve the common. Finally, it did not evaporate into an abstract idealism, but developed into a pragmatic realism, inspiring both the literary and the philosophic realists of modern times.

The transcendental dream renewed the Christian faith that the "kingdom of God" exists within you. It continued the protestant revolt against the corrupt tyrannies of actual institutions. It went beyond earlier protestantism to declare that every individual conscience should be free. But it qualified this principle of individual freedom by emphasizing the complementary principle of external reality. The individual is not romantically free, but is subject to the time and place in which he lives. His freedom is further limited by the freedom of others. And finally, his possession of "the kingdom of God" within implies his responsibility of realizing that ideal actively. From religious protest, through democratic faith, toward pragmatic realization, the transcendental dream has developed in America.

4. EMERSON

I

EMERSON's most famous address described his ideal of "The American Scholar"—"man thinking" in America. It also described the ideal by which he patterned his own life. That he wished to become an ideal scholar is clear, but that he wished to, and did become a representative American is less generally recognized. Judging him by his own standards, "Let us" (to use his own words) "see him in his school, and consider him in reference to the main influences he receives."

Upon Emerson, as upon the mind of his imaginary scholar, the first influence to be exerted was that of nature. "Every day, the sun; and, after sunset, Night and her stars. . . . Every day, men and women, conversing—beholding and beholden." The term "nature" includes not only the sun and the stars, or wild nature, but human nature—the whole environment of man.[1] Born as he was in the middle of the city of Boston, the human environment acted upon Emerson first. The America in which he lived exerted the most significant influence upon both his life and his writing.

To think of Emerson as one of the New England group of writers who flourished a century ago is to misrepresent him at the start. He was born to that group, but grew beyond it. By experience and by sympathy, he became a citizen of a larger America. Lowell declared that two men, Lincoln and Emerson, stood preeminent as products of American democracy.[2] Because modern Americans have been unwilling to couple Emerson with Lincoln, they have too often overlooked the fact that Emerson was wholly a product of democracy. Mr. James Truslow Adams, who rather distrusts Emerson, yet recognizes that "in no other author can we get so close to the whole of the American spirit."[3]

To begin with, a long established myth must be destroyed. It has been repeated so often that Emerson was descended from seven generations of Puritan ministers that men have come to believe the statement literally. But only by a careful hand-picking of the branches of his family tree can the assertion be justified, as Holmes, who originated it, cheerfully admitted. Emerson's mother was the daughter of a "cooper and distiller," and his maternal ancestors were largely innocent of ministerial proclivities.[4] In the direct line of his paternal descent a merchant and a baker intrude. The only generalization that can be made to include all his ancestors is that they were Americans for seven generations and that they shared between them almost all the experiences common to American pioneers. Thomas Emerson, the baker,[5] emigrated to New England in 1635, obtained a grant of land, and founded the family. His son, the Reverend Joseph Emerson, barely escaped with his life when the town of Mendon was destroyed by the Indians. His son, Edward Emerson, was a merchant. His grandson, Ralph Waldo's grandfather, William Emerson of Concord, died of camp fever while serving as chaplain in the patriot army of the Revolution. Lastly, the Reverend William Emerson of Boston, besides serving as chaplain of the Massachusetts Senate, delivered the official Fourth of July oration in Boston in 1802, the year before his son Ralph Waldo was born. In conversation with Bret Harte in 1872, Emerson could argue with justice that he "spoke also from Pilgrim experience." With the blood of seven generations of American pioneers and patriots running in his veins, Emerson came naturally by the pioneer American philosophy of Self-Reliance.

The Boston into which Emerson was born was, perhaps, a Massachusetts town—in his youth, he used to lead the family cow to pasture on the common. But he lived to see Boston become a modern city, and a leader in the change from an agricultural to an industrial America. In his early years he saw it expand (very much as Chicago is doing today) by building new territory out of the sea, creating what is now called Back Bay. He saw the railroad bind together the outlying districts, and make possible a metropolitan center. He saw the influx of Irish immigrants challenge the supremacy of the old Yankee stock, and himself defended the rights of these immigrants against the one-hundred-per-centers of his day. It is false to project him against the conservatism of a modern Boston, and to imagine that he took his tone from that.

Emerson grew to maturity in a new America. The War of 1812 found him in school, with Boston in constant fear of British invasion. One day his class was asked to help throw up earthworks in Boston harbor for the defense of the city. Although the attack never came, it roused him and his generation to a consciousness of their common life, so that after the war a new patriotism had developed. After the war also, he saw the great wave of Western migration begin. At the age of nineteen he dedicated his Journal to "the spirit of America," using all the high-flown phrases of youth, but expressing the sincerity of a deeply felt conviction.

This local patriotism soon expanded to include in its horizon not only Massachusetts, but also the new West that was then opening up. In 1823 he faced squarely the problem of a frontier,[6] with its opportunities and its dangers:

The vast rapidity with which the desarts and forests of the interior of this country are peopled have led patriots to fear lest the nation grow *too fast* for its virtue and its peace. . . . Good men desire, and the great cause of human nature demands, that this abundant and overflowing richness wherewith God has blessed this country be not misapplied and made a curse of. . . . How to effect the check proposed is an object of momentous importance. And in view of an object of such magnitude, I know not who he is, that can complain that motive is lacking in this latter age, whereby men should become great.[7]

America was to supply the motive whereby Emerson became great.

Against the background of this enthusiasm for the new land, Emerson's "American Scholar" was projected. He devoted his life to the study of the "rapidity" of the American tempo. If, in youth, he often seemed to share the conservatives' desire for a "check" upon it, as soon as he began to think for himself, he realized that the best check for thoughtless expansion lay in the application of the intelligence of American scholars to it. Not by halting the car of progress would he save America, but by guiding it well. "Hitch your wagon to a star." All of his essays had as their main theme the application of the scholarship, or wisdom of man, to the problems of the present. He too turned to the present, writing in his Journal: "The dead sleep in their moonless night; my business is with the living."

At the time of the American Scholar address, two new factors were beginning to operate in America, and the nation was being forced to think seriously about the problems which her growth was creating. In 1828 the election of Jackson had focused attention on the problem of the West, while five years later the formation of the Anti-Slavery Society had emphasized the danger of slavery, and foreshadowed the conflict of the North with the South. In both these problems Emerson took a deep interest, but the excitement and the crusading spirit of reform which they engendered excited him even more. His relation to this spirit is vividly described by Lowell in his essay on "Thoreau," while Emerson's own attitude is expressed in his occasional essays, and in his Journals. Indeed, it may be said that Emerson was related to these momentous times both as cause and as effect; his addresses and essays were stimulating the young minds of Thoreau, Lowell, Holmes, and many lesser men, while at the same time the excitement of the times was urging him on to his best work. In his introductory essay to the *Dial,* he justified the new magazine as a vehicle of "a new spirit," and pointed out "the progress of revolution" among the people of New England.[8]

Although Emerson's first knowledge of the West had come through books and travelers' reports, his intimate experience of the life of the nation was not limited to New England, or even to the East. In college he had roomed with a Southern student, and in early manhood made an extended trip to Florida for his health. Frequently thereafter he toured the Eastern states, delivering lectures in New York, Philadelphia, and Washington. Gradually he outgrew the natural provincialism of his youth. The years from the delivery of "The American Scholar" in 1837 to that of "The Young American" in 1844 were filled with new experiences and new thoughts. In the latter address he emphasized the importance of the newly constructed railroads, by means of which "the nervous, rocky West is intruding a new and continental element into the national mind, and we shall yet have an American genius." Beginning in the 1840's, as the railroads pushed their way over the mountains, Emerson followed them farther and farther West, delivering his lectures, first in Pittsburgh and Cincinnati (where his earliest poems had already been published in James Freeman Clarke's *Western Messenger*), then in Chicago and Milwaukee, and finally across the Mississippi in Iowa. On December 31, 1855, he noted in his Journal: "I have crossed the Mississippi on foot three times." And in 1871, at the age of sixty-eight, he travelled to California, delivering several lectures there.

Emerson's life was lived in the days of Westward expansion. It included the War of 1812, the Annexation of Texas, the Gold Rush, the Civil War, and the completion of the Union Pacific Railroad. He was intensely aware of all these events. Only in the light of them can the significance of his writings be appreciated, for before being a scholar, he was first of all an American.

II

But if Emerson was first of all an American, his Americanism was of a particular kind. His philosophy of self-reliance was related to American pioneer experience, but derived from his own personal experiences. His optimism also was related to national expansion, but derived first from his own religious background. His life helps to explain not only his own writing, but the "optimism" of the American dream, as well.

In a famous passage of his essay on "Domestic Life," Emerson drew upon his own experience. Speaking of himself and his brothers, he asked: "What is the hoop that holds them staunch? It is the iron hand of poverty, of necessity, of austerity. . . . The angels that dwell with them and are weaving the laurels of life for their youthful brows, are Toil and Want, Truth and Mutual Faith."[9] These words are important, as they suggest both the usual and the unusual aspects of Emerson's life. "Toil and Want" were always present, so that poverty was one of the driving forces of his life, as it has been in the lives of many young Americans. But "Truth and Mutual Faith" were also present in an unusual degree, and gave his character the simplicity and sincerity which distinguishes it.

Emerson was a poor boy. Unlike Longfellow and Lowell and Holmes, he was never one of the true "Brahmins" of Boston. Socially, he did not belong to "The Genteel Tradition." In 1854 he exclaimed to his Journal: "If Socrates were here, we could go and talk with him; but Longfellow, we cannot talk with; there is a palace, and servants, and a row of bottles of different coloured wines, and wine glasses, and fine coats." Emerson's family had always been poor, and, in spite of success in later life, he always avoided luxury. In his essay on "Napoleon," he criticized the "man of the world" as one who, when he had made all the money he needed, did not know what to do with it, and could find satisfaction only in making more money. Emerson knew the value of poverty as a driving force, spurring the individual to his best efforts, and disciplining him in the school of "necessity and austerity." And he also knew the value of money, which makes social independence possible. So he was able to enjoy the advantages of both, keeping the balance between them. Throughout his life he practiced a self-reliant poverty. He concluded his essay on "Self-Reliance": "So use all that is called Fortune. Most men gamble with her, and gain all, and lose all, as her wheel rolls. But do thou leave as unlawful these winnings, and deal with Cause and Effect, the chancellors of God."

Together with poverty, his domestic life trained him in the virtues of "Truth and Mutual Faith." Here the many generations of puritan ancestry exerted themselves to inculcate the personal integrity which had always been their highest ideal. Anyone reading his Journals must be impressed with his remarkable honesty, both with himself and with other men. He always faced the facts of his life squarely, without evasion. Indeed, in his efforts not to deceive himself, or others, he often criticized himself too severely. At the early age of ten years, he wrote to his Aunt Mary,[10] describing his daily routine of life, and confessing to the faults of occasional anger at his brothers, and a desire to play during the time that should have been devoted to reading. In his later life, he criticized himself not so much for his lack of the puritan virtues, as for his possession of the puritan faults. The famous passage beginning "I was born cold" has been quoted too often. At the start of his essay on "Experience," he criticized himself, in this case unduly, for his inability to feel grief at the death of his eldest son. His absolute honesty with himself and with the world is one of his outstanding characteristics. It is interesting to speculate whether his knowledge of his own faults did not overbalance those faults. A man may perhaps see the world steadily and whole, even with a defect of vision, if he recognizes his defect sufficiently to make exact allowances for it.

Emerson's training in a self-reliant poverty, and his training in truthfulness and sincerity, are two of the keys to his personality and philosophy. They help to explain his optimism, and his wisdom. Considered together they may be taken to illustrate one of the central principles of religious truth—"Blessed are the poor in spirit, for theirs is the kingdom of heaven." Trained in poverty, Emerson knew that unlimited "prosperity" was not only not possible, but not advisable. Trained in truthfulness and self-knowledge, he knew the faults of men too well to be proud.

But one does not usually think of the philosopher of self-reliance as "poor in spirit." He did not try, like Franklin, to "imitate Jesus," and cultivate humility. Rather, he "took himself for better or for worse as his portion in life," cheerfully. But he remained poor in spirit because he did not ask too much of life. He accepted thankfully whatever good was offered him as pure gain. In the language of materialism, he did not list his stock at a par of one hundred, and then despair when its value depreciated; rather he listed it at zero, and rejoiced if his efforts made it climb above that point. His own words, in his essay on "Experience," explain this attitude most clearly, and also explain why his optimism was so at variance with the pessimism of "the modern temper," both in our time and in his own:

The fine young people despise life but . . . I am thankful for small mercies. I compared notes with one of my friends who expects everything of the universe, and is disappointed when anything is less than the best, and I found that I begin at the other extreme, expecting nothing, and am always full of thanks for moderate good.

"Expecting nothing from the universe," Emerson was always optimistic. Trained to live simply, he was easily contented. Knowing his faults, and those of other men, he did not wish for too much. "Ask nothing of men, and, in the endless mutation, thou only firm column must presently appear the upholder of all that surrounds thee."[11] Thus it happened that Emerson himself became one of the "firm columns" of the pantheon of American literature. He did not dream that America would become Utopia.

III

But Emerson did dream that America would develop new ways of life different from the old ways of Europe. He dreamed that the new world would progressively realize the ideals of freedom and democracy enunciated by the Declaration of Independence. And he believed that these American ideals would be realized, not because they were ideal, but because they were appropriate to the facts of American life and to the laws of modern science which were shaping that life. His writing gave expression to the American revolt from the genteel tradition of the European past, to the celebration of the democratic ideals of the American present, and to the formulation of the natural laws and pragmatic attitudes which these implied for the future.

Emerson's "transcendental" philosophy, therefore, was not something borrowed from the abstract ideas of Kant or Carlyle, but something concretely suggested by his own American experience. His revolutionary addresses to the "American Scholar" and the Divinity School reflected his own revolt from the genteel tradition of his youth. His celebration of the discipline of "Nature" and the mysteries of "The Over-Soul" resulted from his own experiences of religious conflict and illumination. And his preaching of active "Self-Reliance," and the facing of "Experience" resulted from his own American experience, and foreshadowed the pragmatism and experimentalism of modern science.

For the first twenty-nine years of his life, Emerson remained a traditionalist of the old school. He studied in the Harvard Divinity School, and for three years preached successfully to one of the most important congregations of Boston. Like his father he was chaplain of the State Senate. His sermons were universally accepted and admired, and as a visiting preacher he was much in demand. He did not leave the Christian ministry because of any failure on his own part to measure up to the conventional standards of his congregation, or because of any misunderstanding. He resigned from it because, as he began to think things out for himself, he saw that he could not continue to believe its traditional tenets.

The most important expression of his early ideas is his extraordinary farewell sermon on "The Lord's Supper."[12] This shows him in the moment of transition from the old religion to the new, when he was still conforming to the rules of the old. Specifically, he had based his resignation on his objection to administering the bread and wine of the sacrament, and in this sermon he argued, from theological grounds, that the Lord's Supper had no justification in scripture or in practice. For the only time in his career as a writer, he played the game according to the rules of the traditionalists, arguing from text to text, and from precedent to historical precedent. He displayed the greatest shrewdness and logical precision in this, and composed the most convincing proof possible of the fact that he did not abandon traditional theology and logical exposition because he was incapable of them. For twenty-nine years he had conformed, had become proficient, and had gained success. For the rest of his life he was to follow his own path and describe truth at first-hand, as he observed and experienced it.

This break from the tradition of the past was largely caused by an increasing preoccupation with the events and ideas of the present— especially the ideas of modern science. He felt that the truths of the old religion must be fused with those of science and that this was possible only if the forms of the old religion were modified. The year before he resigned his ministry he read widely in science, especially in the astronomy of the time.[13] Shortly before making his decision to resign he wrote significantly in his Journal: "The Religion that is afraid of science dishonours God and commits suicide." He himself opened his arms to science, and on his trip to Europe visited many scientific museums and lectures with increasing interest, until standing in the Jardin des Plantes in Paris, he thought to himself: "I am moved by strange sympathies: I say continually, 'I will be a naturalist.' "[14] Of course he never carried out this resolve to the letter, but throughout his life he read continually of the new theories and discoveries of science, constantly coloring his own thought with them.

Emerson's major writing began with his book on *Nature* which, by intention at least, celebrated the modern scientific attitude toward life, and attacked the traditional attitude. He began by protesting that "Our age is retrospective. It builds the sepulchre of the fathers." He then demanded a "philosophy of insight and not of tradition," with "action proportioned to nature." And he exclaimed: "Why should we grope among the dry bones of the past? Let us demand our own works and laws and worship." In this first paragraph of his first book, he attacked tradition in the name of the American present and the laws of nature. The "transcendentalism" of his language has long misled many into believing that he was anti-scientific and anti-modern. But the exact reverse was his intention.

Emerson's attack on the old tradition, thus announced in *Nature*, found clearest expression in his address on "The American Scholar." And here it became most clearly an attack on America's cultural dependence on traditional Europe. What had been a generalized denunciation of "the dry bones of the past," became a specific declaration of American independence from the European past: "Our day of dependence, our long apprenticeship to the learning of other lands, draws to a close." And in the famous peroration declaring "We have listened too long to the courtly muses of Europe," he equated the "European" tradition, with the genteel, aristocratic, "courtly" tradition everywhere.

More specifically, Emerson's "American Scholar" suggested that the new American idea was to be democratic and realistic, in contrast to the "courtly" tradition. Emphasizing the "difference in the ideas which predominate over successive epochs," he called attention to "auspicious signs of the coming days." These included "the elevation of what was called the lowest class in the state," and the celebration of "the near, the low, the common, instead of the sublime and beautiful." In the spirit of the realistic literature of the century which was to follow, he proclaimed that "the literature of the poor, the feelings of the child, the philosophy of the street, the meaning of household life, are the topics of the time." Even while attacking the genteel tradition of Europe, he was projecting his dream of an independent, realistic, democratic America.

Later, in his most famous essay on "Self-Reliance," this revolt from the genteel tradition and this celebration of the democratic present reached its climax. "Trust thyself," he proclaimed; and more specifically, he emphasized the democratic nature of this "self." "Accept the place the divine providence has found for you, the society of your contemporaries, the connection of events. Great men have always done so, and confided themselves childlike to the genius of their age." Consciously, the genius of his age dominated his philosophy, and the American experience gave form to his idealism. Condemning "a dead church, a dead Bible-society," he celebrated rather "a sturdy lad from New Hampshire or Vermont, who in turn tries all professions, who *teams it, farms it, peddles it,* keeps a school, preaches, edits a newspaper . . . and so forth, and always like a cat falls on his feet."

This "sturdy lad" was, of course, Emerson's ideal, American self. If he personally had never "teamed it," or "farmed it," he had kept a school and had preached; while his transcendental friend Bronson Alcott had "peddled it." The discipline of "Nature" and of experience gave form to his transcendentalism. "The genius of his age" inspired it. And, finally, for justification he appealed to the ages to come: "Greatness appeals to the future."

What makes Emerson's idealism typically American—and not genteel, like Alcott, nor romantic, like Poe's—is its close relation to the common experience of his own time, and its appeal to the American experience of the future. Later (as we shall see) the pragmatic and realistic writers found in his work the germs of their new ideas, and remembered him as "the philosopher of democracy."

The common denominator of Emerson's idealism and the later realism is to be found in the idea of experience, defined in the broadest terms. All Emerson's critics[15] agree that this idea is fundamental to his philosophy. He described "experience" inclusively, celebrating both the mystical and the sensuous. There were "spiritual facts" and "physical facts," and like William James, he based his mysticism on the evidence of what he called "God the phenomenon."[16] In his essay on "Experience," he described life as "sensations *and* states of mind," unified by the consciousness of man. By considering the objective *and* the subjective aspects of life, he avoided both absolute idealism, which denied experience, and narrow "empiricism," which denied human ideals.

What separated Emerson's transcendentalism from past empiricism, but related it to the "Radical Empiricism" of James, was his emphasis on the different values of the different kinds of experience. He rejected quantitative empiricism, but celebrated the qualitative empiricism which valued some experiences above others. Thus he introduced "The Over-Soul:"

There is a difference between one and another hour of life in their authority and subsequent effect. Our faith comes in moments; . . . yet there is a depth in those brief moments which constrains us to ascribe more reality to them than to all other experiences.

And later he urged men to follow those who "speak *from within,* or from experience."

Emerson rejected the authority of tradition—which was essentially a formulation of other people's past experiences—primarily because he believed the conditions of modern American life were so different from those of the "courtly" or "feudal" past as to make the old traditions invalid for the new times. He emphasized the need of intuition and of self-reliance for modern men because the new laws and "traditions" of the new world had not yet been formulated. Rejecting all "paltry empiricism," he appealed, like William James, to "the universal impulse to believe" in "this new yet unapproachable America I have found in the West."

Revolting against past tradition, reflecting present experience, appealing of necessity to the future, Emerson's thought became typically the American philosophy, or "dream." For America was founded by men who held an irrational and fundamentally mystical belief in the potentialities of life in the New World. The Declaration of Independence was written by an idealist, and its principles were based on an act of faith. Liberty and equality were originally transcendental ideas.[17] These ideas have been experimentally tested by succeeding generations of Americans, and are still being so tested. But fundamentally they are mystical. As Mr. J. T. Adams writes: "The American Dream was not a logical concept of thought. Like every great thought that has stirred and advanced humanity, it was a religious emotion, a great act of faith, a courageous leap into the dark unknown. As long as that dream persists to strengthen the heart of man, Emerson will remain one of its prophets."[18]

5. BRONSON ALCOTT:
GENTEEL TRANSCENDENTALIST

I

IN THE autumn of 1847, Emerson commissioned Alcott to build a rustic summer-house, and persuaded Thoreau to care for his Concord household during the coming winter. Having thus provided for his two best friends, he departed on a lecture tour of Europe. It is recorded that Thoreau performed his duties cheerfully, gave Emerson's children hilarious pick-a-back rides, and wrote homely letters to their father telling of the fun. But it was Alcott who enjoyed his new work to the utmost.

Emerson's rustic summer-house was to be Alcott's supreme artistic creation. It was to be a labor of love, devoted to the master, and a symbol of all their ideal aspirations. More than any other task which he ever undertook, it absorbed him.[1] By day he worked on it and by night he dreamed of it. When a skeptical neighbor called it "the strangest thing I ever saw," Alcott merely compared it with "the finest work of M. Angelo."[2] In visible and tangible form it expressed his inmost ideas.

Unfortunately, this summer-house also expressed the confusion of Alcott's ideas. Describing the building in his Journal, he suggested the symbolism of it. "The edifice seems to be upheld by the broad cornice, the rafters aspiring in handsome curves to their apex and uniting at the ridge-pole, with broad weather-boards and the bending brackets depending therefrom, as if to find the ground and take root therein."[3] Indeed, the description might also apply to Alcott himself. Did not his own nature aspire in "handsome curves" toward the ethereal ideal? And did not his own intellectual roots "depend" from the upper atmosphere, "as if to find the ground and take root therein?" Alcott's description may suggest to the modern reader the image of a tree on stilts. And these stilts, or "upright joists," as he called them, were nine, "to form the corners for the nine Muses to this poet's bower."

Alcott's symbolic summer-house was important, and the confusion of it significant, because it gave expression to a state of mind common to many American idealists. Seeking to divorce his high aspirations from the base element of earth, Alcott set them on the stilts of

30

the genteel tradition. The nine Greek muses separated his creative thought from the American soil. And so, although he could outsoar Emerson in his idealism, he could never sink his own roots into the vulgar reality of America. He could, for instance, never bring himself to use the "coarse" images which he recognized as contributing to Emerson's power.[4] He could never bring himself to accept Thoreau's "wildness," though he could admire his independence. To the end of his days, he remained a country gentleman of the intellect, building idealistic summer-houses beside the realistic shanties of Thoreau, and the homely cottages of Emerson.

As the friend of Emerson and Thoreau, and as "the father of Little Women," Alcott's fame has always rested upon firm foundations. Moreover, he possessed an original mind and a lovable personality: he was known as "the good Alcott." More than this he did not seriously pretend (although he always hoped) to be. Therefore, it is unfortunate that his biographer and his critics have claimed more for him. They have called him: "the one complete representative of American Transcendentalism,"[5] a "frontiersman of the mind,"[6] and even "a typical American."[7]

But Alcott was none of these things. He was not a "complete representative of American transcendentalism," although he developed one aspect of transcendentalism. He did not dwell in "the Western lands of the mind and soul," although he occasionally visited them. And certainly he was not a typical American, although it may well be true that most Americans are idealists. There are ideas—and ideas.

To Alcott, all ideas were beautiful. Therefore, he described many incongruous ideas beautifully. The suggested image of the tree on stilts will serve: his separate thoughts were often fine, but they did not seem to belong together. Indeed, the jumbled variety of his mind forces us to define the logical implications of these literary ideas.— What was "American Transcendentalism?" What are "the Western lands of the mind?" And what is "a typical American" in life or in literature? Alcott's miscellaneous Journals suggest clues to the solution of these problems.

II

"Transcendentalism" has often been defined as "pure idealism." It asserted the primacy of "ideas, which did not come by experience, but through which experience was acquired."[8] This definition has been traced directly to Kant, and indirectly to Plato. Thus defined, it merely preferred ideas to experience—intuitions to the senses. It did not necessarily distinguish between different ideas, or relate them to actual experiences. And thus defined, Alcott was a complete transcendentalist. "I set out from the ground of Spirit," he wrote. "This is. All else is its manifestation."[9]

But transcendentalism was also "practical idealism." Originally Kant had developed his philosophy to justify the moral ideas of "God, freedom and immortality," and had emphasized the importance of the Practical Reason. In its wider aspects transcendentalism has generally been recognized as the philosophical counterpart of "that great movement for the liberation of humanity which swept over Europe at the end of the eighteenth and the beginning of the nineteenth century."[10] It asserted both the primacy of abstract *ideas,* and the supremacy of moral *ideals.* It sought to make "law for man" prevail over "law for thing."

In America, and particularly in New England, this practical aspect of transcendentalism became dominant. Perhaps its first American historian emphasized this aspect too greatly: "With some truth it may be said that there never was such a thing as Transcendentalism out of New England. In Germany and France there was a transcendental philosophy, held by cultivated men, taught in schools, and professed by many thoughtful and earnest people; but it never affected society in its organized institutions or practical interests."[11] But Emerson also recognized it, defining transcendentalism as "Idealism as it appears in 1842," and warning of its potential radicalism: "In action he [the transcendentalist] . . . may contravene every written commandment."—"Build therefore your own world!" he concluded.

Certainly American transcendentalism participated more actively than its European counterpart in the libertarian movements of the time. It preached independence from "the courtly muses of Europe." It worked enthusiastically for the political movement for emancipation. And it praised the pioneer settlement of the American West (although it opposed the blind materialism of many pioneers). In short, it gave classic expression to "the American Dream"[12] of a new society in the new world.

Specifically, these American ideals of cultural independence, individual liberty, and pioneer initiative found expression in the transcendental morality of self-reliance. In fact, this new morality rather than the abstract philosophy of the schools (which few Americans of the time understood) *was* American transcendentalism. And this new idealism opposed sharply the traditionalism, the classicism, and the orthodoxy of that European way of life, which, surviving in America, has become known as "the genteel tradition."[13]

Among the American transcendentalists, Emerson and Thoreau consistently preached this new morality of self-reliance, and opposed the genteel tradition; using "coarse" words, thinking "wild" thoughts, and (intellectually at least) refusing to compromise with society. But Alcott, who had preached self-reliance before Emerson, and had practised independence before Thoreau, frequently sought to compromise (both intellectually and practically) with the genteel tradition. In earliest youth, for instance, he had written: "To dare to think, to think for oneself, is denominated pride and arrogance. And millions of human minds are in this state of slavery and tyranny.— How shall they escape? Rebel! Think for themselves!" But soon after this, he had cautioned himself: "We may have mistaken arrogance for independence, imagination for reality. Let us be careful."[14] All his life, it is true, Alcott preferred transcendental *ideas* to practical experiences. But all his life he was to vacillate between the transcendental *ideal* of self-reliance and the conservative ideal of tradition and conformity. Therefore, he cannot be considered a complete or typical representative of American Transcendentalism.

Nor did Alcott dwell in "the Western lands of the mind." For the morality of self-reliance was close to that of the frontier.[15] Like pioneer individualism, it sought to go beyond existing society and the conservative tradition. But Alcott distrusted individualism and steeped himself in tradition. He remained an Easterner of the mind, who made occasional excursions to the Western frontiers. Like Emerson, he lectured frequently beyond the Alleghenies and gained many disciples there. He showed genuine sympathy for "that slovenly West,"[16] as it did for him. But he sought rather to teach the West, than to learn from it. He considered himself primarily a citizen of "the ancient society, the Old England of the New England,"[17] whose function was to carry the old culture to the new territories.

"The western lands of the mind" are, of course, impossible to define exactly. But certainly they are not made up of all the ideas of all the people who happen to have lived in the West. Rather, they consist of those ideas which have been formed by the life of the West, as that differs from the life of the East. These frontier lands are not colonies established by Eastern idealists, but independent states of the mind springing from the soil and customs of the frontier.

"The West of the mind," which the transcendentalism of Emerson

and Thoreau sought to interpret, may perhaps be defined as the opposite of that "genteel tradition" which New England had imported
from Old England, and which the "new humanists" have recently
reaffirmed. In the words of Santayana, these "two mentalities" have
long co-existed in America: "the one a survival of the beliefs and
standards of the fathers, the other an expression of the instincts,
practice, and discoveries of the younger generation."[18]

Alcott's Journals illustrate this dichotomy between the new, Western thought and the old, genteel tradition, in detail. His mind embraced an almost endless number of irreconcilable opposites. He
praised self-reliance and tradition; radicalism and conservatism;
protestantism and orthodoxy; individualism and society; rural simplicity and urban gentility; progressive education and the worship of
ancestry; populism and privilege; frankness and reticence; manual
labor and the idealist's superiority to labor; instinctive freedom and
well-bred civility; the West and the East; Concord and Beacon Hill.
Sometimes he praised these in the same breath, unconscious of their
opposition; sometimes alternately, vacillating between the two;
sometimes changing slowly from the one to the other, as his mind
changed.[19]

Indeed, Alcott's confused love of opposites might seem to constitute him "a typical American" but for his utter lack of that pragmatic common sense which usually mediates between the two American extremes. He alternated between two opposing ideals, refusing
to accept the clarification of experience. Unlike Emerson,[20] who
learned the lessons of "nature" and foreshadowed the pragmatism of
James and Dewey, Alcott stuck resolutely to his abstractions. "I am
an Idea without hands,"[21] he lamented. "I find no body for my
thought amidst the materials of this age." But this was only half true.
His thought did lack hands and a body, but many idealists have been
equally theoretical. The trouble was that his lack of a body prevented
him from recognizing that his thought had two faces. He was, really,
"two ideas without hands."

These two contrasting ideas become more clear when one examines
the specific contradictions of his thought.

III

Alcott early recognized the presence of irreconcilable ideas in his
mind, and often regretted it. Shortly after his first enthusiasm for
self-reliance, he wrote, "We are . . . too vacillating in our feelings

and character to secure the full confidence of those with whom we associate."[22] And a year later he repeated: "There mingles in my reflections a desire to accomplish something worthy the purposes of my existence . . . with the weakness of ignorance. . . . I plod on my way, hoping and regretting."[23] At times he recognized the superficial manifestations of this "weakness" and sought to cure them. But he never recognized the cause of the fundamental dichotomy or the need of curing it.

To Alcott, gentility seemed merely a matter of literary style. Brought up in the atmosphere of post-Puritan New England, he did succeed in purging his writing of its self-conscious gentility. His references to "my friend, Miss May," and to their "pure and sentimental acquaintance" soon stopped. Gradually, he qualified his ideas about the "philanthropic purity" of Boston. The adjectives "gentle," "pure," "sentimental," and "good" became less frequent. In 1871 he even referred to his own early style as "vicious." But the stock literary echoes always persisted in his writing, and with them the old genteel standards. Late in life he still valued the Western people primarily for their "cultivation" and "gentility,"[24] imported from old New England.

In his literary friendships, perhaps, Alcott escaped most completely from the genteel tradition. His intimacy with Emerson and Thoreau was unique: no more fruitful relationship is recorded in American literary history. Many other New England authors profited from his stimulation and encouragement. And Walt Whitman drew forth his most courageous and independent admiration. Where Emerson had qualified his enthusiasm for Whitman, and where Thoreau had regarded the expansive poet with distrust, Alcott held to his literary convictions, despite Walt's frank treatment of sex. In his criticism of literature, Alcott divorced himself from the genteel tradition.

But in his ideals of conduct, Alcott inclined more and more toward gentility. His attitudes toward education, for instance, reveal the instability of his mind. As a writer, under the influence of Emerson, he had changed slowly from traditionalist to modernist. But as an educator, under the influence of his English friends and his wife, he changed from progressive to aristocratic traditionalist.

No modern reader can fail to sympathize with young Alcott's courage in conducting the Temple School. That his mild "Conversations on the Gospels" should have been called "one-third nonsense, one-third blasphemous, and the rest obscene,"[25] seems praise to us now. Indeed, all his early faith in the power of education to create a more just society coincided with the faith of American democracy. His fame as an educator has grown from that faith. But as early as 1842 he abandoned it for the belief that heredity determines character. In 1852 he became a genealogist, rummaging among the dead bones of the past. He impressed an English visitor by claiming descent from "Bishop Alcock." And thus, from a believer in the democratizing power of education, he became an advocate of the aristocracy of racial inheritance. "We are, with slight deviations, copies of our ancestors,"[26] he wrote.

Professor Shepard has brilliantly suggested that Alcott's feeling of aristocracy derived from his lack of youthful contact with the American "lower middle class."[27] Born among rural farmers who were almost "peasants," he idealized himself as one of the intellectual *élite*. While Thoreau worked for his intellectual independence, Alcott assumed that the world owed him a living.

> And what he needed for his fee
> To live, he borrowed graciously.[28]

But he resembled Robinson's "Flammonde" psychologically, as well as economically. A "small satanic[29] sort of kink" existed in his brain also, to hold him back from the "high destinies/ That came so near to being his." And this "kink" was caused by the radical confusion between his aristocratic and his libertarian ideals.

The aristocratic tradition had sometimes assumed that society owed its writers a living, and (as a corollary) that these writers should conform, and not preach revolution. But the morality of self-reliance assumed that writers should support themselves, and thus earn the freedom to preach reform or revolution as they chose. "If I devote myself to . . . contemplations, I must first see, at least, that I do not pursue them sitting upon another man's shoulders," wrote Thoreau. But Alcott rode graciously upon other men's shoulders, whenever he needed a lift.

Therefore his attitude towards labor became hopelessly confused. As a young man he had pursued many laborious occupations without complaint. But after his marriage and the failure of his social experiments, he retired toward gentility.[30] His brother-in-law argued: "His friends have to labor. Why should not he?" And his wife admitted that "his unwillingness to be employed in the usual way produces great doubt in the minds of his friends as to the righteousness of his life, because he partakes of the wages of others occupied in the same way."[31] And so Alcott compromised by working occasionally. But to his Journals he complained: "What a distance between the company of such as [Emerson], and the labourers with whom I am now brought into closest communication in my daily callings!"[32]

His resultant theory of labor was a genteel compromise: labor is good, if it is unnecessary. In one mood he could exclaim: "Labour educates the world. There is no education without it,"[33] and again: "I deem sodding / A sternest godding." But this labor must be voluntary. He opposed gardening "for the appetites."

> Sweet is the toil and swift the hours glide by
> While I my grounds delight to beautify.[34]

"The gardener distinguishes himself as man cultivating the ground by choice, not from necessity and in bondage to his wants. He deals duteously with it by humanizing it, so to speak."[35]

These phrases help to clarify the two ideals which divided Alcott's mind. On the one hand, he preached and practised rebellious protestantism—refusing to abandon his high ideals, and refusing to serve Mammon. But on the other hand, he also preached and practised the traditional ideals of that very orthodoxy against which he imagined himself to be rebelling. His language, as well as his thought, implied his participation in the aristocratic tradition. He spelled, and described, "labour" in the English manner. He delighted to "beautify," but scorned to work usefully. And he emphasized man's "duty" to "humanize" nature. Where Emerson celebrated the educational discipline of all nature, including even "debt, grinding debt . . . whose lessons cannot be foregone,"[36] Alcott praised only that part of nature which could be "humanized" and "beautified."

These are neither the words nor the deeds of a "frontiersman of the mind." And yet Alcott had explored the unknown West before Emerson; he had preached self-reliance, the potential divinity of the common man, the power of education, and the tyranny of organized government. Even more boldly than Emerson, he had acted upon these beliefs. He had braved the anger of society in his Temple School, in his "Conversations on the Gospels," and in his championship of William Lloyd Garrison. The image of Alcott, his cane raised and his gray hair blowing, leading a crowd up the courthouse steps to free a fugitive slave, remains vivid. His eyes had seen the glory.

But having explored the frontiers of the mind, Alcott retreated to the conservative East. Intellectually, he became a "back-trailer." He abandoned self-reliance for society. He came to place heredity above individual education. Denying the value of necessary labor and "the discipline of nature," he retired to the traditionalism of Beacon Hill.

There, symbolically, he spent his last days in the "Chamber Looking East."[37]

IV

"True 'progress,' in Alcott's belief," writes Professor Shepard, "involves not an interminable pioneering . . . but a thoughtful return upon a course once traversed."[38] We may agree that intellectual progress involves more than "interminable pioneering," but not that it involves a "return" of any kind. Such a return is usually an admission of spiritual defeat. After the pioneer should come the homesteader. For "progress" involves first, exploration, then settlement—whether of land or of ideas. It involves clarification, cultivation, and development: the slow process of living with, and making fruitful. The Westerner of the mind will not return, however thoughtfully, to the ideas of the past. He will cultivate his new ideas to make them blossom. But Alcott never developed the ideas which he had imagined in the intellectual West. He merely abandoned them and returned East.

The three dominant processes of historic American life may be compared to the three dominant American philosophies. The ideals of the explorer and the pioneer may be compared to the self-reliant transcendentalism of Emerson and Thoreau; those of the settler and farmer to the pragmatism of James and Dewey; and those of the back-trailer to the later Journals of Alcott, and the new humanism of Babbitt and More. Like Emerson, Alcott recognized that pure individualism and interminable pioneering were not enough. But Emerson lived with his new ideas, developed them, and perfected them by the pragmatic test of experience,[39] while Alcott often abandoned his ideas for the traditions of the past.

Alcott lacked utterly the pragmatic respect for experience which is perhaps the chief characteristic of the typical American, and even of the typical American transcendentalist. Like Emerson and Thoreau, Alcott followed his intuitions and explored new ideas in the "West." But unlike them, he refused to plow the wilderness of the mind. Instead, he touched it with his magic wand, commanding it to bloom. When it did not, he declared it barren.

Alcott's anti-pragmatic bias has seldom been recognized, because he often clothed his thought in the words of the later pragmatism. For instance, his early exhortations to self-reliance repeated the words "practise," "act," "do," "practical thought," and "principles of action"; and his later Journals were still demanding "instrumental action for theism," and declaring "the dread facts of the Personality." But what he called "the dread facts" were never "facts experienced individually," as were those of Emerson.[40]

Alcott has been called a proponent of "progressive education," and certainly his educational theories and practice contributed richly to the movement we know by that name. But neither his theories nor his practice were consistently "progressive"—they often became reactionary. In 1847, long after the failure of his Temple School, he attended a meeting of "The Teachers' Institute, under the supervision of Horace Mann, . . . to see what the State is doing for the rising generation."[41] His comment was typical: "The time was passed in an exhibition of methods," he complained, "with the least reference to the principles of the mind or the philosophy of culture; and the hope of improving the state of mankind by these tardy and circuitous means seemed visionary." Profoundly scornful of such base considerations as means and methods, Alcott reversed the ordinary standards of value. To him, the pragmatists seemed visionary, and the absolutists practical. Desiring to speak to this Teachers' Institute, he was informed that his "political opinions were deemed hostile to the existence of the State." Like many absolute idealists, he rejected, and found himself rejected by, the progressive pragmatists.

Alcott had ideas, and sometimes had the courage to act upon them. But he refused to modify them when they seemed impracticable, or to consider the means by which they might eventually be realized. Thus he denied the principle common to Emerson and to pragmatists: "by mutual reaction of thought and life, to make thought solid, and life wise."[42] Instead, he offered his ideas to "life," and when "life" rejected them, he himself reluctantly rejected them. A tentative frontiersman of the mind, he never sank his roots into Western soil, but returned to the genteel traditions of the conservative East.

6. WALT WHITMAN'S EIDOLON

The prophet and the bard,
Shall yet maintain themselves, in higher stages yet,
Shall mediate to the Modern, to Democracy, interpret yet to them,
God and eidolons.

And thee my soul,
Joys, ceaseless exercises, exaltations,
Thy yearning amply fed at least, prepared to meet,
Thy mates, eidolons.

Thy body permanent,
The body lurking there within thy body,
The only purport of the form thou art, the real I myself,
An image, an eidolon.

FROM THE BEGINNING Walt Whitman has been a controversial figure. If the enthusiasm which Emerson and Swinburne first felt soon gave way to doubt, the doubt of others has given way to measured appreciation. In the sixty years since his death he has been accepted as our greatest poet, in spite of the attacks of critics and the instinctive reservations of many readers.

But the controversy has become more acute and the attacks have gained in force through the discovery of startling facts concerning his actual life. And these facts have been interpreted by the theories of Freudian psychology and reinforced by inferences drawn from his poetry. Briefly, it is charged that Walt Whitman was a fake.[1] Although he wrote some fine poetry, his personality and his moral ideas were false. "Purely as a writer," Mark Van Doren concludes, "he will always loom a gigantic and beautiful figure. . . . The claims originally made for him as man and moralist promise to disappear."[2]

I shall argue that poetry and morality are not wholly separable, and I shall interpret Whitman's poetry in terms of his moral ideas. This involves a reconsideration of the recently discovered facts concerning the poet and the charges based upon them. A more favorable interpretation of these facts is suggested by Whitman's own statements concerning the purpose of his poetry. And this leads to a new definition of his moral ideas. For, above all, Whitman was a moralist:

"His purpose, the moral elevation of humanity" (an early interviewer reported), "he trusts is apparent upon every page of his book."[3]

I

It has long been known that Whitman wrote favorable reviews of his own *Leaves of Grass* and published them anonymously in contemporary newspapers and magazines. His unauthorized printing of Emerson's personal letter in the second edition of the *Leaves* is notorious. Often he deceived his own best friends concerning his literary and his financial actions. To the very end of his life he continued to accept small charities, while investing two thousand dollars in a marble mausoleum for himself in the local cemetery. No one could be sure if such a man was telling the truth. Nevertheless, the general facts of his life have seemed clear, until recently.

But in 1924 it was proved that the early chapters of John Burroughs' biography of him had actually been written by Whitman himself.[4] Therefore, the "facts" of his early life came to seem mere myths which Whitman had wished to have believed concerning himself. All his statements became suspect, and some open to absolute disproof. These suspicions and proved falsehoods were then summarized in a brilliant article by Harvey O'Higgins: "Alias Walt Whitman." "Walter" Whitman (the argument went) had actually been a weak, undistinguished young man, who later adopted the alias "Walt" in order to puff himself up to the fantastic proportions of the poet whom the public knew. These charges, in turn, were repeated in a book, *Walt Whitman's Pose*,[5] and combined with the new discovery that the "source" of Whitman's *Leaves of Grass* was an obscure novel by George Sand. Adding this new fact to the others, the critic argued that Whitman borrowed both his inspiration and his false picture of himself from a minor French novel and foisted them upon a credulous American public.

These facts are mostly true—and others besides. The Walter Whitman who lived about New York until 1855 and who copyrighted *Leaves of Grass* was certainly a different person from the "Walt" who celebrated himself in that book, for the early Walter had been something of a dandy and an aesthete—a "debonair young man from Brooklyn" who "usually wore a frock coat and a high hat, carried a small cane" and had "the lapel of his coat almost invariably ornamented with a boutonnière." But the poetic Walt described himself (in one of his own reviews) as "a rude child of the people—likes the ungenteel ways of laborers—is not prejudiced one mite against the Irish[6]—talks readily with them—talks readily with niggers—does not make a stand on being a gentleman, nor on learning nor manners."

Moreover, the young Walter had been a "good" boy with few bad habits—sometimes almost an ascetic. Throughout his life he never smoked. In his early twenties he wrote *Franklin Evans, or the Inebriate,* a novel designed "to aid the great work of reform and to rescue young men from the demon of Intemperance." And, although he later declared that he had written this novel in the Tammany Reading Room and in Pfaff's Bar, "punctuated by gin cocktails," the suspicion remains that he was originally much more of a reformer than a bohemian.

Most important, the young Walter Whitman—and even the more mature Walt of actual life—seems to have been a diffident, modest, and almost chaste individual. His friends have described him as scrupulously polite and reserved with women, and never the "sensual Walt Whitman, eating, drinking, and breeding," of his poetry. The romantic self-portrait of the young man whose life had been "jolly bodily" and who had got "six illegitimate children" has faded: no children or grandchildren have ever appeared; and if he had the alleged love affair in New Orleans, it was not, as he said, with a lady of fashion. The facts are cloudy. But it is probably true that Whitman was, as his critic charges, "neither sensual, nor rough and rugged, nor lusty, nor even very masculine"; but rather a "mother's boy," whose celebration of sex in poetry was partly an overcompensation for his repression of sex in actual experience. The Walter Whitman of Brooklyn was clearly not of the "children of Adam" whom the poet celebrated.

Finally, this Whitman described himself as a "bard," or folk poet. During the writing of the *Leaves of Grass* he experienced an "illumination," during which he gained the belief that he was to be "the prophet of democracy." But he has never been accepted as a popular poet, and his "prophecy" has often seemed bombastic. "From the time of his Great Illumination, Whitman became a poseur, always pretending to be what he was not."[7] So the indictment runs.

II

All these "facts" are true. It is quite possible to interpret Whitman as a charlatan. If you are a strict realist, this is the only possible explanation. If you are a moralist of the old school, it is the only satisfactory one. But it is also possible to interpret "Walt Whitman's pose" idealistically. The poetic "Walt" of the *Leaves of Grass* was the "eidolon" which Walter Whitman imagined for himself and which he strove to realize, first in his poetry and next in his actual life. [This ideal "Walt" was a personification of that democratic dream which Emerson had earlier described abstractly.] And this "eidolon"—this "body lurking there within thy body"—was, in the ancient language of idealism, the *real* Walt Whitman—"the real I myself." "Walt Whitman's pose" was therefore the only true reality.

But this simple idealistic explanation is complicated by the fact that the actual Walter Whitman struggled not only to realize the ideal "Walt" in his poetry but also to actualize him in his own flesh. He strove to make himself over utterly in the image of his ideal. And in this he was only partly successful. He was always bothered by stubborn discrepancies between his early, actual self and his later, ideal self. And, mistakenly, he sought to hide these discrepancies not only from the eyes of the literary public but also from the eyes of his closest friends. Therefore, the ideal Walt Whitman of the poetry has become merged with the composite Walter-Walt of actuality, until the valid imaginative "eidolon" has become suspect, because of the apparent duplicity and confusion of the actual person.

For instance, when the actual Whitman wrote anonymous reviews of *Leaves of Grass,* his purpose was clearly to describe more realistically the poetic "eidolon" which he had imagined. And he did achieve this purpose in part: the reviews make the imaginary "Walt" seem more real. The biography of his early life which he wrote for John Burroughs remains valuable as an imaginative document. But the deception practiced upon his public and upon his friends was false. Similarly, Walt's desire to monumentalize himself in marble would be justifiable if only he had not sought to swindle his disciples in the process.

Concerning his literary "plagiarism," the case is even clearer. All writers have borrowed from their predecessors, and many have rewritten old tales for new magazines. Again it is the element of deception which is bad. If Walt had not tried to cover up his literary trail with such cunning, no one would have bothered about it. If he read in George Sand's novel a generalized description of the bardic poet whom he was later to personify in detail—what of it? That is how literature is created. But his pious pretense of absolute originality and his falsification of the evidence of his literary sources are not defensible.

Most damning of all, perhaps, is Whitman's genial boast concerning his "six illegitimate children," because here the deception seems most disingenuous and the fantasy most infantile. Clearly, he was trying to cover up the fact of his own psychological abnormality and to allay the suspicion of homosexuality which was troubling John Addington Symonds and has troubled many of his later readers. But clearly this fact cannot be covered up, nor can this abnormality be denied. And it need not be, because from this psychological weakness came his poetic strength, and from this personal abnormality his extraordinarily intense imaginative power developed. If only Whitman had not stooped to subterfuge, he might have become a supremely great man, for he did succeed in so sublimating his psychological obsession that it became the means of his achieving immortality.

To put it differently, Whitman's strange power of merging himself with other people gives his poetry its unique excellence. It wholly explains and even partly justifies his attempts to deceive the public concerning his actual life, for he did, in very truth, succeed partly in making himself over, incarnating in his own flesh the ideal Walt Whitman of his dream. To a degree unequaled in literary history, he actually became what he imagined himself to be. This fact is also true.

His imaginative power of transforming himself into another person is best illustrated by his lines on a fugitive slave:

> The hounded slave that flags in the race, leans by the
>   fence, blowing, covered with sweat,
> The twinges that sting like needles his legs and neck, the
>   murderous buckshot and the bullets—
> All these I feel or am.
> I am the hounded slave, I wince at the bite of the dogs;
> Hell and despair are upon me, crack and again crack
>   the marksmen;
> I clutch the rails of the fence, my gore dribs, thinn'd
>   with the ooze of my skin;
> I fall on the weeds and stones.
> The riders spur their unwilling horses, haul close,
> Taunt my dizzy ears, and beat me violently over the
>   head with whip stocks.
> Agonies are one of my changes of garments.
> I do not ask the wounded person how he feels; I
>   myself become the wounded person;
> My hurts turn livid upon me as I lean on a cane
>   and observe.[8]

Thus he could "become" another person.

In imagination utterly, and partly in actual fact, Walter Whitman became the ideal "Walt." That he did succeed, pragmatically, in becoming the man whom he had imagined is a fact verified by countless witnesses. The same average men and common laborers to whom he appealed in his poetry actually accepted the ministrations of Walt Whitman in the flesh, were grateful to him, and remembered him throughout their lives. The soldiers whom he nursed in the hospitals of the Civil War, the workers whom he met on the streets of Manhattan, and the travelers with whom he visited upon the open road have borne witness to him. He realized his ideal wholly in his poetry. And he partly succeeded in incarnating his ideal in the flesh.

III

Walt Whitman's "pose" and his literary deceptions may thus be interpreted as a kind of "idealism"—as an attempt to realize his ideal in actuality. Progressively he struggled to reduce his stubborn, fractional flesh to spiritual unity. But if he had striven to do this only, it is doubtful whether he would have been misunderstood and attacked as he has been, for most of his attackers have themselves been moral idealists. The difficulty has been not so much the fact of his idealism as the character of the ideal which he sought to realize. Not only did the ideal "Walt" differ from, and come into conflict with, the actual Walter Whitman, but his ideal differed from and came into conflict with the genteel tradition which cultured Americans had been taught to revere.

For "Walt" Whitman personified, in poetry and in life, the American dream of popular democracy, in so far as that differed from, and came into conflict with, the genteel tradition of the American past, in which the young Walter had been reared. The conflict between Walter and "Walt" may therefore be interpreted as the conflict between two American ideals. The most bitter opponents of the poet have also been the most bitter opponents of that equalitarian dream which he sought to realize, both in life and in poetry.

Aggressively Walt Whitman announced his challenge to the genteel tradition: "I sound my barbaric yawp o'er the roofs of the world." Specifically, he attacked the polite manners of cultured society: "I wear my hat as I please indoors or out." His ideal was the very antithesis of gentility: his rudeness was purposeful. In order to counteract the polite tradition which the young Walter Whitman had personified, with its "frock coat, high hat, small cane, and boutonnière," Walt Whitman described himself as the "rude child of the people" who liked the "ungenteel ways of laborers" and who did "not make a stand on being a gentleman."

This positive defiance of the genteel tradition motivated Walt and informed every page of the *Leaves of Grass*. Was there anything which the aristocratic culture of the past called good? Walt would celebrate its opposite. Because the old tradition had expressed the very spirit of European civilization, Walt celebrated American "barbarism." Because it had praised cultural humanism and aristocracy, Walt celebrated naturalism and popular democracy. Because it had preached sexual chastity and reticence, Walt celebrated an unashamed sexuality. And, finally, because the old orthodoxy had condemned all revolt and sin as works of the devil, Walt sang the praises of revolt and sin and even of Satan himself.

Whitman's moral ideals have already been described brilliantly and analyzed clearly.[9] It remains to suggest how he formulated these ideals by conscious opposition to the genteel idealism of the past. His "consistency" derived from the consistency of the orthodox creed from which he revolted. For every thesis that it had formulated, he proclaimed the exact antithesis.

First, his ideal of America was the antithesis of Europe. Like Emerson's "American Scholar," who had rejected "the courtly muses of Europe," he called on his muse to "migrate from Greece and Ionia." He, too, praised America for its lack of "feudal" institutions and sang paeans to pioneers. He, too, roamed the continent, in fact and in imagination, from "Kanada" to California. And this wild America seemed good to him because it offered freedom from the European past and opportunity for the future. As Santayana recognized, he first of all denied the traditional culture of Europe. But also, as Santayana failed to recognize, he celebrated in its place the positive democratic dream of the new world.

This democratic dream took form in his poetry by contrast to the traditional ideal of aristocracy. Not the superior, but the average man seemed divine to him because he possessed the qualities most common to all man. Against the old ideal of selection, he set up the new ideal of equalization. Exclusiveness became the great evil. Even the animals seemed to him praiseworthy, because "not one is respectable or unhappy over the whole earth." And he named his poetry for the commonest living thing in all nature—the grass.

Even more clearly in opposition to the aristocratic idealism of the past, Whitman celebrated physical sensualism. And here, perhaps, the critical confusion has been greatest: because he praised the physical he seemed to deny the ideal. But, actually, he tried to establish a contrasting "ideal" of frank sensuality. Because sex was one of the most common, natural functions of life, and—even more—because it was *the* function which the genteel tradition had most severely repressed, he praised it most vehemently. Not his own physical "sensuality," but his intensely idealistic opposition to the old genteel orthodoxy motivated him. And in this he became most original and most "modern." In this he transcended Emerson's "gentility" and foreshadowed the naturalism of modern Americans such as Wolfe and Steinbeck.

Finally, Whitman's defiant celebration of sex led him to an equally defiant celebration of sin itself, for sex had long been synonymous with sin in the land of *The Scarlet Letter*. "I am the poet of sin," he said, "for I do not believe in sin."[10] And he went on to celebrate all the evil forms of natural life. "Newts, crawling things in slime and mud, poisons, / The barren soil, the evil men, the slag and hideous rot." In his "Rounded Catalogue Divine Complete" he praised evil, precisely because traditional orthodoxy had always excluded evil from divinity.

Logically, this led Whitman to the celebration of that personification of evil, the devil. "I am the God of revolt—deathless, sorrowful, vast," he wrote. Indeed, his celebration of Satan merely completed the series of contrasts, or antitheses, which his earlier poetry had described more concretely. If the devil embodied the spirit of revolt, Whitman's ideal America was the country of revolt. "*Resist much, obey little*," was his advice to the states. And the devil, like Whitman, loved the rude and the earthly. Had not Satan tempted Adam with the carnal sin, which "Walt" now celebrated? Whitman's pose, according to the conventional critics, was that of being the very devil of a fellow. And his morality, according to the orthodox moralists, was the morality of diabolism.

IV

There is truth in this. Just as Whitman's personal deceptions gave support to the charge that his ideal "Walt" was a mere pose, so his exaggerated attack on the genteel tradition gave support to the charge that his ideal was merely immoral. Just as he struggled, with imperfect success, to make himself over into the image of his poetic ideal and to destroy all evidences of his earlier self, so he struggled, with imperfect success, to create a wholly new ideal, in utter contrast to the old orthodoxy. If this rebellious ideal had been merely the opposite of conventional goodness, his poetry would have been false and his ideal immoral. But it was much more than this.

Walt's "eidolon" had two aspects: that of revolt, and that of reconstruction. Against the old, genteel orthodoxy he proclaimed not only a new, radical democracy but also the more universal ideal of the brotherhood of man. Against the authoritarian God of orthodox religion he celebrated not only the rebellious Satan but also the inclusive God of universal religion. In opposition to the traditional European thesis he described first the American antithesis and then the universal synthesis.

But the second, more universal aspects of Walt's poetic ideal had also been implied by the first and had developed from it: the synthesis had been suggested by the statement of the antithesis. In the "Song of Myself," he had prefaced his "barbaric yawp" by noting:

> Creeds and schools in abeyance,
> Retiring back a while sufficed at what they are,
>   but never forgotten. . . .

That is to say, he had consciously postponed his poetic consideration of the orthodox "creeds and schools." First he had celebrated "Nature without check with original energy," and then, in his later poems, the universal harmony of nature and man. It is this harmony (whether implied or explicit) which makes his poetry—and the moral idealism which informs the poetry—great.

In "Passage to India" he described symbolically the reconciliation of the European tradition and the American dream. Where his early poetry had seemed nationalistic in its opposition to the past, he now celebrated America, not as a nation, but as the latest link in the cycle of civilizations which had encircled the earth. Where formerly he had celebrated the pioneers for their physical prowess, now he celebrated them as symbols of all spiritual daring. In place of material progress, "Americanism" became the symbol of spiritual discovery. In a sense, even his American idealism now proclaimed a return to the past: first Asia, then Europe, then America, and now the return to Asia.

> Passage indeed O soul to primal thought,
> Not lands and seas alone. . . .

Against traditionalism he still revolted, praising the American pioneer spirit ("reckless, O soul, exploring"), but now he praised also "the infinite greatness of the past" as the source and the end of all striving.

In "Passage to India," also, Whitman proclaimed the reconciliation of "Nature" and "Man" in a new all-embracing nature. If he
had formerly celebrated wild nature in opposition to the genteel humanism of the past, now he criticized "this separate Nature so un-
natural." The union of the new world with the old suggested to him
the union of Nature and Man:

> He shall indeed pass the straits and conquer the mountains,
> He shall double the cape of Good Hope to some purpose,
> Nature and Man shall be disjoin'd and diffused no more,
> The true son of God shall absolutely fuse them.

Thus the poet—the true son of God—preached this new, yet old,
religion.

The inclusive religion of past and present—of old world and new—
of man and nature combined—received clearest expression in Whitman's "Chanting the Square Deific." In place of the old "trinity" of
Father, Son, and Holy Ghost, Whitman proclaimed a new "Square
Deific," which included the devil with these three. Where his early
poems had sometimes praised the devil in protest against orthodox
goodness, now he praised Satan as a part of the divine scheme. Past
and present, man and nature, goodness and evil—all were accepted
as parts of the whole. And it is suggestive that the bibles of ancient
India, to whose primal thought he proclaimed his return, had also
preached the union of these opposites.

The question remains: Did Whitman really succeed in reconciling
his contradictions? In actual life he did not entirely succeed. But in
poetic dream, perhaps, he did. If he did not always see life steadily,
he did achieve the vision of the whole which his divine "Square"
describes formally. Unlike many libertarians and democrats who
preached merely a diabolic revolt against the orthodox "God"—unlike Mark Twain, who paid despairing homage to "the Mysterious
Stranger," and unlike William Vaughan Moody, who described Satan's reconquest of the hill of heaven—Whitman deified the spirit of
revolt without proclaiming its victory or supposing the destruction
of all goodness. In his poetry he accepted all those natural energies
of "evil" which orthodoxy had denied, but he did not grant them
dominance. Rejecting equally the exclusive "goodness" of the orthodox tradition and the blind diabolism of the romantics, he
achieved wholeness.

> Thy yearning amply fed at last, prepared to meet
> Thy mates, eidolons.

In his poetry, if not in his actual life, he merged himself with his ideal opposite and became something greater than either—an interpreter not only of the democratic "eidolon" but also of the universal God.

PART III

7. THE GENTEEL TRADITION: A RE-INTERPRETATION

SOME FORTY years ago, George Santayana first named and described "The Genteel Tradition."[1] Since then many men have repeated his words:

> America is not simply a young country with an old mentality: it is a country with two mentalities, one a survival of the beliefs and standards of the fathers, the other an expression of the instincts, practices and discoveries of the younger generations. . . . The one is all aggressive enterprise; the other is all genteel tradition.[2]

The persistent popularity of his description suggests that it is essentially true. But the partisan violence which it has engendered suggests that its meaning is confused. Santayana described truly the general conflict between aristocratic tradition and democratic practice in American life and thought. But he misunderstood the historic origins of this conflict, and he misinterpreted its modern manifestations. During the last generation, the terms of the dualism have become clearer.

In naming the genteel tradition, Santayana fathered two major confusions. First, he identified this tradition with Puritanism,[3] and traced the genteel mentality to Calvinistic theology. This accentuated the confusion in general usage between "puritanism" as a state of mind, and Puritanism as a historical movement. Second, Santayana denied that the ideal opposite of the genteel tradition was really a "mentality" at all. "Instincts, practices, and discoveries," he called it, and added that "in all the higher things of the mind—in religion, in literature, in the moral emotions—it is the hereditary spirit that prevails."[4] Specifically he charged that Walt Whitman possessed nothing more than "sensations,"[5] and that William James possessed no consistent philosophy.[6] Identifying the genteel tradition with Puritan theology, he also denied that popular democracy had any clear ideal basis.

These two opinions may be disproved. The genteel tradition which Santayana named was something less—and something more—than

51

Puritanism in America. Historically, it derived only from the conservative half of the Puritan religion. And beyond Puritanism, it derived from the traditionally aristocratic culture of the Central and Southern States, as well.[7] It may be defined broadly as the traditionalist mentality in America, as that has been influenced by Puritan morality and aristocratic culture.

Historically, the genteel tradition sprang from Puritanism, but only from one half of that religion. For the Puritanism of early New England had included a liberal, and even radical, element. The most conservative theocrat recognized that "the unknown God" did not always follow the customs of traditional morality. "Moral living" was good, but "divine grace" was infinitely better. The stern realism that recognized this unpalatable truth, and the intense "piety"[8] which positively gloried in it, gave greatness to the old faith. But the narrow traditionalism and intolerant moralism which we often call puritan, resulted in its later decadence.

In opposition to the genteel tradition, this radical element of the earlier Puritanism developed into the Transcendentalism of later New England: the Transcendental idealists worshiped the unknown God with intense piety. Although Santayana called them genteel, these transcendentalists were neither traditional nor moralistic. Emerson prophesied a new America, and Whitman continued his prophecy. Even the later pragmatists stemmed from this root. The worst confusion of American thought is that which seeks to divorce the idealism of the early Puritans and the Transcendentalists from the idealism of the later democrats and pragmatists. Not only Santayana but many popular critics have furthered this interpretation. Yet Emerson did more than any other single writer to discredit the genteel tradition or orthodox morality: in him Transcendentalism became "the philosophy of democracy,"[9] and the arch enemy of conservatism. It stemmed from Puritan piety, but repudiated the authoritarian moralism of the past.

Neither the intense piety of the old Puritanism, nor the enthusiasm of the later Transcendental idealists was traditional, or "genteel." But from this point of view, the anti-transcendental morality of Hawthorne was; and the tragic vision of Melville also described the futility of the transcendental ideal. In *The Scarlet Letter* Hawthorne recognized a certain heroism in self-reliance, but emphasized its greater evil. And in *Moby Dick*, Melville described the heroism of Ahab, but also his fanatical delusion. In their later novels, both authors denounced the libertarian heresy and returned to traditional orthodoxy: although they borrowed the new techniques to describe the liberal emotions, their moral philosophy remained traditional. Therefore they illustrate the genteel tradition at its best, recognizing the beauty and the heroism of the Transcendental ideal but denouncing its romantic extravagances.

Through three centuries of American life, this genteel tradition has developed and changed. From the early Puritans to the new humanists, its champions have denounced as utopian all dreams of a new world. But from the early Puritans to the modern pragmatists, the democratic dreamers have opposed, or "transcended" this tradition.

I

Like most Americans, the early Puritans really worshiped two Gods: they worshiped an absolute and unknown God, whose will was secret and whose face was hidden; [10] but also they worshiped the God of revelation or tradition, whose will was declared in the Bible, and whose face was turned toward man. Between the great "I Am" of piety and the revealed "I Ought" of morality, they admitted no discrepancy, in theory. The few sought the grace of the hidden God, while the many obeyed literally the laws laid down. The Bible, and after the Bible, literature, revealed this God to the populace.

The narrow puritanism against which the modern mind has revolted is that traditional half of historic Puritanism which deduced inflexible moral law from Biblical revelation. What we call the genteel tradition has elevated past precept into omnipotence, and conversely, has minimized the difficult truth which Calvin taught: that divine grace may supersede traditional precept. Looking back, the modern historian can see that "the space between the revealed will and the secret will . . . was the portal through which ran the highway of intellectual development."[11] But although the greater Puritans gloried in the unknown God and kept the portal open, their gentler descendants institutionalized revelation and sought to close the gate.

Moralistic "Puritanism" and secular "humanism," therefore, both sought to interpret and to apply God's will as revealed in the Bible and the classics. They disagreed only in the supreme authority which Puritanism granted to the Bible. They agreed that "the Revival of Letters . . . prepared the World for the Reformation of Religion."[12] They both appealed to logic and human reason to interpret the Bible and the classics. They both applied their interpretations primarily to the fields of morality and human conduct. And they agreed that art (in its broadest sense) was all-important: "Perhaps we have laid bare the innermost essence of the Puritan mind when we find that its highest philosophical reach was a systematic delineation of the liberal arts."[13] The arts direct conduct, and therefore man should imitate art. "Nature is inchoate art; art is nature consummated."[14] The nature of God may never be understood, but the Book of man may be.

This all-too-human half of Puritanism reached its nadir in eighteenth-century New England when the old piety became mere complacency, and the old morality, ritual:

> Our churches turn genteel:
> Our parsons grow trim and trig,
> With wealth, wine and wig
> And their heads are covered with meal.[15]

Of the old religion, only the moral and churchly forms remained. But these forms were, and always had been, important: the new "gentility" was no "reversal" of the Puritan philosophy, as has been asserted,[16] but rather a distortion of it, through exaggeration of the formal element. The old revelation had merely become absolutely systematized.

This moralistic puritanism, on the other hand, reached its most mature development in the proverbial wisdom of Benjamin Franklin. Wholly "emancipated" from the old Puritan piety, Franklin reasserted the Puritan morality in its simplest terms: "Revelation had indeed no weight with me, as such; but I entertained an opinion, that, though certain actions might not be bad, *because* they were forbidden by it . . . ; yet probably these actions might be forbidden *because* they were bad for us."[17] Having freed himself, that is, from the dead hand of the past, he nevertheless returned to the past for wisdom.

This was valid. Tradition is good. As Stuart Sherman has pointed out,[18] "tradition" also includes the tradition of revolt, of progress, and of change. It is good, therefore, as long as it includes all the wisdom of the past, and not merely the prudential part. But when tradition excludes novelty and freedom, it becomes genteel. It denies the unknown God in the name of the God of Moses.

Franklin himself escaped this narrow traditionalism by virtue of his broad tolerance, his instinctive democracy, and his scientific spirit. But his wisdom remained partial. He emphasized the traditional morality so exclusively that he seemed to deny the religious idealism. In his phrase, "health, wealth, and wisdom" became the ideal ends of life. And this fairly translated one-half of the Puritan gospel. But the other half—"the Covenant of Grace" and the practice of piety—he omitted. The intense devotion to the unknown God which motivated Jonathan Edwards would have to wait for the advent of Transcendentalism. Then the religious ideals of "God, freedom, and immortality" would compete anew with the moralistic ideals of "health, wealth, and wisdom" for the devotion of the descendants of the Puritans. Then the mind of America would revolt against the too-narrow Puritan morality with a violence fathered by the almost forgotten Puritan piety.

II

Considered politically, of course, Transcendentalism was not necessarily a liberal philosophy. It might result either in revolt or in reaction, for "God, freedom, and immortality" were not partisan ideals. The thought of Kant, developing through Hegel, resulted eventually in a justification of the totalitarian state. Only in America did the alliance of Transcendentalism with the antislavery movement and with Western democracy produce complete liberalism.

But considered intellectually, Transcendentalism was liberalism itself. It was "the newness." It was the revolt of the younger generation against the forces of conservative tradition. It was the deification of the undiscovered. It was the worship of the unknown God.

Therefore Transcendentalism stood opposed to all forms of traditionalism. As Santayana recognized, it "embodied, in a radical form, the spirit of Protestantism as distinguished from its inherited doctrines; it was autonomous, undismayed, calmly revolutionary."[19] But this historic Transcendentalism had no new system to offer, specifically, in place of the old. Therefore it often resulted in "the dilemma of the liberated." By reaction, it sometimes caused a blind return to tradition. "Similarly in Italy, during the Renaissance, the Catholic tradition could not be banished from the intellect, since there was nothing articulate to take its place."[20] Therefore Santayana considered Transcendentalism a failure. And modern American humanists have sought to escape this frustration by a return to tradition—to religion—to authority—even to Catholicism.[21]

It is true that the negative or anti-authoritarian element of Transcendentalism gave grounds for this negative, or anti-liberal, reaction against it. If the old idealism had resulted only in emptiness and denial, the reaction of the traditional humanists would have been wholly justified. But even the hostile Santayana recognized that Walt

Whitman had developed an inarticulate democracy in place of the old moralism, and that William James had developed a more articulate pragmatism. These developments were positive and progressive. But the reactions of nineteenth-century traditionalists against "the newness" were more obvious.

By far the greatest of the latter-day puritans were two who escaped the smugness of gentility through their intense sympathy with the followers of the unknown God. Having been tempted, like Faust, with the desire for freedom, they did not imagine all apostates from traditional morality to be absolute sinners—rather they described them as the dupes of a romantic idealism. In *The Scarlet Letter* Hawthorne recognized the integrity of his transcendental heroine, even though he condemned her. And in *Moby Dick* Melville realized the magnificence of Ahab, even while describing the inevitable destruction of his romantic ideal. Although these two writers went beyond the genteel tradition to pay homage to the unknown God, they returned to tradition, arguing that men should follow a known God rather than seek a fancied perfection.

Perhaps Hawthorne was the most typical, as well as one of the greatest, writers of the genteel tradition. Born in puritan Salem, in an atmosphere of genteel poverty, he learned to revere as well as to hate his heritage. If he accepted for himself the curse of Maule, which he described in *The House of the Seven Gables,* he did not accept it blindly. In *The Scarlet Letter* he followed in imagination the alternative of individual freedom to its end, and concluded that, like Dimmesdale, it was not for him. In *The Blithedale Romance* he rejected the alternative of social liberalism. And finally, in *The Marble Faun,* his imagination sought refuge in Rome, the source of all orthodox tradition. Through the character of Hilda, who worshiped at the shrine of the Virgin Mary and became "almost a Catholic," he prophesied the return of modern Americans such as T. S. Eliot to the Catholic faith. But Hawthorne remained true to his own tradition, and ended his days in ancestral New England. Rejecting the two living religions of militant liberalism and of Roman Catholicism, he resigned himself, without hope, to his own puritan traditionalism.

Less genteel and less puritan than Hawthorne, Melville followed a less familiar path to the same end. Where Hawthorne experimented with freedom at Brook Farm and in imagination, Melville actually pursued this ideal over the seven seas. But in *Mardi* he concluded that ideal freedom was empty, and in *Pierre* that it was immoral. In *Clarel* he recorded his pilgrimage to the traditional Holy Land. And in *Billy Budd* he reaffirmed the justice of the established morality, even when it condemned a righteous man to death. With the sad eyes of a reformed romantic, he accepted as inevitable the defeat of human freedom. And like Hawthorne, he too resigned himself to fate.

Thus Transcendental liberty caused reaction: to escape the apparent emptiness following the new revolt from tradition, Hawthorne returned to the Puritan past and Melville to the stern old morality. Hawthorne even suggested that the vacuum might be filled by the Roman Catholic faith. But meanwhile other descendants of the Puritans sought to fill it instead with the rich culture of a humanistic past. If the religion of liberty seemed empty, if the religion of Puritanism was outmoded, and the religion of Rome alien, there remained the religion of human culture. This was more credible than Calvinism, and more universal than Catholicism. The immense popularity of the writings of Longfellow and Lowell bears witness to the genuine spiritual need which their gentility satisfied. If the narrow Puritan humanism had failed, the broad classical humanism might succeed.

To be exact, Puritan humanism now expanded to become classical humanism; the religion of the Bible became the religion of Books. Lowell felt this continuity when he prophesied, with characteristically heavy humor, that "the broad foreheads and the long heads will win the day at last . . . , and it will be enough if we feel as keenly as our Puritan founders did that those organs of empire may be broadened and lengthened by culture."[22] Although it is significant that he described culture as a means to empire, it is even more significant that he traced it to the Puritan past and that he made it a continuing means to salvation: "It will be enough."

As a religion, genteel humanism had two aspects, the first moralistic, the second pious (in the more modern sense of the word). The first found expression in Longfellow's famous "Psalm of Life," and second in his "The Day is Done." Although the first bore a certain resemblance to the Transcendental faith, it preached a morality not of self-reliance but of dutiful acceptance: "With a heart for any fate . . . Learn to labor and to wait." And the second preached the religion of culture, that literature has power to make life acceptable:

> . . . songs have power to quiet
> The restless pulse of care
>   And come like the benediction
> That follows after prayer.

But the purpose of both poems was religious, like the purpose of Puritan humanism. Either poetry inspires, like a psalm, or else it consoles, like a prayer. To take the place of the Puritan faith which had faded, Longfellow substituted a more humanistic piety.

For this reason, perhaps, Longfellow was greater than Lowell: where the critic merely preached the culture of the classical past, the poet made it live. He filled the spiritual emptiness which the Transcendental revolt from tradition had caused. He invoked the gods of Olympus and of Valhalla to reinforce the old Puritan God. And in a twilight realm of poetry, his fabulous heroes kept the faith. Lowell was to make clear the implications of that faith.

Like Hawthorne and Melville, Lowell had shared in the Transcendental dream. His essay on Thoreau describes this enthusiasm from the mature perspective of *My Study Windows*. There was something good in it, of course: "the Puritanism that cannot die" had produced Emerson. But there was more that was bad in it; Thoreau reflected its selfishness, its moral emptiness, and its morbid escape to nature.

Instead of this naturalism with its worship of newness, Lowell sought to substitute the solid wisdom of the human past: "What a sense of security in an old book that Time has criticised for us!" From the confusion of modern thought, he turned to the "sane and balanced" writers before Rousseau. More liberal than his follower, Irving Babbitt, he agreed that Rousseau "is as consistent as a man who admits new ideas can ever be." But his conclusion is clear: what is new cannot be consistent, and what is traditional is good. "Democracy" is good, he said, because "properly understood, it is a conservative force." And America, the child of Great Britain, is "a democracy with conservative instincts." To strengthen this hereditary conservatism the genteel descendant of the Puritans preached a religion of humanistic culture: *Among My Books*.

III

Following Lowell, a host of minor gentlemen refined the old tradition still further. Thomas Bailey Aldrich, E. C. Stedman, E. P. Whipple, and Charles Eliot Norton became so exclusively "genteel," indeed, that they hardly remained human. Were it not for their far-reaching influence—first, on the thought of the new humanists, and secondly, on popular taste—they might now be forgotten. But they helped carry the old ideas to their logical conclusions.

While this gentility was developing, the meaning of words was changing, and narrowing. For instance, "puritanism" was slowly coming to mean an exclusive, moral traditionalism. And "humanism" was coming to mean an equally exclusive cultural traditionalism. The content of "puritanism" and of "humanism" was being divided in half. Reacting against the Transcendental enthusiasm, gentility was supplanting the old gods with half-gods; soon, only the cultured would be human.

The exclusive aspect of this "new humanism" found its clearest expression in the first book of Irving Babbitt, in which the young author specifically avowed his debt to the gentle Charles Eliot Norton. In *Literature and the American College,* Babbitt outlined all his major ideas. The Renaissance humanists, he said, had taken for their motto Terence's *"humani nihil a me alienum puto,"* and had embraced everything human. But they had missed true (*i.e.,* classical) humanism because they had denied "the idea of selection," which Aristotle had first established. "Very few of the early humanists were really humane . . . Rabelais, for instance, is neither decorous nor select."[23] So the new humanist emphasized selection rather than humanity—classical culture rather than human sympathy. Rejecting the indecorous elements of the broadly humanistic past, he sought to establish a strict cultural tradition, just as the latter-day puritans had rejected the unknown God to establish a strict moral tradition.

As Santayana was to point out, this was really not humanism at all, but supernaturalism.[24] It was the degradation of one half of humanity and the deification of the other half, an attempt "to sacrifice ruthlessly one set of passions merely in order to intensify another set." That the virtuous set of passions were called "human," and were even denied the name of "passions" made little difference. Essentially this new humanism sought to reinforce a passionate conservatism by an appeal to the quasi-religious authority of classical literature. It made cultural absolutism the cloak for moral absolutism. "The new humanism" was really the old Puritan moralism in new clothes.

The virtue of this new humanism was that it recaptured some of the religious enthusiasm and logical rigor of the old Puritan theology. Unlike the urbane Lowell and the genteel Norton, Babbitt fought for his convictions against all comers, using all the weapons of the intellect. Let an opponent once admit his premises, and his conclusions were inescapable. The only way to conquer him (besides ignoring him, as many critics did) was to attack his first principles (as Santayana did). His logic was powerful.

The weakness of Babbitt's "humanism" was partly the narrowness of his moral principles, but even more the rigidity with which he applied them to literature. If his moral philosophy was authoritarian, it was nevertheless based upon a classical tradition. But his literary applications of this moral philosophy were wholly negative: he damned every important modern writer since Rousseau. Where others had been content to describe the failure of the romantic enthusiasm, he sought utterly to eradicate it. Where Hawthorne, Melville, and even Lowell, had sympathized while they condemned, Babbitt denied all human value to Romance. He insisted not only that literature should inculcate strict morality, but also that it should refrain from treating the romantic passions with sympathy. *Moby Dick* seemed to him bad because the character of Ahab lacked all self-restraint, or "decorum": that it described the self-destruction of the monomaniac hero was not enough.

Clearly, this narrow "humanism" implied "puritanism," and even a genteel censorship: it would not merely condemn all unrestrained emotion in literature but would wholly exclude it. Against this narrowness, therefore, other "humanists" objected. Paul Elmer More sought to apply Babbitt's standards with greater tolerance, although with less precision. Yvor Winters showed how even the romantic heroism of Melville's Ahab and of Hawthorne's Hester implied a traditional morality. And a recent humanist has suggested that, although Babbitt's ethical or moral criticism was usually excellent, his literary criticism was merely negative.[25]

Thus the genteel tradition which began as Puritan moralism, has returned to orthodox morality as the source of all judgment and the end of all argument. It has rejected, therefore, the Puritan piety which admitted the omnipotence of a hidden God. It has rejected the Transcendental enthusiasm which sought to discover the hidden God, even in defiance of established morality. It has rejected the naturalistic science which has called all revealed truth into question. It has rejected even that part of the humanistic tradition which gloried in the natural instincts of man. Although it has recognized the strength, and even the beauty, of the human instinct of liberty and desire for newness, it has opposed this liberalism in the name of morality and of law.

IV

If the genteel tradition is narrow, illiberal, and opposed to everything modern, why is it so strong? Santayana prophesied its death, but lived to describe its renaissance. A Marxian critic has attacked it as "fantastic," but has approved T. S. Eliot's statement that only this tradition and Marxian socialism offer living faiths to modern man.[26] In American universities, even in the untraditional West, the tradition continues to flourish. And it continues to govern popular taste, as evidenced by the best-seller lists and by the frequent outbursts of "moral" censorship by elected authorities. The genteel tradition is not dead, nor is it dying.

The reason for this vitality is suggested by the words of a hostile critic: "In the plainest, least evasive of words, gentility is conservatism. It is the moral and social orthodoxy of the bourgeois who has, so to speak, been 'refined.' "[27] But if the genteel tradition is conservatism, a fair majority of Americans are genteel; a recent poll of public opinion showed that fifty-three per cent of all American citizens consider themselves "conservative," rather than "liberal." And if the genteel tradition is "bourgeois," a majority of Americans believe that they belong to the middle class. Finally, most middle-class Americans still desire to become "refined," as well: the old cultural ideal remains popular in our political democracy.

Actually, the genteel tradition has developed from historic American beginnings, and remains widely popular today. But beyond these clear facts, the tradition also includes permanent values. It reaffirms the truth of those humanistic ideals which were preliminary, and therefore remain necessary, even to the naturalistic philosophy of a scientific age. And it reaffirms the eternal necessity of ideals, or "standards" of some sort, to every age: it challenges democratic naturalism to define its own new standards.

The old Puritan and humanistic virtues of hard work, discipline, moderation, and the rest (which Franklin formulated and which Irving Babbitt reaffirmed) can never be discarded. Emerson and Whitman did not deny them, but rather relegated them to the realm of unconscious habit, and then went on to emphasize that imagination, invention, and artistic creation are greater virtues than these. But in the process of revolt from the extreme discipline of the old morality, Transcendental self-reliance and equalitarian democracy often neglected, and often still neglect, the preliminary needs of discipline and routine. The old Puritans and the new humanists have wisely emphasized the evil consequences of this neglect.

The genteel tradition has recently found imaginative embodiment in the character of Henry Pulham, Esquire, hero of John Marquand's novel. As the personnel director of a New York advertising firm says of him: "There is something basic there."[28] Among the "idea-men" and high-pressure salesmen of the modern metropolis, this genteel and conscientious routineer remains indispensable. And the solid strength of his character emphasizes the unstable weakness of his associates'.

But when this typical Henry Pulham, Esquire, returns to his ancestral Boston to fill the niche which his father has occupied in the mahogany offices of a securities investment firm, he becomes merely genteel. He cuts himself off from the struggle of modern life to take refuge in a decadent security. He denies the potentialities of growth which have always lain dormant in his character, until what was "basic" becomes merely solid. The fundamentals of human morality which he has embodied become fundamentalism. And in him, "the great tradition" of American life forgets the principle of growth and change, and becomes merely "the genteel tradition."

To summarize: this genteel tradition of American humanism has become reactionary only when it has divorced itself from the forces of change and renewal; just as the old Puritan moralism became decadent only when divorced from the old Puritan piety. When gentlemen have sought to impose a rigidly classical culture upon a growing, democratic society; when conservatives have sought to impede the processes of democratic change; when "puritans" have denied the possibility of a more liberal morality than the old, and when "humanists" have taken refuge from the unknown God of high religion and of science in the revealed literature of the past—then the great tradition has become decadent and partial. Often has this been so. But when the old tradition has married the new idealism and merged itself in the larger life of the country, it has contributed "something basic" and indispensable, and has ceased to be "genteel."

8. SCARLET A MINUS

FROM THE first *The Scarlet Letter* has been considered a classic. It has appealed not only to the critics but to the reading public as well. The young Henry James described the feeling of mystery and terror which it aroused in his childish mind—a feeling not easily definable, but reaching to the depths of his nature. The scarlet letter has seemed the very symbol of all sin, translating into living terms the eternal problem of evil. And in 1850 the book was timely as well as timeless: it specifically suggested the nineteenth-century answer to the eternal problem. "Sin" might sometimes be noble, and "virtue" ignoble. Rousseau himself might have defined the scarlet letter as the stigma which society puts upon the natural instincts of man.

But in modern times *The Scarlet Letter* has come to seem less than perfect. Other novels, like *Anna Karenina,* have treated the same problem with a richer humanity and a greater realism. If the book remains a classic, it is of a minor order. Indeed, it now seems not quite perfect even of its own kind. Its logic is ambiguous, and its conclusion moralistic. The ambiguity is interesting, of course, and the moralizing slight, but the imperfection persists.

In one sense the very imperfection of *The Scarlet Letter* makes it classic: its ambiguity illustrates a fundamental confusion in modern thought. To the question "Was the action symbolized by the scarlet letter wholly sinful?" it suggests a variety of answers: "Yes," reply the traditional moralists; "Hester Prynne broke the Commandments." But the romantic enthusiasts answer: "No; Hester merely acted according to the deepest of human instincts." And the transcendental idealists reply: "In part; Hester truly sinned against the morality which her lover believed in, but did not sin against her own morality, because she believed in a 'higher law.' To her own self, Hester Prynne remained true."

From the perspective of a hundred years we may reconsider these three answers to the problem of evil suggested by *The Scarlet Letter*. The traditional answer remains clear, but the romantic and the idealistic have usually been confused. Perhaps the imperfection of the novel arises from Hawthorne's own confusion between his heroine's transcendental morality and mere immorality. Explicitly, he condemned Hester Prynne as immoral; but implicitly, he glorified her as courageously idealistic. And this confusion between romantic immorality and transcendental idealism has been typical of the genteel tradition in America.

I

According to the traditional moralists, Hester Prynne was truly a sinful woman. Although she sinned less than her hypocritical lover and her vengeful husband, she nevertheless sinned; and, from her sin, death and tragedy resulted. At the end of the novel, Hawthorne himself positively affirmed this interpretation:

Earlier in life, Hester had vainly imagined that she herself might be destined prophetess, but had long since recognized the impossibility that any mission of divine and mysterious truth should be confided to a woman stained with sin.

And so the traditional critics have been well justified. *The Scarlet Letter* explicitly approves the tragic punishment of Hester's sin and explicitly declares the impossibility of salvation for the sinner.

But for the traditionalists there are many kinds and degrees of sin, and *The Scarlet Letter,* like Dante's *Inferno,* describes more than one. According to the orthodox, Hester Prynne belongs with the romantic lovers of the *Inferno,* in the highest circle of Hell. For Hester sinned only through passion, but her lover through passion and concealment, and her husband through "violating, in cold blood, the sanctity of the human heart."[1] Therefore, Hester's sin was the least, and her punishment the lightest.

But Hester sinned, and, according to traditional Puritanism, this act shut her off forever from paradise. Indeed, this archetypal sin and its consequent tragedy have been taken to symbolize the eternal failure of the American dream. Hester suggests "the awakening of the mind to 'moral gloom' after its childish dreams of natural bliss are dissipated."[2] Thus her lover, standing upon the scaffold, exclaimed: "Is this not better than we dreamed of in the forest?" And Hawthorne repeated that Hester recognized the eternal justice of her own damnation. The romantic dream of natural freedom has seemed empty to the traditionalists, because sin and its punishment are eternal and immutable.

That Hester's sin was certain, and her dream of freedom impossible, traditional Catholicism has also agreed. But the Catholic critics object that Hawthorne's Puritanism denies the Christian doctrine of the forgiveness of sin. They believe that Hester expiated her evil by means of repentance and a virtuous later life: "Hester represents the repentant sinner, Dimmesdale the half-repentant sinner, and Chillingworth the unrepentant sinner."[3] Therefore, Hester individually achieved salvation, even though her sin was clear and her dream of universal freedom impossible.

But all the traditionalists agree that Hester's action was wholly sinful. That Hester herself never admitted this accusation and that Hester is never represented as acting blindly in a fit of passion and that Hester never repented of her "sin" are facts which the traditionalists overlook. Moreover, they forget that Hawthorne's condemnation of Hester's sin is never verified by Hester's own words. But of this more later.

Meanwhile, other faults in Hester's character are admitted by the traditional and the liberal alike. Even if she did not do what *she* believed to be evil, Hester nevertheless did tempt her lover to do what *he* believed to be evil and thus caused his death. And because she wished to protect her lover, she consented to a life of deception and concealment which she herself knew to be false. But for the traditional moralists neither her temptation of her lover nor her deception of him was a cardinal sin. Only her act of passion was.

Therefore Hester's passion was the fatal flaw which caused the tragedy. Either because of some womanly weakness which made her unable to resist evil, or because of some pride which made her oppose her own will to the eternal law, she did evil. Her sin was certain, the law she broke was immutable, and the human tragedy was inevitable—according to the traditional moralists.

II

But, according to the romantic enthusiasts, *The Scarlet Letter* points a very different moral. The followers of Rousseau have said that Hester did not sin at all; or that, if she did, she transformed her sin into a virtue. Did not Hawthorne himself describe the radiance of the scarlet letter, shining upon her breast like a symbol of victory? "The tendency of her fate had been to set her free. The scarlet letter was her passport into regions where other women dared not tread." Hester—if we discount Hawthorne's moralistic conclusion—never repented of her "sin" of passion, because she never recognized it as such.

In absolute contrast to the traditionalists, the romantics have described *The Scarlet Letter* as a masterpiece of "Hawthorne's immoralism."[4] Not only Hester but even the Puritan minister becomes "an amoralist and a Nietzschean."[5] "In truth," wrote Hawthorne, "nothing short of a total change of dynasty and moral code in that interior kingdom was adequate to account for the impulses now communicated to the . . . minister." But Hester alone became perfectly immoral, for "the world's law was no law for her mind." She alone dared renounce utterly the dead forms of tradition and dared follow the natural laws of her own instinctive nature to the end.

Therefore, the romantics have praised *The Scarlet Letter* for preaching *"la mystique de l'Amour."*[6] And especially the French critics, following D. H. Lawrence, have spoken of Hawthorne's "gospel of love." "Hester gave everything to love,"[7] they have repeated:

> Give all to love;
> Obey thy heart;
> Friends, kindred, days,
> Estate, good-fame,
> Plans, credit and the muse,—
> Nothing refuse.

As Emerson counseled, so Hester acted. In spite of Hawthorne's moralistic disclaimer, his heroine has seemed to renounce traditional morality and to proclaim the new morality of nature and the human heart.

Therefore, according to the romantics, the tragedy of *The Scarlet Letter* does not result from any tragic flaw in the heroine, for she is romantically without sin. It results, rather, from the intrinsic evil of society. Because the moral law imposes tyrannical restraints upon the natural instincts of man, human happiness is impossible in civilization. *The Scarlet Letter,* therefore, becomes the tragedy of perfection, in which the ideal woman is doomed to defeat by an inflexible moral tradition. Because Hester Prynne was so perfectly loyal and loving that she would never abandon her lover, she was condemned by the Puritans. Not human frailty, therefore, or any tragic imperfection of character, but only the inevitable forces of social determinism caused the disaster described by *The Scarlet Letter*—according to the romantic enthusiasts.

III

Between the orthodox belief that Hester Prynne sinned utterly and the opposite romantic belief that she did not sin at all, the transcendental idealists seek to mediate. Because they deny the authority of the traditional morality, these idealists have sometimes seemed merely romantic. But because they seek to describe a new moral law, they have also seemed moralistic. The confusion of answers to the question of evil suggested by *The Scarlet Letter* arises, in part, from a failure to understand the transcendental ideal.

With the romantics, the transcendentalists[8] agree that Hester did wisely to "give all to love." But they insist that Hester's love was neither blindly passionate nor purposeless. "What we did," Hester exclaims to her lover, "had a consecration of its own." To the transcendental, her love was not sinful because it was disloyal to her evil husband (whom she had never loved) or to the traditional morality (in which she had never believed). Rather her love was purposefully aimed at a permanent union with her lover—witness the fact that it had already endured through seven years of separation and disgrace. Hester did well to "obey her heart," because she felt no conflict between her heart and her head. She was neither romantically immoral nor blindly rebellious against society and its laws.

This element of conscious purpose distinguishes the transcendental Hester Prynne from other, merely romantic heroines. Because she did not deny "the moral law" but went beyond it to a "higher law," Hester transcended both romance and tradition. As if to emphasize this fact, Hawthorne himself declared that she "assumed a freedom of speculation which our forefathers, had they known it, would have held to be a deadlier crime than that stigmatized by the scarlet letter." Unlike her lover, she had explicitly been led "beyond the scope of generally received laws." She had consciously wished to become "the prophetess" of a more liberal morality.

According to the transcendentalists, therefore, Hester's "sin" was not that she broke the Commandments—for, in the sight of God, she had never truly been married. Nor was Hester the blameless victim of society, as the romantics believed. She had sinned in that she had deceived her lover concerning the identity of her husband. And she admitted this clearly:

> "O Arthur," cried she, "forgive me! In all things else, I have striven to be true! Truth was the one virtue to which I might have held fast, and did hold fast, through all extremity; save when thy good . . . . were put in question! Then I consented to a deception. But a lie is never good, even though death threaten on the other side."

Not traditional morality, but transcendental truth, governed the conscience of Hester Prynne. But she had a conscience, and she had sinned against it.

Indeed, Hester Prynne had "sinned," exactly *because* she put romantic "love" ahead of ideal "truth." She had done evil in allowing the "good" of her lover to outweigh the higher law. She had sacrificed her own integrity by giving absolutely everything to her loved one. For Emerson had added a transcendental postscript to his seemingly romantic poem:

> Leave all for love;
> Yet, hear me, yet
>
> . . . . .
>
> Keep thee to-day,
> To-morrow, forever,
> Free as an Arab
> Of thy beloved.
> Heartily know
> When half-gods go,
> The gods arrive.

That is to say: True love is a higher law than merely traditional morality, but, even at best, human love is "daemonic." The highest law of "celestial love" is the law of divine truth.

According to the transcendental idealists, Hester Prynne sinned in that she did not go beyond human love. In seeking to protect her lover by deception, she sinned both against her own "integrity" and against God. If she had told the whole truth in the beginning, she would have been blameless. But she lacked this perfect self-reliance.

Nevertheless, tragedy would have resulted even if Hester Prynne had been transcendentally perfect. For the transcendental ideal implies tragedy. Traditionally, tragedy results from the individual imperfection of some hero. Romantically, it results from the evil of society. But, ideally, it results from a conflict of moral standards or values. The tragedy of *The Scarlet Letter* resulted from the conflict of the orthodox morality of the minister with the transcendental morality of the heroine. For Arthur Dimmesdale, unlike Hester Prynne, did sin blindly through passion, committing an act which he felt to be wrong. And because he sinned against his own morality, he felt himself unable to grasp the freedom which Hester urged. If, on the contrary, he had conscientiously been able to flee with her to a new life on the western frontier, there would have been no tragedy. But:

"It cannot be!" answered the minister, listening as if he were called upon to realize a dream. "I am powerless to go. Wretched and sinful as I am, I have had no other thought than to drag on my earthly existence where Providence hath placed me."

To those who have never believed in it, the American dream of freedom has always seemed utopian and impossible of realization. Tragedy results from this conflict of moralities and this unbelief.

IV

According to the orthodox, Hester Prynne sinned through blind passion, and her sin caused the tragedy. According to the romantic, Hester Prynne heroically "gave all to love," and tragedy resulted from the evil of society. According to the transcendentalists, Hester Prynne sinned through deception, but tragedy resulted from the conflict of her dream of freedom with the traditional creed of her lover. Dramatically, each of these interpretations is possible: *The Scarlet Letter* is rich in suggestion. But Hawthorne the moralist sought to destroy this richness.

The Scarlet Letter achieves greatness in its dramatic, objective presentation of conflicting moralities in action: each character seems at once symbolic, yet real. But this dramatic perfection is flawed by the author's moralistic, subjective criticism of Hester Prynne. And this contradiction results from Hawthorne's apparent confusion between the romantic and the transcendental moralities. While the characters of the novel objectively act out the tragic conflict between the traditional morality and the transcendental dream, Hawthorne subjectively damns the transcendental for being romantically immoral.

Most obviously, Hawthorne imposed a moralistic "Conclusion" upon the drama which his characters had acted. But the artistic and moral falsity of this does not lie in its didacticism or in the personal intrusion of the author, for these were the literary conventions of the age. Rather it lies in the contradiction between the author's moralistic comments and the earlier words and actions of his characters. Having created living protagonists, Hawthorne sought to impose his own will and judgment upon them from the outside. Thus he described Hester as admitting her "sin" of passion and as renouncing her "selfish ends" and as seeking to "expiate" her crime. But Hester herself had never admitted to any sin other than deception and had never acted "selfishly" and had worn her scarlet letter triumphantly, rather than penitently. In his "Conclusion," therefore, Hawthorne did violence to the living character whom he had created.

His artificial and moralistic criticism is concentrated in the "Conclusion." But it also appears in other chapters of the novel. In the scene between Hester and Arthur in the forest, Hawthorne had asserted:

She had wandered, without rule or guidance, in a moral wilderness. . . . .
Shame, Despair, Solitude! These had been her teachers,—stern and wild
ones,—and they had made her strong, but taught her much amiss.

And again Hawthorne imputed "Shame" to Hester, and declared that
her "strength" was immoral.

This scene between Hester and her lover in the forests also suggests the root of Hawthorne's confusion. To the traditional moralists,
the "forest," or "wilderness," or "uncivilized Nature" was the symbolic abode of evil—the very negation of moral law. But to the romantics, wild nature had become the very symbol of freedom. In this
scene, Hawthorne explicitly condemned Hester for her wildness—
for "breathing the wild, free atmosphere of an unredeemed, unchris-
tianized, lawless region." And again he damned her "sympathy" with
"that wild, heathen Nature of the forest, never subjugated by human
law, nor illumined by higher truth." Clearly he hated moral romanticism. And this hatred would have been harmless, if his heroine
had merely been romantic, or immoral.

But Hester Prynne, as revealed in speech and in action was not romantic but transcendental. And Hawthorne failed utterly to distinguish, in his moralistic criticism, between the romantic and the transcendental. For example, he never described the "speculations" of
Hester concerning "freedom" as anything but negative, "wild," "lawless," and "heathen." All "higher truth" for him seemed to reside exclusively in traditional, "civilized" morality. But Hawthorne's contemporaries, Emerson and Thoreau, had specifically described the
"wilderness" (*Life in the Woods*) as the precondition of the new
morality of freedom; and "Nature" as the very abode of "higher
truth": all those transcendental "speculations" which Hawthorne
imputed to his heroine conceived of "Nature" as offering the opportunity for the realization of the higher moral law and for the
development of a "Christianized" society more perfectly illumined
by the divine truth.

Therefore, Hawthorne's moralistic passages never remotely admitted the possible truth of the transcendental ideal which he had
objectively described Hester Prynne as realizing. Having allowed
his imagination to create an idealistic heroine, he did not allow his
conscious mind to justify—or even to describe fairly—her ideal
morality. Rather, he damned the transcendental character whom he
had created, for being romantic and immoral. But the words and
deeds by means of which he had created her contradicted his own
moralistic criticisms.

V

In the last analysis, the greatness of *The Scarlet Letter* lies in the character of Hester Prynne. Because she dared to trust herself and to believe in the possibility of a new morality in the new world, she achieved spiritual greatness in spite of her own human weakness, in spite of the prejudices of her puritan society, and, finally, in spite of the prejudices of her creator himself. For the human weakness which made her deceive her lover in order to protect him makes her seem only the more real. The calm steadfastness with which she endures the ostracism of society makes her heroic. And the clear purpose which she follows, despite the denigrations of Hawthorne, makes her almost ideal.

Hester, almost in spite of Hawthorne, envisions the transcendental ideal of positive freedom, instead of the romantic ideal of mere escape. She urges her lover to create a new life with her in the wilderness: "Doth the universe lie within the compass of yonder town? Whither leads yonder forest track?" And she seeks to arouse him to a pragmatic idealism equal to the task: "Exchange this false life of thine for a true one! . . . . Preach! Write! Act! Do anything save to lie down and die!"

Thus Hester Prynne embodies the authentic American dream of a new life in the wilderness of the new world, and of self-reliant action to realize that ideal. In the Puritan age in which he lived, and in Hawthorne's own nineteenth century, this ideal was actually being realized in practice. Even in our modern society with its more liberal laws, Hester Prynne might hope to live happily with her lover, after winning divorce from her cruel and vengeful husband. But in every century her tragedy would still be the same. It would result from her own deception and from the conflicting moral belief of her lover. But it would not result from her own sense of guilt or shame.

In *The Scarlet Letter* alone among his novels, Hawthorne succeeded in realizing a character embodying the authentic American dream of freedom and independence in the new world. But he succeeded in realizing this ideal emotionally rather than intellectually. And, having completed the novel, he wondered at his work: "I think I have never overcome my adamant in any other instance," he said. Perhaps he added the moralistic "Conclusion" and the various criticisms of Hester, in order to placate his conscience.[9] In any case, he never permitted himself such freedom—or such greatness—again.

Where *The Scarlet Letter* described the greatness as well as the human tragedy which lies implicit in the American dream of freedom, Hawthorne's later novels describe only the romantic delusion which often vitiates it. *The Blithedale Romance* emphasizes the delusion of utopianism, and *The Marble Faun* preaches the falsity of the ideal of "nature" (Donatello). Where Hester Prynne was heroically self-reliant, Zenobia becomes pathetically deluded, and Miriam romantically blind. Hawthorne, rejecting the transcendental idealism which Hester Prynne seems to have realized almost in spite of his own "adamant," piously recanted in his "Conclusion" and took good care that his later "dark" heroines should be romantic, unsympathetic, and (comparatively) unimportant.

9. MELVILLE AND THE MEN-OF-WAR

LITTLE KNOWN in his own lifetime, Herman Melville did not become famous until after the centenary of his birth, in 1919. But from then till the centenary of his first novel, in 1946, his fame has increased a thousand fold.—Why? Perhaps his early critics were imperceptive, or his reading public stupid. Or perhaps his sudden reputation may fade in the future. But there is a better reason. Melville first became a classic after 1919, at the end of the First World War. Since 1946, the end of the Second World War, his stature has increased. Melville had the misfortune to live during the most peaceful of all the civilized centuries, but to think in terms of Armageddon. He conceived the world as a man-of-war.

Born a century too soon, Melville truly prophesied the future. But in a sense he also lived outside of time—like Taji, "eternity is in his eye." He was a prophet, not only in that he foretold the future, but also in that he proclaimed the inner reality of things. He possessed the myth-making imagination: all life became an allegory whose meaning obsessed him. But since most readers prefer simple stories to allegorical fiction, his prophecies fell flat at first. Today their meaning seems important.

That Melville prophesied disaster to a century which expected the millennium, and that he suggested the inner meaning of things to an America concerned first with their utility, are reasons enough for his greatness. But they are also reasons for his weakness. Remonstrating against the blind optimism of his contemporaries, he often exhausted himself in reaction. And searching for the undiscoverable truths of eternity, he often lost himself in speculation. In one book only did he achieve the perfect balance, suggesting the truths of eternity in terms of his own time: *Moby Dick* prophesied the ultimate failure of the American dream, without distortion or confusion. But all his other novels (including even *Billy Budd*) suffered either from the bitterness of his disillusion, or the obscurity of his thought.

That his own literary greatness was bound up with his philosophic meaning, Melville himself repeatedly implied. In *Mardi*, he announced his intention of contriving a "romance" which might, possibly, "be received for a verity." In *Moby Dick*, Ahab suggested his author's purpose to uncover "the features of that reasoning thing"

which lurks "in each event—in the living act, the undoubted deed."
And the allegorical names in *Billy Budd* are obvious.

But more explicitly, Melville included a great deal of pure theoriz-
ing in his novels. The speeches of Babbalanja in *Mardi,* Melville's
own Epilogue to *White Jacket,* his invocation to the "democratic
God" of *Moby Dick,* and the pamphlet of Plotinus Plinlimmon in
Pierre, all declare his conscious philosophic intention.

To trace the symbolic action and to analyze the explicit philosophy of Melville's novels is to make clear their author's avowed purpose and to suggest his importance in the course of American thought.
To show how this philosophic purpose contributed to the greatness of
Moby Dick is to approach literary criticism. And finally, to criticize
the implications of Melville's fiction is also to criticize the implications of the American dream itself.

I

Melville may be described as the greatest critic of the American
dream.[1] In sharp contrast to Emerson and Whitman, who enthusiastically celebrated the dream, Melville's novels suggested its dangers. But Melville was its greatest critic, because he was also most
sympathetic. In contrast to his friend, Hawthorne, who often condemned the dream with scant sympathy, Melville shared it feelingly.
But at last, his lack of any positive faith in the democratic dream
caused him to contrive his plots so as to predetermine its failure. By
so doing, it is true that he placed himself in the great tradition of
catholic Christianity. But by so doing he alienated himself from the
great tradition of protestant Christianity, which has been the chief
source of American idealism.

To put it differently, Melville was a democrat by conviction but
not by faith. He believed, that is, in the value of the American dream,
but not in its victory. In *Clarel,* he stated this position characteristically:

> Conviction is not gone
> Though faith's gone: that which shall not be
> Still ought to be.

Emphatically he put the negative first: the dream of human freedom
"shall not be," though men may be convinced of its ideal truth. And
throughout his life he denied the real possibility of the democratic
dream, even while reaffirming its desirability. By contrast, Emerson
and Whitman affirmed both its possibility and its value, while Haw-

thorne remained doubtful whether individual freedom was truly desirable in this sinful world.

In the ideal realm of values, therefore, Melville always praised democratic freedom, and criticized authoritarian compulsion. Specifically, he celebrated the natural freedom of the Polynesians, the questing spirit of Taji, the frank independence of Jack Chase, the high idealism of Pierre, the brotherly friendliness of Billy Budd, and even the instinctive democracy of Captain Ahab. And he condemned the hypocritical attempts of civilized men to reform the Polynesians, the autocratic cruelty of all men-of-war, the "arbitrary laws" which circumscribed Pierre, and the military necessity which made necessary the execution of good Billy Budd. Always Melville's heart was with the freedom-loving democrat.

But in the world of actuality, Melville increasingly counseled the acceptance of authoritarian laws, and the resignation of personal rights. Only in his early novels did he suggest that the ideal might actually be realized, praising the active Christianity of "Serenia," and in *White Jacket,* declaring that "Our Lord High Admiral will yet interpose" to right the world's wrongs. But beginning with *Moby Dick,* he emphasized the impotence and the blindness of good men. In *Pierre,* he explicitly urged his weak hero to follow "those arbitrary lines of conduct, by which the common world . . . surrounds thee for thine own good." And finally his Billy Budd—the ideally good man—voluntarily assented to his own execution for the sake of maintaining the authoritarian discipline of the world as a man-of-war. With increasing emphasis as he grew older, Melville declared the impossibility of "that which ought to be," even while reaffirming its desirability.

This sharp dualism between the ideal and the real—between the world of democratic values and the world of authority—produced the unique effects of his novels. Its first recognition resulted in the artificial allegory of *Mardi.* Its full realization heightened the tension and increased the terror of the tragedy of *Moby Dick.* In *Pierre,* it caused an absolute despair, and an inability to choose between the impossible ideal and the intolerable real. And in *Billy Budd,* it finally led to a deeply religious resignation which accepted the defeat of goodness as inevitable, and firmly rejected the American dream that something might actually be done about it.

A study of Melville's two greatest novels will suggest most clearly his final criticism of the American dream. In *Moby Dick,* his disbelief in the possibility of actually realizing it found perfect expression; this prophecy remains as eloquent and as unanswerable as any in the Old Testament. But in *Billy Budd,* Melville's writing became more didactic and less inevitable. These two novels embody in terms of living character the central problem, not only of American democracy, but of world Christianity as well.

II

Melville first expressed his criticism of the American dream explicitly in *Mardi,* speaking as: "A Voice from the Gods."

The grand error of this age . . . is the general supposition, that a very special Diabolus is abroad; whereas, the very special Diabolus has been abroad ever since Mardi [the world] began.

And the grand error of your nation . . . seems this—the conceit that Mardi is now in the last scene of the last act of her drama; and that all preceding events were ordained to bring about the catastrophe you believe to be at hand—a universal and permanent Republic.

May it please you, those who hold to these things are fools, and not wise.
. . . . .
There are many, who erewhile believed that the age of pikes and javelins was passed; that after a heady and blustering youth, old Mardi was at last settling down into a serene old age; and that the Indian summer first discovered in your land . . . was the hazy vapour emitted from its tranquil pipe. But it has not so proved. Mardi's peaces are but truces. Long absent, at last the red comets have returned. And return they must, though their periods be ages. And should Mardi endure till mountain melt into mountain, and all the isles form one table-land, yet, would it but expand the old battle-plain.

. . . In no stable democracy do all men govern themselves. Though an army be all volunteers, martial law must prevail. Delegate your power, you leagued mortals must.

But implicitly, Melville's novels had all been informed by this criticism of democracy. Because he believed that war was the one constant fact of human history, he wrote of the world as a man-of-war. And because he believed that this constant of war made it inevitable that martial law should prevail, he embodied this law in the authoritarian discipline of the ship, whose captain's orders were final. About half of his novels were set in actual men-of-war where martial law was absolute, and about half in whaling ships where authoritarian discipline prevailed in a modified form. But all his novels excepting *Pierre* suggested that the authoritarian life of the ship was the microcosm of the life of the nation, and ultimately of the world as a whole.

This setting on shipboard, with the consequent assumption that authoritarian discipline was both natural and necessary, was by all odds the most important feature of Melville's fiction. It made all his captains "leaders," or tyrants of a sort, and all his crews subservient, or impotent. The failure of democracy in Melville's thought-world was predetermined by the nature and necessities of that world. Most of Melville's best novels were set upon whaling ships rather than men-of-war, where authoritarian principles are not absolute and democracy has a chance. *Moby Dick,* of course, is the greatest of these. In the novels set upon men-of-war, democracy exists only in men's souls, but not at all in their governments. The fate of *Billy Budd* is therefore predetermined.

III

Moby Dick achieves much of its greatness by making the captain a democratic leader, who persuades his crew voluntarily to assist in the pursuit of the white whale. Indeed, the first half of the book describes the democratic drama by which Ahab, the eternal demagogue, hypnotizes the crew to do his will. That his will is romantically confused becomes apparent later: the second half of the book (divided from the first by the factual chapters on the whaling industry) describes the drama in which deluded men accomplish their own destruction. This American tragedy is motivated, first, by the weakness of the crew, and second, by the falsity of the ideal which they follow. Unlike Melville's novels in which the tyranny of the captains predetermines the tragedy, the crew of the Pequod bring disaster upon themselves; and unlike the novels (including *Pierre*) in which the naïve heroes suffer tragedy innocently, the crew of the Pequod do what they recognize to be wrong.

The peculiarly democratic nature of the tragedy of *Moby Dick* has never been fully described. Melville's invocation to the "great democratic God" is familiar, with its appeal to the "democratic dignity" of the common man; but the reason for this invocation is important: it is preceded by a long analysis of the weakness of Starbuck, and "the complete abasement of Starbuck's fortitude" before Ahab's fanaticism. Melville, in short, invoked the democratic God to excuse the weakness of democracy as embodied in its most admirable character—Starbuck. Melville's democratic sympathy would "spread a rainbow over his disastrous set of sun."

Later, the chapter on "The Quarter-Deck" derives its drama from the democratic struggle of wills between Ahab and Starbuck. Because Ahab cannot attempt his purpose without the willing help of the crew, this struggle is central. After achieving his victory, Ahab specifically proclaims: "Starbuck now is mine; cannot oppose me now, without rebellion"—the point being, of course, that democratic consent rather than martial law prevails on the Pequod. "I do not order ye; ye will it."

But after the crew of the Pequod have abdicated their democratic rights and voluntarily submitted to their leader, the drama turns upon the nature of the purpose which they all pursue. Doubtful at first, it becomes increasingly clear that this is actually evil. In the chapter on "The Forge," the crew participates in the tempering of the harpoon *"non in nomine patris, sed in nomine diaboli."* And later they jettison the scientific instruments of navigation to emphasize the blind fanaticism of the chase. The ideal of the Pequod's crew is declared to be mad, impossible, and diabolic. Attempting to reverse the eternal nature of things and to conquer evil with evil—they romantically accomplish their own damnation.

Thus the fate of the Pequod becomes a kind of prophecy of the fate of the democratic ship of state. Dedicated to a democratic God and manned by a democratic crew, sailing in search of profit, the Pequod is persuaded by an idealistic captain to give up its democratic rights in order to make total war against the forces of evil. To make the world safe for democracy, it abandons democracy; and to destroy evil, commits evil. Inevitably it sinks at last in "the final Pacific." And, as Ahab exclaims after seeing Moby Dick ram the Pequod: " 'The ship! . . . its wood could only be American!' "

Thus the tragedy of Moby Dick prophesies (in the deepest sense of the word) the tragedy of the democratic dream. Its drama makes real the two great dangers inherent in all democracy: first, the actual danger that men may abandon their freedom of their own free wills; and second, the ideal danger that they may confuse their democratic dream of freedom with the old romantic dream of absolute empire. For all historic democracies—the Roman, for instance—have perished thus: first by voluntarily accepting a Caesar, and second by seeking empire over all the evil of the earth. Thus—Melville had warned—"Romara's free eagles flew over all Mardi, and perched on the topmost diadems of the east."

In its own terms, therefore, the tragedy of *Moby Dick* is unanswerable: it is the tragedy of a weak and romantic democracy. The human weakness of its crew makes its tragedy probable, and the ideal falsity of its romantic purpose makes it inevitable. Unlike Hawthorne's *Scarlet Letter,* whose heroine was neither weak nor romantically deluded, Melville's *Moby Dick* suggests the tragedy of a weak and deluded democracy: if the American dream fails, it will fail either through the carelessness of the common people or through the confusion of its leaders. It will not fail because its freedom is inherently sinful (as Hawthorne often suggested), nor yet because its dream of goodness is wholly impossible (as Melville himself was to suggest, in *Billy Budd*).

IV

Everyone, I think—be he democrat or authoritarian, liberal or traditionalist—will agree that the tragedy of *Moby Dick* is inevitable —given the situation. With a crew as weak as that of the Pequod and a captain as strong as Ahab, with both dedicated to an impossible ideal and set in the totalitarian framework of a ship—given all this, the tragedy is inevitable. If democracy fails, this will be the manner of its failure. But many will disagree with the terms which Melville gave. If the democratic crew had been more self-reliant or the captain less strong-willed, if their purpose had been more moderate or the framework different—if the terms, that is, had been more favorable, the doom might not have been inevitable. The prophetic logic of Moby Dick does not necessarily declare the doom of all democracy. But Melville—both as he had announced himself in *Mardi,* and as he was to make more clear in *Billy Budd*—believed that it did. "Though the army be all volunteers, martial law must prevail."

Where *Moby Dick* was set on a whaling ship, *Billy Budd* was set on a man-of-war. Where the crew of the Pequod were volunteers, the crew of the Indomitable were impressed into service. Where the Pequod's crew voluntarily abdicated their democratic rights, Billy Budd lost his without a hearing. And finally, where the Pequod was an independent American vessel, the Indomitable served "his majesty, the king." The change from *Moby Dick* to *Billy Budd* was the change from a democratic America at peace to a monarchic England at war. This change was momentous.

As the story opens, Billy Budd—the natural democrat—is serving on a merchant ship: the Rights of Man. But England is at war, and on the voyage home the Rights of Man is stopped by the warship Indomitable, and Billy Budd is trans-shipped. On the Indomitable, Billy serves under an evil mate, who unjustly attacks him. In instinctive self-defense, Billy kills the mate. But because the deed occurs on the warship of a country at war, the just Captain Vere condemns Billy to death under martial law, even while recognizing his essential innocence. And Billy accepts the justice of the sentence, exclaiming before his execution: "God bless Captain Vere!" Thus the story describes the military execution of the good man, who has previously been deprived of his civil rights without his own consent.

—Unlike *Moby Dick* where the crew voluntarily abdicated their rights, and where they voluntarily embraced an evil purpose, *Billy Budd* justifies the arbitrary execution of the truly good man: "martial law must prevail."

Captain Vere carefully analyzes the case: Billy is "innocent before God" and "Nature." " 'But do these buttons that we wear attest that our allegiance is to Nature? No, to the King . . . We fight at command . . . Not so much ourselves, as martial law operating through us' " condemns Billy. And " '*for that law and the rigour of it, we are not responsible*.' "[2] Where *Moby Dick* describes the inevitable operation of natural law, *Billy Budd* describes the human operation of martial law.

The tragedy of *Moby Dick* was truly inevitable. And the tragedy of *Billy Budd* has also been called "unanswerable."[3] But there is a fundamental confusion here: natural law is truly inevitable, but human law (including all martial law) is not inevitable. Human law may always be tempered with mercy, especially when it conflicts with natural law. In justifying the execution of Billy Budd, Captain Vere (and Melville) was justifying man's destruction of his own goodness. " 'Struck dead by an angel of God,' " exclaimed Captain Vere of Billy's action: " 'Yet the angel must hang.' "—Melville, in short, was justifying the eternal crucifixion of man by man.

Even more important, Melville was denying the responsibility of man for his own legalized actions: "For that law, we are not responsible." In *Billy Budd,* Melville clearly declared that man is not responsible for the law which man himself has made. The reasons given for this were military necessity, and the absolute power of the authorities who established the law.—The individual's first duty, that is, was to his king and country—duty to God was a poor second. In this final, moral allegory, the earlier worldly advice which Melville had cynically given Pierre finally became serious wisdom: follow "those arbitrary lines of conduct, by which the world surrounds thee for thine own good." Thus Melville finally rejected the democratic principle of active independence, and the protestant belief that disobedience to human law may be obedience to God's law.

V

The problem presented in *Billy Budd* is therefore central, not only to American democratic thought, but to Christian theology as well. The solution presented by Melville is not "unanswerable," but is still orthodox and traditional. It is the solution offered by catholic[4] Christianity from the beginning. But it is a solution which protestant

Christianity has always questioned, and which American democratic thought has commonly rejected. Where orthodoxy has emphasized those words of Christ which declared the absolute dualism of the actual and the ideal: "My Kingdom is not of this world," and "Render unto Caesar . . . "; protestant democracy has emphasized the Christian counsels of active perfection. Where orthodoxy has rejected the hope that the Christian ideal may actually be realized in this world, protestant democracy has dedicated itself to the belief that it ultimately may be realized. Indeed, ideal democracy can almost be defined as the political attempt to realize the Christian ideal. Certainly, Melville so understood it. In rejecting the possibility that the American democratic dream might actively be realized in this world, Melville was merely applying the logic of orthodox Christianity to American life.

Ultimately, the question is theological, and therefore not to be answered simply; but all Melville's fictions offered vivid illustrations of it, and all suggested answers to it. This was their greatness and also their weakness.

Melville's novels remained unpopular for almost a century, partly because they contradicted both the experience and the aspiration of his century. They described war as the normal state of things to a world largely at peace. And they illustrated in different forms the defeat of democracy to a country which had recently triumphed through democracy, and was increasingly thriving under democracy. And they rejected both the "right to rebellion," which had underlain the American Revolution, and the principle of self-reliance, which underlay American pioneer expansion. Where Emerson had denounced the Fugitive Slave Law as evil, and Thoreau had preached "civil disobedience," and Whitman had counseled "resist much, obey little"; Melville denounced all rebellion, and declared that "for the law, we are not responsible." His fiction was set in a man-of-war's world.

Well—ours has become a man-of-war's world in reality: the red comets which Melville foretold have returned. Again we stand ready to "fight at command." Modern American experience has thus far justified Melville's prophecies, and modern idealism is tending toward his philosophy. We are recognizing the weaknesses of democracy and the dangers of the old individualism. We are accepting the eternal truth of the fable of *Moby Dick*.

But even in a world of war, American experience and American idealism both have questioned and qualified the authoritarian philosophy of *Billy Budd*. We have acted upon the principle that even martial law may be tempered with mercy: Lincoln actually pardoned deserters and malingerers in the Civil War, and in the World War conscientious objectors were granted democratic rights. And more broadly, American jurisprudence has actually assumed responsibility for the rigour of its law: Justice Oliver Wendell Holmes, Jr., repeatedly affirmed that not only the precedent but also the probable effect of a law should determine the Supreme Court's approval of it. —In other words, democratic principle has mitigated, and even partially triumphed over martial law, even in an America repeatedly at war—thus far Melville's pessimistic prophecies have been proved wrong.

Melville remains the greatest critic of the democratic dream. Whether our democracy ultimately triumphs and proves his forebodings false, depends in part on how well it heeds Melville's own warnings in *Moby Dick*. But the submission to traditional authority and the rejection of individual responsibility which Melville approved in *Billy Budd* runs counter both to American experience and to American idealism.

PART IV

10. THE PRAGMATIC REALIZATION

"THE CLOSE of the American frontier marked the end of an era," say the textbooks.—For three centuries the land had offered unlimited opportunities to pioneers and homesteaders. Expansion had been the rule, individualism necessary, and freedom natural. Most of the great writers of "the golden day" imagined a sure progress toward an ultimate perfection, and American experience seemed to justify their hopes. Jefferson, who believed that the free land would last for centuries, was the prophet of this America, Emerson the philosopher, and Whitman the poet. Their words gave expression to the great American dream.

Then the closing of the frontier put an end to this era of unlimited opportunities. Expansion slowed, pioneering became obsolete, and free land disappeared; independence gave way to inter-dependence, and freedom to regulation. Most of the writers of modern America have doubted the earlier dream, because their experience has not justified its high hopes. In literature, realism has replaced romanticism, and naturalism the old idealism. The later writings of Mark Twain reflected this change. From the gentle realism of Howells to the bitter naturalism of Dreiser the cleavage deepened. And the "perfect democracy" of Walt Whitman became the "perishing republic" of Robinson Jeffers. The most typical modern literature has been tragedy.

In the realm of ideas, this new era produced the philosophy of pragmatism. After the transcendental dream came "the pragmatic awakening"; after the romantic idealism, the cold philosophy of facts. The Emersonian metaphysics gave way to the scientific realism of Peirce, the radical empiricism of William James, and the instrumentalism of John Dewey: ideas had "cash value" and were true if they worked. And the high moral faith became, by reaction, the philosophy of "acquiescence."—Or so the indictment runs.

But the true meaning of this change from the old America to the new is not so simple: The popular interpretation has distorted the facts. The cleavage between the two Americas was less fundamental than it has seemed, representing no change of purpose, but only of mood—no denial of the old faith, but a new self-criticism directed toward practical effort. In particular, it can be proved that American pragmatism never preached acquiescence, but attempted to realize the old dream in terms of the new facts. The literary and philosophic realism of our own day is the logical development of the old American idealism.

This realistic philosophy developed from the earlier idealism by gradual stages. First, pragmatism attempted to define and to clarify the old ideas in terms of the new events (or "pragmata"). In his famous essay on "How To Make Our Ideas Clear," Charles Sanders Peirce announced the fundamental pragmatic principle that ideas have no meaning except as they refer to facts. But in this essay, as in all his writing, Peirce also reaffirmed the fundamental importance of ideas. In effect, he made clear the meaning of the old transcendentalism by translating its vague idealism into scientific and practical terms.

Following Peirce, William James gave expression to the second phase of American pragmatism by urging the immediate practical testing and realization of specific ideas. Developing Peirce's maxim that ideas have meaning only as they refer to facts, he narrowed this to mean that ideas can be verified only by their immediate results in "specific" situations. Therefore he rejected Peirce's philosophy of "general" ideas in favor of a philosophy of specific ideas (or "pluralism"); urging that unless ideas work individually, they are invalid. His philosophy emphasized the immediate testing of ideas (with the consequent rejection of those which do not work), and the realization of specific ideas in actual practice. It carried one step farther the pragmatic process of making clear the old idealism, and began the process of its practical realization. If it rejected those "transcendental" ideas which could not specifically be realized, it reaffirmed the value of the old faith, and possible realization of parts of it.

Finally, the "instrumentalism" of John Dewey carried the pragmatic idealism of Peirce and of James to its logical conclusion. Assuming that the old ideas had been made clear and defined in terms of facts, and assuming that the first, obvious steps toward their realization had been taken, Dewey sought to describe the general plans, or "instruments," by which those ideas might eventually and more fully be realized. He accepted the scientific idealism of Peirce, but sought to use it. And he accepted the practicalism of James, but sought to enlarge its application. Going beyond experimental verification and beyond individualistic realization, he preached the gen-

eral, or social realization of the old ideas. And, like the other pragmatists, he assumed the real existence and the practical value of the
American dream.

Because this pragmatic instrumentalism of Dewey has seemed
most completely to deny the transcendental idealism of the golden
day, its classic statement of faith is worth quoting. In the concluding
chapter of his greatest book, *Experience and Nature,* Dewey specifically reaffirmed the earlier dream, and the possibility of its partial
realization:

A mind that has opened itself to experience and that has ripened through
its discipline, . . . knows that its wishes are not final measures of the
universe. . . . But it also knows that its juvenile assumption of power is
not a dream to be wholly forgotten. . . . Fidelity to the nature to which
we belong, as parts however weak, demands that we cherish our ideals till
we have converted them into intelligence, [and] revised them in terms of
the ways and means which nature makes possible.

And so, even while accepting the limitations of experience and admitting the necessity of "revising" the earlier dream, the pragmatic
philosophy has continued the old idealism.

Pragmatism has attempted to translate the Jeffersonian idealism of
pioneer America into modern terms. Recognizing the changes and
the limitations of the modern world, it has also recognized its con-
stancies and its continuing opportunities. In the new philosophy, the
old initiative of the pioneer, the settler and the builder has become
the new initiative of the scientist, the inventor, and the organizer.
And the economy of abundance which Jefferson imagined as resulting from the productive power of the free land, the new pragmatists
have imagined as resulting from the productive power of modern
science and machinery.

"Pragmatism" (as the dictionary defines it) is "the doctrine that
the whole meaning of an idea is to be sought in its practical consequences, and that the purpose of thinking is to develop general
principles of conduct."[1] Pragmatism has interpreted the ideas and
principles of the American past in terms of the conduct which those
principles imply for the American present.

In the following pages we shall consider, first, the historical origins
of this pragmatism in the old idealism. The immediate ancestry of
the philosophy was transcendental, both American and German. It
grew up in the shadow of the earlier New England philosophy and
also avowed debt to Kant and Hegel. Personally and philosophically
Peirce and James knew the New England idealists well. Most enthusiastically of all Dewey described their influence upon his thought.

Informally, the first group of pragmatists (including Peirce, James, and Oliver Wendell Holmes, Jr.) called themselves "The Metaphysical Club." Both consciously and unconsciously, therefore—both formally and informally, pragmatism developed from transcendental idealism.

Second, and more important, we shall see that pragmatism has been idealistic in its presuppositions. But just as the pragmatists sometimes neglected the historic origins of their thought, so they often neglected the idealistic presuppositions of their logic. William James stated these clearly in his later books, and many of his disciples have reaffirmed them. All pragmatism has assumed what may be called "the fact of idealism" (that is, the primary existence of *ideas*), but then has argued that these ideas can best be defined "practically." Similarly, it has assumed the reality of *ideals* (or human purposes); but then has abandoned the language of idealism. By so doing, it has (superficially) seemed to deny its historical and logical debt to the older philosophy.

Finally, we shall follow the development of the pragmatic principles from Peirce, through James, to Dewey. In the course of this development, the transcendental dream has become naturalized in American philosophy.

I

In Cambridge, Massachusetts, forty years after the founding of "The Transcendental Club" in nearby Concord, a new group of young men banded themselves together to discuss the philosophical problems of their world. The leader, Charles Sanders Peirce, thus describes the event:

It was in the earliest seventies that a knot of us young men in Old Cambridge, calling ourselves, half ironically, half defiantly, "The Metaphysical Club"—for agnosticism was then riding its high horse, and was frowning superbly upon all metaphysics—used to meet, sometimes in my study, sometimes in that of William James.[2]

Besides Peirce and James, the group included Oliver Wendell Holmes, Jr., later justice of the Supreme Court, Chauncey Wright, philosopher, John Fiske, historian, and others scarcely less famous. In the course of their discussions, this informal "club" outlined the philosophical ideas which later became known as "pragmatism"; just as the earlier club had outlined the ideas which later became known as "transcendentalism."

Thus the later pragmatism developed in the same region as the earlier idealism and under its influence. By 1871, the old philosophy had become so respectable in New England that Emerson had been invited to lecture at Harvard. And Peirce, then a young instructor there, could describe himself as having grown up "in the neighborhood of Concord"—that is, in Cambridge. In near-by Vermont, John Dewey was also being indoctrinated with transcendentalism by Professor James Marsh. The old, but still radical ideas remained in the air—pervasive and stimulating.

More specifically, the older American transcendentalists taught and influenced the younger pragmatists, personally. Henry James, Senior, had brought his children to Cambridge to be near to Emerson and Thoreau, with whom he had long been intimate. Oliver Wendell Holmes, Senior, had formed a close friendship with Emerson, and later became his biographer. The sons of these fathers grew up under the very eyes of the great man. Young Peirce came also under the influence of Professor F. H. Hedge, an original founder of the "Transcendental Club" (originally known as "Hedge's Club"). Indirectly, through family influence, and directly, through personal contact, the older thinkers taught the younger.

But the personal statements of the chief pragmatists concerning their debt to the older men are most convincing. Peirce, whose thought was closest to theirs, was least specific, yet emphasized the influence of Emerson upon his thought. William James' many statements of indebtedness to Emerson will be described in a later chapter. And O. W. Holmes, Jr. later declared that the three greatest intellectual influences upon his life had been Plato, Emerson, and his friend William James.

But John Dewey, who has seemed farthest from transcendentalism, both personally and philosophically, has offered the greatest tribute to its influence. At a Centenary celebration in Chicago, he declared that, "thinking of Emerson as the one citizen of the New World fit to have his name uttered in the same breath with that of Plato, one may without presumption believe that even if Emerson has no system, none the less he is the prophet and herald of any system which democracy may henceforth construct and hold by."[3] And in reply to a personal inquiry, Professor Dewey wrote: "I have not changed, so far as I am aware, my views on Emerson from those expressed in the article of 1903."[4]

All this evidence suggests a genetic relationship between the transcendentalism of the nineteenth century and the pragmatism of the twentieth. And this genetic relationship is paralleled by a logical relationship less explicit but no less important.

II

Logically, the blood-relationship between modern pragmatism and the earlier idealism may be described in various ways. First, the word "idealism" has many meanings: pragmatism founded its philosophy upon what may be called "the fact of idealism," even while denying the theory of absolute idealism. Second, pragmatism evolved logically from the earlier forms of idealism: William James himself described this evolution in detail, and specifically repudiated "materialism." Third, the recent consequences of pragmatism have been idealistic: contemporary pragmatists have emphasized the "conceptual" basis of thought, and modern "physicalists" have frankly described the ideal foundations of their science.

Pragmatism has always contained this suppressed premise: it has presupposed the fact of idealism, even while it has denied the theory of absolute idealism. This premise is present also in modern science, and in most of the "scientific" philosophies of our times—in realism, naturalism, physicalism, and the rest. This fact can be proved by reference to certain explicit statements of the pragmatists and of their friends, and by analysis of their thought as a whole.

Every philosopher, whether realist or idealist, presupposes the fact of idealism. He finds himself in "the Ego-Centric Predicament"[5] because, clearly, every act of knowledge presupposes an "ego" or knower. All knowledge and science, in this sense, presupposes an "idealist." But this "self-evident fact" of idealism merely defines the means that must be employed for the ultimate solution of the problem. Meanwhile this fact may profitably be ignored, and the ultimate problem "postponed," while philosophy and science deal with more immediate problems. For the solution of these practical problems, the hypothesis of realism (that real things do exist independently of the human ego, or idealist) seems most valuable: we must deal with things on the ideal assumption that they are real, and exist independently of us.

In other words, pragmatism and realism have rejected "idealism" only in so far as idealism has refused to accept the fundamental hypothesis of modern science: that real things exist independently. Only when the idealists have exalted the "fact of idealism" into a "theory of absolute idealism" have they shut the door upon experimental science. William James himself repeatedly emphasized this fact.

In *A Pluralistic Universe*,[6] James described clearly the logical evolution of his pragmatism from the earlier forms of idealism. These forms were two: dualistic, and monistic. Catholic Christianity had always preached a dualistic idealism, sharply separating the kingdom of God from the kingdoms of this world, and urging men to renounce this world. But Protestant Christianity and many modern philosophies had preached a monistic idealism which culminated (according to James) in "post-Kantian or absolute idealism." This philosophy assumed that man and God are essentially one, and therefore that man may hope to know God in this world.

James specifically described this monistic idealism as the parent of his own "pluralism," or pragmatic realism. "The philosophy of the absolute agrees with the pluralistic philosophy . . . in that both identify human substance with divine substance." But his own "pluralism" differed from absolute idealism in that it was more "intimate" with nature: James criticized "the more absolutistic philosophers" for dwelling "on so high a level of abstraction that they never even try to come down."[7] Accepting the idealism of the older philosophy, he concerned himself with the plural differences of nature rather than with its ideal unity. Therefore he attacked "absolute idealism" only when that denied the "real" differences of things.

The true enemy of pragmatism, James emphasized, was not absolute idealism, but "cynical materialism";[8] for both pragmatism and idealism resulted from the "sympathetic temper" in man, but all materialism resulted from "the cynical temper." All idealism, that is, believed in the real existence of laws, or "ideas"; but materialism cynically disbelieved. Above all things, James valued the "will to believe."

Probably the confusion has arisen from the ambiguity of the words "materialism" and "empiricism." If "materialism" means the unintelligibility and uncontrollability of nature, then pragmatism means the opposite. But if "materialism" means the belief that mind is made of the same stuff as matter, is subject to the same ultimate laws, and therefore is able truly to know matter, then pragmatism agrees.— And so with "empiricism": originally the word meant "a practice . . . founded on mere experience, without the aid of science or a knowledge of principles; hence, ignorant and unscientific practice."[9] But James, like all modern philosophers, used "empiricism" to mean exactly the opposite: "the knowledge of principles, or scientific practice."

In his famous essay "Does Consciousness Exist?" James defined his philosophy as "pure empiricism," continuing: "The conception which I am defending does little more than consistently carry out the 'pragmatic' method which . . . [Locke and Berkeley] were the first to use." And he paraphrased Berkeley "that what common sense means by realities is exactly what the philosopher means by ideas."[10] Clearly, therefore, his "empiricism" was merely the earlier idealism redefined in terms of experience and concrete reality.

Even more clearly, the "physicalist" disciples of William James have emphasized the idealistic presuppositions of pragmatism. Answering James' earlier question, "Does Consciousness Exist?" Professor Boring has described: *The Physical Dimensions of Consciousness*. The old dualism of the knower and the thing known "will ultimately be abandoned," he declares; and "consciousness will ultimately be measured in physical dimensions." But the modern "physicalist" can affirm this only because he has first defined "physical reality" as "the conceptual system that yields the most orderly view of nature."[11] In other words, the followers of James have declared that all ideas may ultimately be described in terms of physical science, because physical science itself is ideal. Therefore the new "physicalist" differs from the old "idealist" only in that he believes that the realistic language of physics is proving more clear, more accurate and more useful than the vague language of "idealism." Indeed, modern physics itself is not "materialistic": "Only the naïve scientist believes that science espouses observation and rejects speculation. . . . The valid dichotomy lies between useful hypothesis and dangerous speculation."[12]

Finally, the chief contemporary exponent of "pragmatism," as such, has called his system "conceptual." Tracing his thought behind James to Peirce, Professor C. I. Lewis has described all empiricism as ideal: "Experience must be capable of conceptual interpretation— it could not conceivably be otherwise."[13] Describing the facts of idealism in new ways, the modern pragmatists have increasingly emphasized the ideal basis of their thought. Whether realists, naturalists, physicalists—they have sought to define ideas and ideals in terms of actual practices.

III

Peirce, James and Dewey: these are the great names of modern American philosophy. For practical purposes the writings of these men constitute "pragmatism." In later chapters, we shall consider their ideas in some detail; here, we may summarize the "pragmatic" principles which they developed from the old idealism.

First in time as well as in logic, Peirce was also the most "idealistic"[14] of the group. And the distinctive feature of his thought was its doctrine of absolute novelty, or indeterminism. This belief that "all things are possible" characterized, to a lesser extent, all American transcendentalism and pragmatism and found verification both in pioneer experience and in scientific practice. Like Emerson, Peirce insisted on the genuinely creative power of intuitive "Reason." But unlike Emerson, Peirce described this "Reason" scientifically, as the logic of making hypotheses, and emphasized the importance of verifying, or realizing these intuitive hypotheses in experience. In contrast to traditional science and classical philosophy he celebrated the genuine possibility of the discovery and the realization of new ideas in the modern world.

Where Peirce rejected "idealism," he used the adjectives "mere," or "absolute." He opposed only that formal idealism which excluded the possibility of genuine chance, and newness. Like Emerson, he disbelieved in systems, whether ideal, or practical; and like James, he rejected the "block-universe," whether the "blocks" were ideal or material. But then Peirce, the realist, went beyond transcendental idealism to make clear that ideas and materials alike have a "real" existence outside men's minds: "ideas" are also the patterns and relations and directions of "things" in the world of reality. And so Peirce's philosophy may equally well be described as "objective idealism" or as "logical realism." It sought to naturalize logical ideas.

Like Peirce, and like Emerson before him, William James proclaimed the radical newness of life, and its infinite opportunities. To Santayana,[15] this spontaneity seemed his most striking characteristic, and the mainspring of his revolt from the genteel tradition. But it had also been the distinguishing characteristic of all American transcendentalism before him. And (as Santayana himself recognized) this "pragmatic" spontaneity was "a thousand times more idealistic than academic idealism, which is often simply a way of whitewashing and adoring things as they are."[16] Actually, therefore, the pragmatism of James revolted against the genteel tradition by means of a "spontaneous" idealism.

But James, rebelling from the genteel tradition and distrustful of all its shibboleths, hated the word "idealism." His philosophy would be empirical and realistic. And so he attacked the "block-universe" of idealism, as if all ideals were necessarily inflexible. And he attacked the "general ideas" of Peirce, as if all general ideas were necessarily unreal. By emphasizing the "practical" and the "particular" so exclusively, he alienated many of his natural philosophic allies. Pragmatism became misinterpreted as blind materialism, the gospel of opportunity as the gospel of opportunism, and the old

American dream as the doctrine of manifest destiny. But through this babel of confusion and recrimination, James and the other pragmatists continued their task of testing, and practising, and partially realizing these new ideas.

Near the end of his life, William James defined his pragmatic faith in progress by opposition to the pessimism of "the modern temper." Specifically, he remonstrated with Henry Adams, whose "education" had just ended in despair. Accepting the "ultimate" fate of man as obvious, James nevertheless reaffirmed his belief in man's relative perfectability. Remonstrating with Adams, he declared that the second law of thermodynamics is wholly irrelevant to human history, "save that it sets a terminus—for history is the course of things before that terminus. . . . Though the *ultimate* state of the universe may be its vital and physical extinction, there is nothing in physics to interfere with the hypothesis that the penultimate state might be the millennium."[17]

To the partial achievement of this "millennium" by means of a practical idealism, John Dewey addressed his thought. Drawing his inspiration from Emerson and Peirce as well as from James, he reaffirmed their faith and their logic, but translated it into contemporary terms. And more than any pragmatic philosopher, he made clear the actual implications of the ideal "American dream."

What distinguishes the pragmatism of John Dewey from that of his predecessors is its combination of the militant Americanism of an earlier era with the democratic realism of the twentieth century. Unlike Peirce and James, who considered pragmatism a branch of European philosophy, Dewey emphasized its relation to the new world. He described its position on "the American Intellectual Frontier."[18] Emphasizing the real "newness" of "The New World," he proclaimed the coming-of-age of Emerson's American Scholar: "We are no longer a colony of any European nation nor of them all collectively. We are a new body and a new spirit in the world." Thus he integrated the pioneer American faith in opportunity, the transcendental doctrine of novelty, and the pragmatic concern for the realization of that opportunity and novelty.

But in contrast to James, whose "pluralism" continued the individualism of the nineteenth century, Dewey believed that a pragmatic realization of the American dream could only be achieved by concerted social effort. "Bacon," he affirmed, "did not exaggerate the control of nature to be obtained from the study of nature. But he enormously underestimated that inertia of social forces which would resist free application of the new power to the relief and betterment of the human estate."[19] Therefore, he argued, the main concern of pragmatism should be with social, not individual forces. It should deal with general, not specific, ideas. Like Peirce, he praised rigorous logic. But unlike Peirce, he insisted upon the direct application of that logic. For him, philosophy was "an intellectualized wish, an aspiration subjected to rational discriminations and tests, a social hope reduced to a working program of action."[20]

Thus the first concern of the pragmatism of Peirce, James and Dewey has been with newness, spontaneity, and opportunity. Their first enemy has been traditionalism: "Legalism . . . is the anti-pragmatic 'made' which hinders and perverts our pragmatic makings."[21] Like the transcendental idealists, all the pragmatists have emphasized the genuinely creative power of intellectual ideas. Only secondarily have they concerned themselves, in different ways, with the clarification, the verification, and the active realization of these ideas. The ideal, the "intellectualized wish," the "aspiration" has always come first.—After the transcendental dream, the pragmatic realization.

11. CHARLES SANDERS PEIRCE:
PRAGMATIC TRANSCENDENTALIST

ASK THE average college graduate who Charles Sanders Peirce was and, if he can answer at all, he will say: "the father of pragmatism." Peirce profoundly influenced William James, Josiah Royce, and John Dewey. Professional philosophers are more apt to remember his technical excellence, calling him "America's greatest logician." He was "the most original and versatile" of American philosophers, and the possessor of a "seminal mind."[1]—All these things are true. But an important aspect of Peirce's thought has been overlooked. He continued and developed the old ideas of transcendentalism. Before being a pragmatist, Peirce was an ardent idealist.

Often the break between transcendental idealism and pragmatic naturalism has seemed absolute. William James emphasized the practical aspect of thought so persuasively that pragmatism even came to be interpreted as the gospel of material success. Although this was a mistaken interpretation, there was some reason for it. But Peirce's thought could never have been called materialistic by any stretch of the imagination. As he said, Kant's terms *"praktisch* and *pragmatisch* were as far apart as the two poles."[2] Completely opposed to practical materialism, Peirce developed a pragmatic or experimental idealism.

Technically and consciously, Peirce developed this philosophy from Kant and Hegel. But naturally and often unconsciously, he developed it from the native transcendentalism of Emerson and Thoreau. In a preface to one of his most important papers, he wrote half-humorously:

> I was born and reared in the neighborhood of Concord—I mean in Cambridge—at the time when Emerson, Hedge, and their friends were disseminating ideas. . . . The atmosphere of Cambridge held many an antiseptic against Concord transcendentalism; and I am not conscious of having contracted any of that virus. Nevertheless, it is probable that some cultured bacilli, some benignant form of the disease was implanted in my soul, unawares, and that now, after long incubation, it comes to the surface, modified by mathematical conceptions and by training in physical investigations.[3]

Without attempting to differentiate sharply between the philosophic transcendentalism of Kant and the literary variety of Emerson, I would emphasize Peirce's debt to his American predecessors.

The influence of Emerson appears most concretely—if least attractively—in Peirce's conduct of life. The son of a famous Harvard professor, he was brought up quite literally in the neighborhood of Concord. In the households of such men as Henry James, Senior, and Professor Frederic Henry Hedge, he heard much talk of transcendentalism. In the year 1870–71, he lectured in the same Harvard course of philosophy with Emerson. Thereafter he seems to have practised Emerson's self-reliance without Emerson's self-restraint. Escaping from the narrowness of Cambridge society, he deserted his Cambridge wife and eventually married a French woman. He spent the last years of his life in ostracism and loneliness on a Pennsylvania farm. His self-willed independence of life exaggerated and distorted his originality of thought. But during his lifetime society took vengeance upon him for his self-will. After his death his ideas, more disciplined than his actions, grew in stature and multiplied in influence.

In the realm of the mind, Peirce was neighbor to Emerson also. Particularly when he most disagreed with the pragmatism of his friend William James, he most completely agreed with the transcendentalism of Concord. Unlike James, he believed that ideas were preliminary to actions. As a platonic realist he opposed all forms of nominalism, valuing the general above the particular. Emphatically he considered himself a monist, rather than pluralist. In these fundamentals he agreed with Emerson, and in most of them he disagreed with James.

Even when Peirce foreshadowed the distinctive ideas of pragmatism, he often developed and translated the intuitions of Emerson's transcendentalism. Action, he argued, is essential to thought, and to man thinking. *Vice versa,* thought influences action; intelligence is creative. And most important, America's "greatest logician" argued that thought need not be conscious and formal. He valued instinctive insights as the source of all intellection, and translated the Emersonian "intuitions" into the "hypotheses" of modern science. Just as thought realizes itself in action, so unconscious intuition realizes itself in conscious thought. Thus the "anti-intellectualism" of the transcendental philosophy became one of the foundations of the new pragmatism.

Finally, Peirce developed the transcendental idea of morality in new ways. He opposed equally religious absolutism and pragmatic humanism. He believed in the power of the human will to direct man's destiny; but he thought that progress would best be achieved, not by fighting against evil but by developing human intelligence.

Therefore he took issue with William James in the name of pure science. While accepting humanistic morality as a starting point, he denied its final authority. He interpreted self-reliance in terms of scientific open-mindedness. He accepted as his ultimate ideal the discovery and realization of the unknown laws of an impersonal God, rather than obedience to the laws of a God already revealed. Where James preached morality, Peirce preached science.

The thought of Charles Sanders Peirce bridges the gap between the nineteenth century and the twentieth. He translated the vague idealism of our romantic pioneer period into the scientific realism of modern America. He remained true to the spirit, and sometimes even to the letter, of the old philosophy; but he helped mightily to create the new. To compare his thought with historic transcendentalism on the one hand, and with modern pragmatism on the other, may help to make ideas clear. Even though he did not consciously derive from Emerson, and even though he repudiated much of William James, these two were his nearest of philosophic kin.

I

Peirce was an idealist in almost every sense of the word. William James, it is true, believed in the supremacy of moral ideals, but he denied the supremacy of intellectual ideas, and even their real existence. Peirce argued long and earnestly with him on this point. In the beginning he had described pragmatism as a theory of "How to Make Our Ideas Clear," by relating them to their practical consequences in action. But James had repeatedly emphasized the practical consequences, to the neglect of the ideas. In 1902, Peirce remonstrated forcefully with his friend:

Pragmatism is correct doctrine only in so far as it is recognized that material action is the mere husk of ideas. The brute element exists, and must not be explained away, as Hegel seeks to do. But the end of thought is action, only in so far as the end of action is another thought.[4]

James would not agree, and would not "correct" his doctrine. And so Peirce publicly disowned the new pragmatism of James, coining the term "pragmaticism" to describe his original variety of idealism.[5] "If pragmaticism really made Doing the Be-all and End-all of life, that would be its death. For to say that we live for the mere sake of action, regardless of the thought it carries out, would be to say that there is no such thing as rational purport."[6]

Peirce, then, agreed with the transcendentalists in preaching the superiority of ideas to actions—a doctrine derived directly from Kant and Hegel. But where the Germans had denied the reality of the brute element altogether, Emerson had explained it as the necessary preliminary to thought. "The preamble of thought, the transition through which it passes from the unconscious to the conscious, is action. Only so much do I know as I have lived."[7] Peirce now formulated this pragmatic modification of German transcendentalism in logical language. But James chose, consciously, to emphasize the practical, even at the danger of confusing it with the materialistic. Pointing to this danger, Peirce reaffirmed his idealism.

Moreover, Peirce emphatically opposed the "selfishness" toward which the pragmatic materialism of James was tending. Like Emerson, he reverenced abstract ideas because they transcended the personal and the particular: they denied all forms of privilege. In his "Divinity School Address," Emerson had attacked the idea of the "personality" of God as too narrow and limiting. In his *Varieties of Religious Experience*, James, in turn, attacked Emerson's "worship of mere abstract laws," as vague and unhuman. But Peirce rejected James's view and defended Emerson's. Speaking to a Cambridge audience which included James, he denounced that philosopher's concern with "vitally important topics":

For the only vitally important matter is *my* concern, business, and duty— or yours. Now you and I—what are we? Mere cells of the social organism. Our deepest sentiment pronounces the verdict of our own insignificance. Psychological analysis shows that there is nothing which distinguishes my personal identity except my faults and my limitations. . . . To pursue "topics of vital importance" as the first and best . . . can only lead . . . to what is called, I hope not justly, Americanism, the worship of business. . . .[8]

Impersonal ideas and abstract laws therefore seemed all-important to Peirce. But impersonality and abstraction need not keep ideas from being useful. Active life can be lived "according to principle." The architect's blueprint is abstract, but can be copied repeatedly in the world of materials. At the end of *Walden,* Thoreau had written: "If you have built castles in the air, your work need not be lost. That is where they should be. Now put the foundations under them." Peirce enlarged upon the idea:

People who build castles in the air do not, for the most part, accomplish much, . . . but every man who does accomplish great things is given to building elaborate castles in the air and then painfully copying them on solid ground. Indeed, the whole business of ratiocination, and all that makes us intellectual beings, is performed in imagination. Vigorous men are wont to hold mere imagination in contempt; and in that they would be right if there were such a thing. . . . Mere imagination would indeed be mere trifling; only no imagination is *mere*. "More than all that is in thy custody, watch over thy phantasy," said Solomon, "For out of it are the issues of life."[9]

Thus Peirce developed and explained the idealism of Emerson and Thoreau, and like them, refused to rest in "mere" idealism. Ideas, he urged, were superior to actions, but ideas could be made clear and realized only by means of actions. In the last analysis the two were inseparable: just as no imagination was merely ideal, so no action was merely physical. What Peirce opposed was the separation of individual actions from the general pattern of social activity as a whole. A single act, he believed, has meaning only as it contributes to the moral habits of the individual or to the laws of the social group. Therefore no truth can be tested by the success of any particular individual. All that Peirce meant by an "idea" was a general habit or pattern of action. Where he most disagreed with James was in his emphasis upon the general pattern as opposed to the particular act.

Even when James fathered pragmatism upon Peirce, he substituted a different idea for the original: "I should prefer," he wrote, "to express Peirce's principle by saying that the effective meaning of any philosophic proposition can always be brought down to some particular consequence, . . . the point lying rather in the fact that the experience must be particular, than in the fact that it must be active."[10] But Peirce's principle had been as different from this as white from black. "The pragmaticist maxim says nothing of single experiments or of single experimental phenomena," he replied, "but only speaks of *general kinds* of experimental phenomena."[11] And these "general kinds" of phenomena corresponded to the general ideas of the mind.

Because Peirce's practical idealism identified abstract ideas, or laws, with general modes of action, it stood at the crossroads of American thought. Emerson and Thoreau had suggested this identification. Peirce formulated the idea as "pragmatism." James tried to change it. But John Dewey and contemporary pragmatists, such as Sidney Hook and C. I. Lewis, have returned to the thought of Peirce.

Developing Peirce's idea, Dewey has suggested the final fusion of transcendental idealism and scientific pragmatism. "Insistence upon ever growing continuity, or generality of ways of action," he wrote, "differentiates the pragmatism of Peirce, from that of James. . . . To Peirce habits of reasonable action, or general modes of action, were the end of knowledge. . . . Knowledge tends to produce ways of action, and these ways of acting are immensely more important than is any particular result effected by the action."[12] The American hankering after practical results is a form of materialism, misnamed pragmatism. The American attempt to practise the principle of experimental liberalism is the form of idealism originally, and justly, named pragmatism.

But this idealism is experimental, and realistic. It always attempts to clarify its ideas by experiment and to realize them by action. It conceives of ideas as necessarily deriving from experience and returning to it. Indeed, mind and matter seem continuous to it, and not separate; neither can exist without the other. Emerson wrote, "words and deeds are indifferent modes of the divine energy." That Peirce actually did develop his scientific idealism partly from the Concord transcendentalism is suggested by the fact that he referred to Emerson in introducing his scientific paper on "The Law of Mind," in which he proclaimed his monism.

The world is *one*, Peirce argued, because all parts of it are continuous. "Consider a gob of protoplasm, say an amoeba or a slime-mould." This "matter" is capable of taking the impress of habit, and of reacting in certain ways not essentially different from those of an intellectual organism. "What we call matter," he concluded, "is not completely dead, but is merely hidebound with habits."[13] Therefore "the one intelligible theory of the universe is that of objective idealism, that matter is effete mind, inveterate habits becoming physical laws."[14]

Because mind is not separate from matter, it is capable of remaking the effete materials according to the ideal pattern. So Emerson's "orphic poet" had urged: "Nature is not fixed but fluid. Spirit alters, moulds, makes it. The immobility or bruteness of nature is the absence of spirit. . . . Build therefore your own world." Peirce translated Emerson's "spirit" into "Reason," and identified the individual's "own" world with that of the Over Soul, or the evolutionary God. But his ultimate ideal was much the same:

> The creation of the universe, which did not take place during a certain busy week in the year 4004 B.C., but is going on today and never will be done, is the very development of Reason. . . . Under this conception, the ideal of conduct will be to execute our little function in the operation of the creation by giving a hand toward rendering the world more reasonable.[15]

The pragmatist was modest where the transcendentalist had been magniloquent, but both argued the existence of an ideal which the individual can help to realize by means of intelligent action.

II

Opposing Kant and Hegel, and agreeing with Emerson, Peirce emphasized the pragmatic necessity of action to the philosopher. But going beyond Emerson, he emphasized also the necessity of cold, abstract, logical thought. Himself a consummate logician, he could hardly have done otherwise. But this "logic" of his was new, and strange. In opposition to the old, narrow, traditional logic, Peirce became even more violent than Emerson had ever been.

Traditional logic had recognized only two types of reasoning: deduction and induction. To these Peirce, the great originator, added a third: "The three main classes of logical inference are Deduction, Induction, and Hypothesis. These correspond to three chief modes of action of the human soul."[16] Later he devoted himself to this new logic of hypothesis. But first he paid his ironic respects to the traditional logic of deduction:

In deduction the mind is under the dominion of a habit or association, by virtue of which a general idea suggests in each case a corresponding reaction. . . . That is the way the hind legs of a frog, separated from the rest of the body, reason, when you pinch them. It is the lowest form of psychical manifestation.[17]

Deductive reasoning by the hind legs of a frog!—Romantic anti-intellectualism could hardly have gone farther. But it was all part of his philosophy: deductive logic, *separated from living thought,* is valueless. Peirce could even refer to Euclid as "that eminently bad reasoner."[18]

Having thus disposed of the merely traditional logic, Peirce went on to the new. Time after time, he sought to describe the logic of making hypotheses. Time after time he failed. But in his failures he achieved more than most men in their successes. For by "hypothesis" he meant "the whole logic of science," including much of pragmatism, transcendentalism, positivism, and many other cross currents of modern thought.

First he coined new words to describe this "logic of hypothesis," calling it alternatively "abduction" and "retroduction": "Abduction is the process of forming an explanatory hypothesis." Then he suggested its supreme importance: "It is the only logical operation which introduces any new idea."[19]

The American transcendentalists had opposed "logic," because it excluded the faculties of "imagination" and "originality." Peirce now

sought to enlarge logic to include these very faculties. In this attempt he was driven to explore the frontiers between conscious and unconscious thought. Groping in this dim borderland, he stumbled upon clues suggesting inner relations between science, literature, and logic. Needless to say, he could do no more than describe these clues tentatively. But suggestions may be more valuable than linked logic.

Much of the creative power of Peirce's thought lies in his recognition of the instinctive quality of what men call "reason." As opposed to traditional logic, Peirce's "reason" is instinct, corrected by experience and by criticism, resulting in abduction, or the power of making valid hypotheses. And "if you consider carefully the question of pragmatism, you will see that it is nothing else than the question of the logic of abduction."[20]

If the eighteenth century had been "the age of reason," the nineteenth became "the age of reason redefined." Following Kant, the romantic writers contrasted the intuitive "Reason" with the mechanical "understanding." What had been a regulative principle in the first "age of reason" became a creative principle in the second. But most romantic writers, like Coleridge, defined this new "Reason" merely as religious insight, separating it from the phenomenal world. Sometimes Emerson followed their examples, but sometimes also he naturalized "Reason," by identifying it with animal "instinct."[21] Peirce took the final step, consistently identifying this transcendental "Reason" with natural instinct and declaring it to be the basis of all scientific and pragmatic thought.

> This Faculty is of the general nature of Instinct, resembling the instincts of the animals in . . . its directing us as if we were in possession of facts entirely beyond the reach of our senses. . . .
>
> If you ask an investigator why he does not try this or that wild theory, he will say, "It does not seem *reasonable*." It is curious that we seldom use this word where the strict logic of our procedure is clearly seen. . . . We call that opinion reasonable whose only support is instinct.[22]

Thus transcendental "Reason" became the basis of the pragmatic logic of science.

But Peirce sought more than scientific knowledge. Rather he sought to formulate the rules of "our instinctive logic."[23] This led him to define pragmatism. For experimental action not only corrects our external knowledge but also leads the mind back to the internal springs of thought. "It is in action that logical energy returns to the uncontrolled and uncriticizable parts of the mind."[24] Peirce therefore sought to describe the pragmatic training of the instinctive mind.

Thus abstract logic, of which he was an acknowledged master, at last led him back to the springs of imagination. First he discarded deduction, when divorced from creative thought. Next he welcomed action, not merely as a corrective to abstract thought but also as a stimulant to the creation of hypotheses. And finally he celebrated the subconscious mind, disciplined by action and by criticism, as the source of all science, philosophy, and literature.

III

Perhaps the key-word in Peirce's writing is "secular." He used this in an unusual sense, suggesting the synonyms "cosmic," "public," and "long-term."[25] Thus he exactly reproduced Emerson's use of the term to describe "periods in which mortal lifetime is lost."[26] Both men chose the word to suggest a paradox. In the sense of "long-term" or "cyclical," "secular" implies opposition to the short-term or practical humanism of James and Schiller, while in the sense of "anti-clerical," it implies opposition to the "eternal" absolutism of traditional religion. Against the immediately practical, Peirce opposed, not a religious absolutism but a temporal idealism.

Peirce described the "real" as that which is to be.[27] But, as we have seen, he did not believe that this future reality was yet created. Therefore he opposed Royce's theory of "absolute pragmatism" and in its stead substituted a theory of "evolutionary love." Although no absolute ideal yet exists, man should seek to make the world "more reasonable" by working to realize the long-term tendencies of history. More often than not, this ideal lead him to oppose the practical tendencies of his own time, but in the long run this should prove the most "practical" course of all.

Specifically, Peirce's ideal of secular or evolutionary love involved a transcendental morality, in opposition to the humanistic morality of William James. "As darkness is merely the defect of light, so hatred and evil are mere imperfect stages of . . . love and loveliness,"[28] he wrote. He opposed this theory to that of William James but consciously derived it from the writings of William James's father: "Henry James, the Swedenborgian . . . [who] discloses for the problem of evil its everlasting solution."[29] Thus again, he developed the idealism of the predecessors of James rather than the practicalism of his followers.

It is interesting to go behind transcendentalism to trace the development of this non-humanistic morality in American thought. Before Emerson, Edwards had preached that man cannot be saved by "works," or particular attempts to fight against human evil, but only by divine "election" as evidenced by the individual's "love of God."[30] Although this preaching seemed to deny the value of human volition and action, making religious love the end of life, actually it often "converted" men from an obedience to worldly authority to a reliance upon the God within them. Even if these converts did not actively fight against evil or strive directly to reform society, they "bore witness" to their own illumination and acted independently of society.

Where Edwards had preached that only a few may be "elected" for salvation, Emerson believed that every man could be saved by planting himself "indomitably on his instincts." He translated the "love of God" or "inner light" into man's "instincts" in order to imply the presence of the divine in every individual. But like Edwards, Emerson preached that man should not fight against external evil but rather should perfect his own soul. In his essay "New England Reformers," he opposed salvation by works as a partial and negative doctrine; the reformer perishes in his attempt to clear away past rubbish. Instead he preached self- or God-reliance, and Thoreau illustrated the idea in practice. Although these men held aloof from active social reform, they preached an active individual "life according to principle" rather than obedience to worldly authority. Social evil would gradually disappear, they believed, if each individual would remain true to himself and rely upon the God within him.

Like Emerson, Peirce believed that human evil was not a positive force but merely a defect of divine love. Therefore he also opposed a merely humanistic morality, preaching non-resistance to evil and quoting John's Gospel: "God sent not his son into the world to judge the world; but that the world through him should be saved."[31] More specifically than Edwards or Emerson, he preached the active practice of "evolutionary love" and identified this with the spirit of science. First, he made clear that humanistic morality was highly necessary as a preliminary—calling it "the folklore of right conduct."[32] But then he pointed out that it involved "an element which can become bad"—namely, a conservatism which will oppose all free inquiry. Therefore, "the whole moral weight of such a [conservative] community will be cast against science." The votaries of science, refusing to accept orthodox morality as final, must "surrender themselves at discretion to experimental inquiry, in advance of knowing what its decisions may be."[33] Therefore, the self-reliant scientist will deny the final authority of humanistic or conservative morality and will continue his free inquiry for—as Edwards would have phrased it—the glory of God.

In Edwards the old transcendental doctrine had been theological, or miraculous. God elected men either to good or to evil, arbitrarily. The mark of the good man was disinterested love—"the love of Being in general";[34] and no interested practice of morality toward particular beings could make men "good." In Emerson, this transcendental doctrine became more secular or ethical. Men might achieve goodness by following the instinctive God within them, in opposition to the dictates of worldly society. But again, no conscious practice of morality or particular acts of reform could make them truly good. In Peirce, this transcendental doctrine became scientific and pragmatic. Men might achieve goodness by devoting themselves disinterestedly to scientific inquiry, making clear the laws of God through hypothesis and experiment. Thus the element of experimental action, which Edwards and Emerson had partially neglected, became specifically a means to salvation. But once again, salvation by works—by moral reform and "the folklore of right conduct"— was denied. Only by selfless devotion to the cosmic God whose purposes transcend human interests and moralities, can man be saved.

12. WILLIAM JAMES AND EMERSON

WILLIAM JAMES was closer to Emerson and to the transcendental group than were any of the other pragmatists. Emerson had been an intimate friend of his father's, and had often visited the James household. William had heard Emerson's essays read aloud, and later often read them to himself. At Harvard he was to dedicate "Emerson Hall," and at Concord to deliver a laudatory address on the centenary of Emerson's birth. Both his family heritage and his New England home placed him in the transcendental tradition.

But philosophically, William James attacked Emerson and his transcendentalism more sharply than did any of the other pragmatists. In his published writings he often quoted from Emerson unfavorably, and opposed his philosophy. In his letters he deprecated Emerson's easy optimism. Moreover, he reached his own philosophic conclusions by way of British empiricism, rather than the idealism of the Germans and Americans: where Peirce and Dewey had been trained in the earlier transcendental school and often avowed their debt to it, James ignored his. And so it has often seemed that the pragmatism of James (which is also the pragmatism of popular America) represented rather a reaction from the old transcendental dream than a realization of it: the first historian of American thought[1] called pragmatism "a recoil against transcendentalism."

The historical importance of William James, and the popular influence of his philosophy makes this question central to an understanding of the American mind. Where Peirce was obviously an idealist, and where Dewey has repeatedly affirmed his admiration of Emerson and the earlier idealism, James has seemed to deny his heritage. In considering Peirce and Dewey, we may deal with general ideas: in considering James, particular evidence and specific comparison is important.

Fortunately, William James was both particular and specific. Unlike Peirce and Dewey his writing abounds in detailed quotation and in personal reference. He wrote voluminous letters, and kept many notes on his reading. We shall recall the history of his father's friendship with Emerson, and of his own youthful contacts. In his early maturity he himself read and annotated Emerson's essays in detail. Later he reread them, and commented on their thought in careful marginal notes. Besides quoting from Emerson directly, he often did him the honor of indirect citation: echoes of word and thought throughout his writing confirm the evidence of his notes. Repeatedly, his personal letters describe his enthusiasm for Emerson, as well as his irritation. And finally his Centenary Address expresses his most obvious admiration for the "beloved master." We shall consider in detail the specific personal and philosophical relations between William James and Emerson. These point to the more general relations between the transcendental dreamers of the earlier America, and the pragmatic realists of modern times.

All the evidence of these relations suggests the conclusion that James, in spite of his frequent disagreements, was as close to Emerson philosophically as he was personally. His philosophy often took over the earlier transcendental ideas unconsciously. His earlier thought was more directly influenced by transcendentalism than his later. His criticism was usually directed at Emerson's method (or lack of it), and at the vagueness of his generalizations rather than at the substance of his thought. His own pragmatism often sought to describe the earlier transcendental ideas specifically and to apply them practically, rather than to deny them. When he attacked Emerson, he attacked him for being too facile, or too abstract. When he praised him, he praised many of his own distinctive ideas.

I

William James was born in 1842. "Henry James, Senior . . . named the boy William, and a few days later, brought his friend Ralph Waldo Emerson to admire and give his blessing to the little philosopher-to-be."[2] For the next thirty years Emerson remained an intimate of the James family. From birth to maturity, William came directly, even if unconsciously, under the influence of "the sage of Concord." In 1870–71, when the young man was going through his acute spiritual crisis, he again heard and read Emerson repeatedly.

The philosophical as well as the personal intimacy of this family relationship is evidenced by the many letters which the father and Emerson exchanged.[3] And it is significant that the father felt the same reservations that the son was to feel, addressing: "The Invisible Emerson, the Emerson that thinks and feels and lives . . . ; and not the Emerson that . . . bewitches one out of his serious thought . . . " The influence on both father and son seems to have been pervasive and almost unconscious. The atmosphere of their friendship is suggested by Henry James, the younger, who remembered "the winter firelight of our back-parlour at dusk, and the great Emerson—I knew he was great, greater than any of our friends—sitting between my parents, before the lamps had been lighted, as a visitor consentingly housed only could have done."[4]

After Emerson, the other American transcendentalists also became intimate with the James family. So Henry Thoreau visited them during his year in New York, and admired the father greatly. Margaret Fuller, Bronson Alcott, and later Walt Whitman made their acquaintance. And in time the father moved his family to Cambridge, to be nearer to the hub of intellectual America and to these men. Through Emerson, Henry James, Senior became a member of the famous "Saturday Club," and met Oliver Wendell Holmes, Senior and Junior. And through Emerson, of all people, both William and his father became honorary members of Phi Beta Kappa. In all the intellectual relationships of life, the James family and the transcendental group became intimate.

This intellectual intimacy became most conscious and most significant in the years 1870–71, when William James was living at home in Cambridge, struggling with the problem of his own vocation—much as Emerson had done forty years before him. Besides the usual personal visits, we find the family reading Emerson's essays aloud. In 1870, the father wrote:

My dear Emerson,—

Many thanks for *Society and Solitude,* of which I have read many chapters with hearty liking. But unfortunately just before the new volume arrived, we had got a handsomely bound copy of the new edition of the old essays, and I had been reading them aloud in the evening to Mama and Willy and Alice with such delectation on all sides, that it was vain to attempt renewing the experience.[5]

And during the next year, William acquired the first two volumes of essays for his own library, and annotated them for himself. In this year also Emerson gave his first public lectures at Harvard. And this year marked the founding by Charles Sanders Peirce, Oliver Wendell Holmes, Jr., William James, and others of the "Metaphysical Club" which was to result eventually in the formulation of "pragmatism."

In 1870 and 1871—crucial years of ferment, during which the shape both of his own career and of the future pragmatic philosophy was being determined—William James both heard Emerson and read and annotated his books repeatedly. These personal and philosophical relationships produced practical results.

II

The philosophical library of William James,[6] consisting of some three hundred books, has been preserved as a whole in the Houghton

Library at Harvard. In this collection are included nine volumes by Emerson, and one about Emerson.[7] These volumes have been marked, annotated, and carefully cross-referenced by James. They describe his enthusiasm for certain aspects of the Emersonian philosophy. And they also describe his disagreement with other aspects of it.

The first two volumes of Emerson's writings are inscribed: "William James, Scarboro, July 5, 1871." These have obviously been read many times, for they contain notes, references, and markings, entered successively in pencil, pen, and blue pencil. Two flyleaves at the end of each are scribbled with indexes, quotations, and comments of all varieties. Clearly these have been revised, altered and added to on different occasions. Almost every page of the text is underlined or annotated in such a way as to make clear James's interest.

Of the other volumes, only one is inscribed. His copy of *Lectures and Biographical Sketches,* printed in 1884, bears the words: "William James, from his Wife, Quincy St., Cambridge, June, 1879 (*sic*)," on the first flyleaf. The remainder of the volumes may have been purchased later, at some time before the centenary address of 1903. Each of these contains about ten or twelve quotations and references entered on the flyleaves, and numerous marks along the margins of the text. The most striking fact which these reveal is that James literally read almost everything which Emerson wrote. Only a few of the essays at the end of *Natural History of Intellect* have not been marked. When James wrote his brother that "The reading of the divine Emerson, volume after volume, has done me a lot of good," he was not exaggerating the thoroughness of this reading.

In general James's remarks about Emerson's essays fall into three classes. The first includes passages which James considered typical of the author, or particularly revealing of "Emerson's singularity." These he usually indexed under the initials "R. W. E." But since he used many of these in the later composition of his centenary address without further comment, their interest is comparatively small.

The second group includes passages from Emerson which James considered "against my philosophy." For the most part he indexed these under such titles as "monism," "abstract unity," "the ONE," and "transcendental." Some of these reappear—often with his disapproving comments omitted—in *The Varieties of Religious Experience.* Sometimes these passages are mingled with other Emersonian passages of which he approved. They seem to have irritated him either because of their abstractness, or their denial of "pluralism."

The third group of passages, which James wholeheartedly ap-

proved, is the most interesting, the most various, and the most revealing. Under the title of "pragmatism" he indexed many paragraphs, usually containing the words "action" or "deeds." Related
to these are other sections emphasizing "the present tense," and
the word "to-day." Another group of marked passages celebrates "the
common man," "the poor," and "the laborer"; and condemns the
"puny, protected person." Still others describe "the creative I," "psy-
chic energy," and "expansiveness" or power in general. Lastly, James
underlined and approved many of Emerson's sentences for their
"concrete style." All in all, James's enthusiasms were more important
and more suggestive than his criticisms.

The form in which James's comments are scribbled suggests that
he first read Emerson's text for its general interest and stimulation,
without specific reference to his own thought. Many passages were
indexed, without comment. At some later date he returned to the
text, noted that some of these passages were "against my philosophy," and added: "but see pp. — for pragmatism." Then he again
wrote: "pragmatism," in connection with other page references, formerly listed without specific comment. Although he carried out this
procedure only for the first two volumes of Emerson's work, his comments are sufficiently numerous to be significant.

As might have been expected, the passages specifically "against my
philosophy" appear in the chapter on "Idealism," in Emerson's
Nature; while the neighboring chapters on "Discipline," and "Pros-
pects" contain suggestions of "pragmatism." Most pragmatic, however, was the section on "Action," in "The American Scholar": "The
great soul will be strong to live. . . . Thinking is a partial act. Let
the grandeur of justice shine in his affairs."[8] And in "Literary
Ethics," he underlined several pragmatic passages: "Let him (the
man of letters) endeavor . . . to solve the problem of that life
which is set before *him*. And this by punctual action, and not by
promises or dreams. . . . Feudalism and Orientalism had long
enough thought it majestic to do nothing; the modern majesty consists in work."[9]

These passages appealed to James as celebrating "pragmatism,"
or "the superiority of action." But he found these mixed with other
passages which declared "the superiority of what is intellectualized."
Therefore he indexed the two contrasting series of statements, and
referred specifically to certain paragraphs which contained "both
close together." Obviously James considered Emerson's remarks
ambiguous, if not contradictory. Which did Emerson consider superior—deeds or thoughts; actions or ideas? If the answer were

"ideas," James called Emerson "transcendental"; if "actions," Emerson was "pragmatic."

It might be argued that Emerson was essentially a transcendentalist, because he commonly set ideas above actions. "Action is with the scholar subordinate, but it is essential," he wrote. Certainly he called himself an idealist, and certainly he emphasized ideas as the ultimate concern of the American Scholar. In this he disagreed with James, who emphasized particular acts. In a later essay on "Nominalist and Realist," Emerson definitely classed himself with the Platonic realists. But was this attitude inconsistent with his incipient "pragmatism"?

The answer depends upon the definition of "pragmatism," and takes us beyond the philosophy of James. For pragmatism originated as a theory of ideas, in Peirce's historic essay: "How to Make Our Ideas Clear."[10] It declared that an idea, or conception, consisted simply in the sum total of its conceivable relations to practical experience: "The elements of every concept enter into logical thought at the gate of perception and make their exit at the gate of purposive action; and whatever cannot show its passports at both those gates is to be arrested as unauthorized by reason."[11] In general terms, pragmatism declared the doctrine of the necessary interrelation of ideas and active experience. We may adopt this broad definition, both because it was prior to the more specific definitions of James, and because it suggests the philosophic continuity between Emerson and James.

Pragmatism, then, declared ideas to be meaningless except as they related themselves to experience—to perception and to action. In this it contradicted the transcendentalism of the German philosophers who declared the dichotomy between ideas and actions. But Emerson, in as much as he repeatedly proclaimed the necessary interaction of thought and experience, was pragmatic, and James frequently recognized the fact. Thus he labeled as "pragmatism" Emerson's exhortation: "Let the scholar first learn the things. . . . Let him know how the thing stands; in the use of all means, and most in the reverence of the humble commerce and humble needs of life, —to hearken what *they* say, and so, by mutual reaction of thought and life, to make thought solid, and life wise."[12] "The mutual reaction of thought and life"—had not Emerson founded his thought upon this principle? In other words, he had described it as "the uses of nature," ascending from the use of nature as the brute material for experience, to the use of nature as the material for purposive action: "Build therefore your own world." "The secret of Emerson," as one of his best biographers has observed, "lies in the superlative value which he found in the unit of experience, the direct, momentary, individual act of consciousness."[13] And, as even the unsympathetic Santayana recognized: "he coveted truth, and returned to experience."[14]

III

Although William James found in Emerson many suggestions of his own "pragmatism," he usually considered him a "transcendentalist," and often objected to expressions of this philosophy in his reading. These objections are significant. But even more significant are the echoes of this same "transcendentalism" which James incorporated (often unconsciously) into his own thinking and writing.

Emerson had called himself a "transcendentalist," had written an essay on the subject, and had become associated with that "philosophic" sect, in the popular mind. James was to discuss transcendental idealism as an important philosophic example of *The Varieties of Religious Experience,* and was to declare its logical inadequacy. Therefore it was natural for him to overlook, for the purposes of philosophic argument, the connections between transcendentalism and pragmatism.

In an early chapter of this book, James described at length the peculiarly Emersonian variety of religious experience, and suggested his own mixed attitude toward it: "Modern transcendental idealism, Emersonianism, for instance, also seems to let God evaporate into abstract Ideality. . . . In that address to the graduating class at Divinity College in 1838 which made Emerson famous, the frank expression of this worship of mere abstract laws was what made the scandal of the performance."[15] In other words, the abstractness of Emerson's transcendentalism constituted both its power and its danger. In his copy of Emerson, James had underlined: "Beware when the great God lets loose a thinker on this planet." James clearly approved Emerson's celebration of the effective power of thought. But, after quoting two pages of the Divinity School Address in his book, he objected to the vagueness of Emerson's abstract over-soul: "It quivers on the boundary of these things, sometimes leaning one way, sometimes the other, to suit the literary rather than the philosophic need." To him, the transcendental over-soul was bad because it was vague. But it was also good, because it was effective: "Whatever it is, though, it is active. As much as if it were God, we can trust it to protect all ideal interests, and keep the world's balance straight. The sentences in which Emerson, to the very end, gave utterance to this faith, are as fine as anything in literature."[16]

These remarks of James are suggestive. They conform his enthusiasm for Emerson's active "pragmatism." And they suggest that his disapproval of Emerson's "transcendentalism" was caused not by any suspicion of its ultimate ideals, or ends; but partly by the mere abstractness of those ideals, and partly by its failure to describe any method—other than that of intuitional self-reliance—by which those ideals might be realized.

Emerson repeatedly declared truth to be ideal, indefinable, and abstract; while James declared it to be specific, definable, and embodied in concrete objects. But, at the end, the two men agreed upon one and perhaps the most important question. Emerson phrased it: "If you ask, 'How can any rules be given for the attainment of gifts so sublime?' " and answered: "I shall only remark that . . . the one condition coupled with the gift of truth is its use. . . . The only way into nature is to enact our best insight. . . . Do what you know, and perception is converted into character." James underlined these pragmatic sentences. But the bad taste remained. He indexed the last of them under the title of: "his optimism."

Emerson's transcendence of sensuous experience disturbed James most when it appeared in the essay on "Self-Reliance," for there it seemed to vitiate much that was best in the Emersonian gospel. The essay first described the need for self-reliance in eloquent language, which James copied. But it then based this reliance on personal intuition. "And now at last the highest truth on this subject remains unsaid; probably cannot be said; for all that we say is the far-off remembering of the intuition. . . . It shall exclude example and experience."[17] This angered James. On his first reading he called it: "The anaesthetic revelation," although he commonly used this phrase only to describe mystical trances induced by drugs, or other artificial means.[18] Then, on a second reading, he indexed the same passage as: "the tasteless water of souls."

"—It shall exclude experience. . . ." But had not Emerson himself celebrated "experience," many times? James explained Emerson's thought as: "sometimes leaning one way, sometimes the other, to suit the literary rather than the philosophic need." He separated Emerson's pragmatism, or empiricism from his transcendentalism, or intuitionalism. But are the two necessarily exclusive? Are they not rather complementary? Are they not different aspects of the same life-process? Emerson suggested this by distinguishing the inventive, creative, "spiritual act," from the routine, mechanical act. C. S. Peirce developed a similar distinction between "abductive" or intuitive thought, which originates ideas, and inductive and deductive thought which merely tests ideas. He identified this intuitive "abduction" with the scientific method of hypothetic inference. Later philosophers have confirmed his interpretations, using different terminology. All have recognized that the creative, inventive mind works rather by intuition than by "example and experience."

Emerson's transcendentalism denied common experience when, and only when, it sought to describe the pure, creative act of consciousness—as, of course, it often did. Then it praised a "perfect self-reliance," as the only means of originating new ideas. It always, however, started from the more common, routine "uses of nature." And it always returned to experience, in order to enact its insights—"to convert thought into truth." James, the experimentalist, approved the pragmatic action. James, the spiritualist, often sympathized with the transcendental enthusiasm for the conception of new ideas. But James, the moralist, felt instinctively the danger of too much uncontrolled transcendentalism. He distrusted the run-away intellect.

IV

In reading Emerson, James approved many suggestions of "pragmatism," and disapproved many expressions of "transcendentalism." Unconsciously, however, he often accepted many of Emerson's most "transcendental" ideas and sentences. Besides his specific and formal comments on Emerson, his published philosophic writings reveal many evidences of his relationship to transcendentalism.

James criticized Emerson for sometimes preferring words to deeds —ideas to actions. And yet James himself, in his earliest book on *Psychology,* had suggested the explanation of Emerson's "idealism," and its relation to his own "pragmatism." In his central chapter on the "Will," he showed how the two philosophies could be reconciled:

> The essential achievement of the will is to attend to a difficult object and hold it fast before the mind. The so doing is the *fiat*; and it is a mere psychological incident that when the object is thus attended to, immediate motor consequences should ensue. A *resolve, . . .* involves all the psychic elements of a motor fiat except the word "now."

Before the pragmatic act comes the will, and before the will comes belief. In a significant passage of Emerson's essay on "Experience," William James found this "belief" described, in italics, as *"the universal impulse to believe."* This phrase alone, with its italics and its carefully chosen phraseology, would suggest the relation between James's pragmatism and Emerson's transcendentalism.

But James further copied Emerson's phraseology in coining the word "over-belief," to describe his faith that "characteristically divine facts" exist.[19] And again, James's phrases are reminiscent when he asserts the reality of the religious experience, saying: "The axis of reality runs solely through the egoistic places—they are strung upon it like so many beads."[20] For Emerson had written: "Life is a train of moods like a string of beads. . . . Temperament is the iron wire on which the beads are strung."[21]

Finally, James borrowed Emerson's exact phrase to describe his own highest intellectual ideal. Emerson had early described the American Scholar as "man thinking"; and always liked to consider himself in that role. James, in his essay on "Philosophy and its Critics," described philosophy as "in the full sense only *man thinking* (the italics are James's)—thinking about generalities rather than about particulars." And James, for his part, liked to consider himself as a philosopher. The ideal of each writer was the same: "*man thinking*."

The passages in which James echoes Emerson's words and ideas are neither casual, nor random. They lie at the very heart of James's philosophy, and suggest how he converted the vague ideas of transcendentalism into the stuff of his own thought. They even suggest that the philosophic inconsistency which he saw in Emerson, reappeared in his own writing. For he also could praise both words and deeds—both general ideas and specification—both philosophy and practicality. He also could celebrate "over-beliefs" and religious ideals. He could even describe the ideal philosopher as "*man thinking* about generalities rather than particulars."

V

William James and his pragmatism owed more to Emerson and his transcendentalism than James was conscious of, or was willing to admit. His attitude was somewhat ambivalent, and may partly be explained by his family background. For Emerson had been a friend of his father—a great man in his way, but one of an older generation. Emerson's writings were familiar to him—so familiar that they did not seem very important. And after all, Emerson had been a transcendentalist—one of a philosophic species now extinct. Therefore, he could now forget him.

But in 1903 the Emerson Centenary forced James to read Emerson's Works through once more, from cover to cover. As professor of philosophy at Harvard he was asked to prepare an address for the occasion. And although his address was laudatory, of necessity, his personal letters at the time reveal his genuine, and somewhat surprised admiration.

To his brother Henry he wrote: "The reading of the divine Emerson, volume after volume, has done me a lot of good, and, strange to say, has thrown a strong practical light on my own path." And shortly afterwards: "Emerson is exquisite . . . !—You too have been leading an Emersonian life—though the environment differs." And again: "I have just been reading Emerson's 'Representative Men.' What luminous truths he communicates!"[22]

Then, after the occasion of the Centenary, James wrote of . . . "my address. I let R. W. E. speak for himself, and I find now, hearing much from others of him, that there are only a few things that can be said of him. . . . Reading the whole of him over again continuously has made me feel his real greatness as I never did before. He's really a critter to be thankful for."[23]

Shortly afterwards, however, in a letter to H. W. Rankin, who was an enthusiastic admirer of Emerson, James qualified his praise with the following statements:

I myself believe that the orthodox theology contains elements that are permanently true, and that such writers as Emerson, by reason of their extraordinary healthy-mindedness and once-bornness, are incapable of appreciating. . . . Rereading him *in extenso,* almost *in toto,* lately, has made him loom larger than ever as a human being, but I feel a distinct lack in him of too little understanding of the morbid side of life.[24]

And later still he repeated to W. C. Brownell his "light estimate of (Emerson's) monistic metaphysics, and his Platonic philosophy in general."[25]

William James developed and clarified many ideas of Emerson's philosophy. Some of these ideas were genuinely pragmatic; others were apparently transcendental. Often he was unaware of the recurrent "transcendentalism" in his own thought. He made these ideas his own by describing them concretely, and by shifting the emphasis from general to particular. He contradicted and denied some of Emerson's doctrines. An important disagreement, both philosophic and temperamental, remained to the end. But the surprising thing is not the disagreement, but rather the fundamental agreement between the two men and their philosophies.

13. SINCLAIR LEWIS AND
THE FORTRESS OF REALITY

DURING THE decade of the 1920's the novels of Sinclair Lewis achieved an acclaim unequaled in the history of American literature. First *Main Street,* then *Babbitt* and *Arrowsmith* appealed to popular imagination and to critical judgment alike, each selling hundreds of thousands of copies. By general agreement Sinclair Lewis became spokesman of a new renaissance in American writing, and finally won world recognition with the first award to an American of the Nobel Prize for literature, in 1930. No such immediate success, combining the popular and the critical, the national and the international, has fallen to the lot of any American before or since. As recently as August 5, 1944, the distinguished contributors to the *Saturday Review of Literature* for the past twenty years voted *Arrowsmith* the most important novel of the period.

But following the award of the Nobel Prize in 1930, the reputation of Sinclair Lewis steadily declined. By popular and by critical agreement, his novels written after then became progressively bad. As literary fashions shifted from realism to symbolism, and popular attitudes from individualism to conservatism, critics began to ask: "How Good Is Sinclair Lewis?" In 1948 Warren Beck denounced the 1930 award of the Nobel Prize as "outrageous."[1] And Bernard De Voto accused Lewis of defaming the American character, calling the conception of *Arrowsmith* itself: "romantic, sentimental, and, above all, trivial."[2] Increasingly, even Lewis's admirers began to wonder: Why had his later novels become so bad? Had his earlier novels ever really been so good? Once again they saw illustrated in his career the fate of "the artist in America." For, beyond any possible question, Sinclair Lewis had been the representative American artist of his era.

In his Stockholm address on receiving the Nobel Prize, Lewis had described "the American novelist" as working "alone, in confusion, unassisted save by his own integrity."[3] And the words accurately described Lewis himself. The confusion of values in which he worked may explain both his successes and his failures. When he was able to describe this confusion objectively, as in *Babbitt,* or to project his own integrity in a character such as that of Arrowsmith, he approached greatness. But as he grew older he found himself progressively involved in the confusion. The representative American artist progressively failed to understand, and so to transcend the confusion of his society.

The confusion of values which Lewis imputed to American society, and which he himself shared, is suggested by a sentence from one of his last (and worst) novels. *The God-Seeker*, published in 1950, told of a young missionary to the Sioux Indians in 1850, who finally decided to abandon his search for God in the wilderness in order to lead his new bride "back in the fortress of reality," to St. Paul. Safe there from the insecurity of the frontier, this early "God-Seeker" became a successful contractor, and the fictional ancestor of George F. Babbitt. Like his creator, this Lewisian hero early sought God in the "Free Air" of the western wilderness, and regarded the stodgy business men with a satiric eye. But like his creator, he later went "back in the fortress of reality," and regarded his early idealism as romantically unreal.

Like many Americans and most realists, Lewis conceived of Reality in two ways.[4] The first Reality included all the facts of life—both the material and the ideal, the ugly and the beautiful, the dull and the romantic. But the second "reality" included only the status quo of existing society—usually materialistic, and ugly, and unromantic. Following the tradition of nineteenth century "realism," the early Lewis described existing society as materialistic and ugly, in order to urge the reform of this narrow "reality." But the later Lewis increasingly identified this partial "reality" with total Reality, and therefore rejected as unreal both that idealism which would reform society and that romance which would escape its existing conventions.

As late as 1935, Lewis could retrospectively describe the years 1885–1935 as "This Golden Half-Century,"[5] when "there was romance everywhere, and life, instead of being a dusty routine, was exciting with hope and courage and adventure." For Lewis had been born a romantic and a liberal idealist. "For all his modernity," wrote Vernon Parrington in 1927, "Sinclair Lewis is still an echo of Jean Jacques and the golden hopes of the enlightenment." In his youth he had attended the utopian "Helicon Hall" of Upton Sinclair. And always his heart had sympathized with the rebellious Carol Kennicot, the romantic Babbitt, and the God-seeking scientist, Martin Arrowsmith. The greatness of these earlier novels lay in the romance and idealism which he described as implicit even in the ugly "reality" of Main Street and Zenith.

But progressively as he grew older, Lewis praised those unromantic social realities which he had earlier satirized—although, to be sure, he had always valued them grudgingly. For even in celebrating the youthful enthusiasm of Carol Kennicut, he had valued the unromantic realism of her doctor-husband. And even in sympathizing with the romantic dreams of George F. Babbitt, he had realistically returned him to the fortress of his family at last. Only with his ideal Martin Arrowsmith had he dared to pursue individual freedom to a cabin in the wilderness, and there, like Thoreau, his ideal hero suffered exile from social "reality." But after *Arrowsmith,* Lewis described all his idealistic heroes as either returning to "the fortress of reality," or as failing. So Dodsworth and his wife sought romance in Europe, but found it empty and alien. Ann Vickers sought to reform society, but finally married the realistic judge whom she had earlier sought to indict. And *Work of Art* celebrated a work-a-day hero who abandoned his earlier ideal of creating the perfect hotel in order to make a living for his family in the real world.

All Lewis's novels described the conflict of men's ideals or dreams with the "reality" of things as they are. Some of his earlier novels achieved a measure of greatness by describing these conflicts vividly, and showing why the romantic dreams failed or how the ideals sometimes achieved success. But all the later novels failed by denying the value or the "reality" of those earlier ideals. By deporting romance to Europe and idealism to Utopia, they made "reality" safe for America. But in so doing, they themselves became unreal.

*   *   *   *   *

Disillusionment with the romantic idealism of the nineteenth century has been typical of the realism of the twentieth. But just as the earlier idealism was sometimes confused, so the disillusion has been. For sometimes the earlier idealism was pragmatic, and directed towards the reform or control of "reality": the ideals of the pioneer and the aviator, of the scientist and the doctor, were all realistic. But sometimes the earlier idealism was merely romantic, and directed toward escape from "reality": the dreams of the great lover and the world traveler, of the esthete and the perfectionist, were all unrealistic. When modern realism has described the falsity of the merely romantic ideals of escape, it has been valid. But when it has described all ideals as false, it has become confused and empty.

Lewis's first adult novel described the romantic idealism of *Our Mr. Wrenn,* who dreamed of world travel and free love, and sought them in Europe. But there he met the bohemian Istra Nash, who explained: "When a person is Free, you know, he is never free to be anything but Free." So Mr. Wrenn returned to America, a sadder but wiser man: although his idealism was romantically false, he had learned from it.

Lewis's second adult novel, *The Trail of the Hawk,* described the ideal of the aviator in the modern world. And an early, juvenile novel, *Hike and the Aeroplane,* had also celebrated the romance of flight. But characteristically, *The Hawk* described its hero as an opportunist who failed to realize the pragmatic ideal of man's conquest of the air, and soon lost sight of all his early idealism.

In later years, Lewis compared *The Trail of the Hawk* to the true life-story of Charles Lindbergh, described recently in *The Spirit of St. Louis.* But their differences are more significant than their resemblances. Lewis's Carl Ericson, the "hawk" of Joralemon, Minnesota, was a farm boy of Scandinavian ancestry like the actual Lindbergh, who, like him, turned mechanic, flew in barnstorming exhibitions, and felt and communicated to others the ideal of flight. The first part of *The Trail of the Hawk* vividly prophesies the true story of "the lone eagle." But where Lindbergh focused his energies on his historic conquest of the Atlantic and became an authentic American hero, the fictional Carl Ericson, lacking any focus or heroism, puttered away his life, leaving even aviation at last and ending as a minor promoter. Not only does the second half of *The Trail of the Hawk* fail to realize the heroism of fiction, but it fails to realize the heroism of American reality embodied in "the lone eagle."

With *Main Street* Lewis achieved fame. And *Main Street* begins with romance and idealism. Dedicated to "James Branch Cabell and Joseph Hergesheimer," its heroine is introduced: "On a hill by the Mississippi where Chippewas camped two generations ago," standing with a "quality of suspended freedom." This fictional granddaughter of "The God-Seeker" of 1850 now questions the "comfortable faith" of Main Street, but after failing to convert her "dull neighbors" or to find romance with her unimaginative husband, she flees to New York and Washington in search of culture and freedom. But this freedom proves empty, and when Will Kennicut comes to woo her back, she returns. "It's so much more complicated than I knew when I put on Ground Grippers and started out to reform the world," she admits. She has failed, and returns to reality: "But I have won in this: I've never excused my failures by sneering at my aspirations." *Main Street* ends with the defeat of romantic idealism, but with the reaffirmation of ideals.

Babbitt achieved greater fame than *Main Street* and was a better novel. It enlarged the scope of the American society which it studied, but its scope does not explain its excellence. In *Babbitt,* Lewis almost achieved the realist's goal of allowing the story to tell itself without apparent interference of author. Where Lewis had obviously sympathized with Carol Kennicut, and later almost identified himself with Martin Arrowsmith, Babbitt is neither hero nor villain, but seems to exist in his own right—the natural product of his society. And through him America seems to reveal itself to the reader.

The archetypal American, George F. Babbitt, accepts the standards of his community without question, and when he revolts from them, does so blindly, as an individual or "natural" man. The natural friend of the sensitive Paul Riesling, he resents the crucifixion of Paul by society. With natural decency, he revolts against the political graft which society seems to take for granted. Seeking freedom from the narrow intolerance of his social group, he dares briefly defend the radical leader of the opposition party. Longing for romance, he indulges in a bohemian love affair. But recognizing that he owes both his past success and his present livelihood to the approval of his society, he finally conforms, returns to "reality," and renounces his former rebellions against the standards of his community.

The change from *Main Street* to *Babbitt* is essentially a change of perspective. In *Main Street,* Lewis and his heroine saw society from the outside—in *Babbitt,* from the inside. The sharpness of the contrast between "ideal" freedom and "reality" has become blunted, and the value of the "aspirations" themselves dubious. Babbitt's friend, Paul Riesling, has shot his wife—is friendship for a criminal good? Babbitt's real estate office has prospered by connivance with graft—who is he to cast the first stone? Radicals are "reds," and therefore un-American—is not friendship with them traitorous? And his "romance" with the bohemian Tanis was obviously an escape from his own dull marriage. Therefore the rebellious and romantic idealism of George F. Babbitt seems not only foredefeated, but confused. The greatness of the book is that this confusion reveals itself without the apparent intervention of the author. But the weakness of the book is that the author seems to share the confusion.

Just as *Babbitt* described the life of a typical real estate salesman, so Arthur Miller's recent tragic drama describes *The Death of a Salesman.* A comparison of the two is revealing. Both George Babbitt and Willy Loman are confused in their standards—both dream empty dreams, commit adultery, condone dishonesty. But where Babbitt exists in a society where all values are confused, and men succeed chiefly by dishonesty, the confusion of Willy Loman is contrasted with the clear standards of his neighbors, which bring success. The tragic flaw in Babbitt is also that of his society, but the tragic flaw of Loman is that he has mistaken the compromises of his society for its true standards. In *Babbitt,* "reality" seems to deny idealism; but in *Death of a Salesman* Reality includes idealism, denying only false dreams. The fault of *Babbitt* is that its author seems to accept the standards (or lack of them) of his hero as the American norm; or, to put it differently, that he equates the very confusion of that American society which he describes, with ultimate Reality. He fails to distinguish between romantic escape from, and the ideal criticism of, society.

Arrowsmith, however, seemed to overcome this fault. The "quality of suspended freedom" which Carol Kennicut had failed fully to realize, and which Babbitt had renounced, Martin Arrowsmith now realized to the full. The American idealism which Lewis and his earlier characters had sought constantly in different ways—Lewis himself in Helicon Hall, Mr. Wrenn in European travel, Carl Ericson in the romance of aviation, Una Golden in an independent career, Carol Kennicut in cultural reform, and Babbitt in romantic rebellion —all this idealism Lewis now concentrated in the character of Martin Arrowsmith. Alone among his idealistic heroes, Arrowsmith achieved a measure of success, and even of greatness (Mr. De Voto to the contrary notwithstanding). And not only did this hero achieve fictional greatness, but he achieved the greatness of fiction—the novel became Lewis's best, not because it described his "best" character, but because it realized him most intensely and completely. *Arrowsmith* seemed to embody and to illustrate the ideal values of its author, and to refute the charges of confusion.

Arrowsmith remains Lewis's best novel and—I think—one of the best American novels. Like *Moby Dick* and *Huckleberry Finn,* it achieved a balance and a focus which the earlier and the later novels of these American authors lacked. Like *Moby Dick* it described a heroic quest and, like *Huckleberry Finn,* it spoke the authentic American language. Beyond both, it embodied the modern ideal of the scientist and seeker of truth in a credibly human character. But its minor flaws were also prophetic—like the inflated language of *Moby Dick,* or the confused conclusion of *Huckleberry Finn.* In minor ways *Arrowsmith* suggested that final divorce of idealism and "reality" which was to confuse Lewis's later novels.

As his letters to his publisher repeat, Lewis intended to entitle *Arrowsmith,* "The Barbarian."[6] From his first conception the idealistic character of his hero seemed to him somehow un-American. This pure idealism was inspired by and embodied in the German-born Professor "Gottlieb," whose absolute devotion to truth carried a conviction wholly lacking, for instance, in the later hero of *The God-Seeker*. One of the central conflicts which motivate the story is that between Martin Arrowsmith and the materialistic American society which demands immediate results from his experiments. Probably it is this excessive materialism which prompted Mr. De Voto's charge that *Arrowsmith* gives a distorted picture of the American Public Health Service and of American research foundations in general. And certainly Arrowsmith is presented as an intransigeant individualist, in conflict with American institutions which resemble Booster Clubs rather than research foundations. The hero's devotion to scientific truth is somewhat too pure, and American society's concern with cash results somewhat too blind.

Nevertheless *Arrowsmith's* conception of scientific truth is neither "sentimental," nor "trivial." The conflict between the idealism of the scientist, and society's demand for immediate results has always been real, and was even more intense when the novel was written. Arrowsmith does not ignore the social concept of science—indeed he fails in his attempt to test his "bacteriophage" by means of scientific "control groups," precisely because he is a social being, subject to human weaknesses. When at last he resigns from the "Institute" to devote himself to private research in his cabin-laboratory, he does so without romantic illusions concerning either his own righteousness or his probable success. And on the other hand, his resignation from American "society" repeats that classic pattern of American individualistic idealism, first clearly defined by Thoreau a century earlier.

The minor flaw in the conception of *Arrowsmith*, which was to cause major confusion in the later novels of Sinclair Lewis, is the logical flaw which has lain latent in our American conception of Reality. Social "reality" has often seemed to deny "idealism." Therefore, either the idealist must reject social reality, or he must abandon his ideals and "return to reality." In *Walden*, Thoreau rejected society, and *Arrowsmith* repeats some of his intransigeance. Similarly, the heroes of *Main Street* and *Babbitt* found that society rejected all their ideals as romantic, and each to a different degree abandoned his aspirations and "returned to reality." The workable concept of a Reality which includes and uses ideals in order to change society has often been ignored by American writers. And in his later novels, Lewis conceived of an American "reality" which excluded both romance and idealism completely.

In contrast to *Arrowsmith, Elmer Gantry* described a "hero" who had adopted the opportunist compromises of his society as his ideals. Lacking the scruples of Babbitt, Elmer Gantry took "reality" for his

God, and denounced as communistic that idealism which would try to reform society.

On the other hand, *Dodsworth* carried on Babbitt's submerged idealism, and sought in Europe what *Babbitt* so signally failed to realize in America. But an alien European culture could not fill his life, and for him Europe became an escape from American "reality." After the break-up of his marriage, he returned to his European love, without hope. And in Lewis's last novel, *World So Wide*, Dodsworth finally reappeared, leading an expatriate existence in Italy, and ironically warning the final hero against the unreality of this rootless European life.

After *Dodsworth*, Lewis won the Nobel Prize, and was hailed as the representative American writer. In his Stockholm address, he bewailed that Americans "have no standards . . . no heroes to be followed nor villains to be condemned, no certain ways to be pursued and no dangerous paths to be avoided. . . . The American novelist . . . must work alone, in confusion . . ." And three years after returning to America, Lewis published *Ann Vickers* to document this confusion.

All the earlier heroes of Lewis had been idealists of a sort, and he had described their many conflicts with "reality" in many ways. Sometimes they had succeeded in part, more often they had failed and adjusted to "reality," but always he had sympathized with them. Only when *Elmer Gantry* clearly perverted the "yearning" of American romantics did Lewis scorn his hero. Always the author's emotional sympathy with romance and his moral approval of idealism had remained clear. Now *Ann Vickers* embodied an American idealism more complete than any, except *Arrowsmith*. A feminist and social reformer, Ann lived a free life, fought social corruption in all its forms, and sought love in the confusion of a great city. Clearly her author favored her among his heroines. But at the very end, Ann Vickers—to the consternation both of her associates and of her readers—chose to marry an ex-judge who had just been condemned for accepting graft and condoning dishonesty in office. And clearly Sinclair Lewis approved of his heroine's choice of this manly judge, who had scorned the social reformers, but now found himself beaten by them. His idealistic Ann not only renounced her earlier "idealism," but fell in love with that "realism" which she had formerly condemned. In *Ann Vickers* Lewis reversed himself and rejected the idealism which had inspired Arrowsmith.

Finally, *Work of Art* consciously reversed the earlier standards of *Main Street* and *Babbitt*, and completed Lewis's confusion. Carol

Kennicut had tried vainly to bring art to Gopher Prairie, and Babbitt had embodied that smug philistinism which scorns art. Now *Work of Art* set out to prove fictionally that the art of managing a hotel is just as valid as the art of painting a picture. And the idea was entirely valid. If his hero had embodied that quality of imagination which creates new forms—whether of the fine arts or of business management—*Work of Art* might have become a fine novel. But Lewis's hero, although embodying perfectly the ideal of *Work,* not only lacked, but positively condemned the ideal of *Art,* or creative idealism. And Lewis's notebooks show that this denial of artistic idealism was conscious and purposeful.

The published novel tells the story of a hard-working but unimaginative manager of a series of hotels, and his brother, a romantic poet who scorns work and continually borrows money from his brother. In the published novel, the hero is the epitome of "realism," in its unromantic extreme—honest and plodding but accepting stolidly the dishonesty of the world and making the best of it. And the brother is the epitome of romanticism at its worst—dishonest and flamboyant, denouncing the world but living as a parasite upon it. At the end the hero decides, (wisely, the author implies) to give up his second-rate hotel and start a motel, because that is the way the business is going. He has never created a truly fine hotel, or "work of art," but he has worked hard and gotten along, and adjusted to "reality."

But Lewis's notebooks[7] for *Work of Art* show that he originally conceived of his hero as an idealist who constantly planned to create the perfect hotel. The hero was to have been an artist, who, unlike his romantic brother, wished to create something real. But (Lewis asked himself in his notebook), is not the "artist" who plans to create an impossibly perfect hotel, just as unrealistic as the poet who writes about impossible beauty and romance? Therefore, Lewis consciously converted his hero from an imaginative artist in hotel-making to a realistic worker in hotel-keeping. Rejecting *Art,* Sinclair Lewis idealized *Work.* And in so doing he destroyed not only the significance of this novel, with its challenging title, but of his later novels which followed this pattern. The representative American artist, renouncing vision, retreated into the fortress of reality, and (artistically speaking) perished.

The decline and fall of Sinclair Lewis—typical American novelist—illustrates an American tragedy. The idealist, recognizing that his vision of perfection is impossible, renounces his vision and "returns to reality." Or, clinging to his ideals in spite of their certain defeat, he may become a fanatic—as in *Kingsblood Royal,* or a rootless expatriate—as in *Dodsworth* and *World So Wide.* The realist, on the other hand, denounces all idealism either as romantic, because unrealizable, or because it threatens the "reality" of things as they are. In whatever form, this American tragedy of "all or nothing" exiles the idealist from "reality" and even declares him to be "un-American."

But the earlier novels of Sinclair Lewis—especially those which made him spokesman for his generation—described the conflict of American idealism and materialism in pragmatic or comic terms. Though the cultural enthusiasm of Carol Kennicut was sometimes comically exaggerated, it embodied an impulse not only ideal, but pragmatically possible, so that the Main Streets of today hear more of the music and read more of the books that Carol urged. And though the scientific idealism of Arrowsmith was sometimes narrowly individualistic, his celebration of "pure science" influenced the practice even of modern industrial research, and his realization of the heroism of the "microbe hunters," even though partial, gave modern American fiction one of its few authentic heroes.

Sinclair Lewis lived through "the golden half-century" of America, and realized some of its glory. But when he renounced the glory, and retreated in confusion to the fortress of reality, both he and his America became the poorer.

PART V

14. THE ROMANTIC CONFUSION: THE DEVIL IN AMERICA

THE FRENCH and American revolutions of modern history paralleled the romantic revolution of modern literature. Historically, the French Revolution went to extremes: liberty degenerated into anarchy, and caused the reaction of Napoleonism. But the American Revolution limited its liberty by Constitutional Convention, and defined it in a Bill of Rights. In Europe, unlimited liberty led to the extremes of anarchy and fascism. In America, liberty limited and defined became liberalism, and led to democracy. The romantic revolution of modern literature reflected both these historic revolutionary experiences. But in general, American literature described the limited liberalism of American experience, while European literature often emphasized the more romantic extremes.

The romantic extremes of revolutionary experience and thought found expression in America, of course. There are elements of romantic nihilism throughout American literature. Emerson's affection for the "dear, old devil" has seemed mere diabolism. And so has Whitman's inclusion of Satan in his "Square Deific."—In order to define the difference between democratic liberalism and romantic nihilism, let us trace the history of the devil in modern literature.

The trouble is that God, until recently, has always been an authoritarian, and has often seemed something of a tyrant. During the Puritan Revolution, Milton conceived Satan as unconquered in will, because unconvinced of the justice of God's cause. The "Almighty Power" of *Paradise Lost* proved Himself almighty in battle, but Satan's continued resistance to Him seemed justifiable, because He remained a tyrant. The devil, therefore, became a kind of protestant hero. That he was also a devil, Milton protested almost too much. Unconsciously his Satan came to embody the root-principle of modern liberty.

Every revolutionary, of course, considers himself a champion of freedom. And every libertarian who actively opposes a tyrannical sovereign is a revolutionary. The signers of the Declaration of Independence were all rebels in imminent danger of hanging, and the

American Revolution was a denial of constituted authority. Something, therefore, of Satan's "indomitable will" animated even George Washington. Many of the diabolic virtues described by Milton have always seemed especially attractive to Americans. The devil has gained many converts in this protestant and independent new world.

All this has seemed confusing. Why should the new nation that dreamed of establishing an ideal commonwealth also worship the traditional devil? Why should one of its most influential thinkers declare that if he were the devil's child, he would live then from the devil? Why should Walt Whitman deify the devil, and Mark Twain welcome "The Mysterious Stranger," and William Vaughn Moody write an epic poem on the Serpent's reconquest of heaven? In the modern world, romantic diabolism has flourished side by side with the American dream.

But confusion often attends transition. The new diabolism has also implied a transvaluation of values: American worshipers of the old devil have usually become worshipers of the new, democratic God. The confusion has been caused by our failure to distinguish between two different qualities of the traditional devil. On the one hand, Satan has embodied the quality of liberal criticism; on the other he has embodied the quality of romantic violence and negation.

Traditionally, the devil tempted man with the fruit of the tree of the knowledge of good and evil; and man chose knowledge, including the qualities of criticism and of free experiment. To Catholicism this choice has seemed wholly evil. To Protestantism it has seemed partly good. But confusion has resulted from the protestant failure to distinguish between liberal criticism, or the protest against unjust authority, and romantic nihilism, or the denial of all authority. This failure has caused some moderns to worship the devil in all his forms, and others to despair utterly of the damned human race.

Logically, four solutions are possible to this Christian problem of evil. The Catholic solution condemns both protestant liberty and romantic rebellion. The orthodox-protestant praises liberty only when it is governed by written law. The liberal-protestant, or democratic, welcomes protest and criticism as preliminary to a more liberal law. But the extreme romantic praises violent rebellion, even while doubting that the dream of liberty can ever be realized.

Most modern European writers have chosen either the orthodox-protestant or the romantic philosophies of evil—either moderate liberalism or fascist nihilism. Most modern Americans, on the other hand, have divided between the orthodox-protestant and the liberal-democratic philosophies—between moderate liberalism and radical democracy. We shall consider first the development of the protestant idea of evil in Europe, as that has found embodiment in the famous devils of European literature; and then the parallel development of the idea of evil in American literature. In more detail, other chapters describe the contrasting conceptions of the devil and the ideas of evil embodied in the writings of Walt Whitman, Eugene O'Neill, and Robinson Jeffers.

I

The devil has had a long history.[1] But his first important European appearance was in the nethermost pit of Dante's *Inferno*. There he was an ideal Catholic devil, ugly and impotent, his legs frozen into the foundations of the earth, and his monstrous wings flailing the empty air. No creature could better have exemplified the futility of protest and of revolt in medieval Europe. The unity of faith which Henry Adams so admired found no question there—the absolute authority of the Church no protest. Doubt and negation, science and revolution, were equally unthinkable.

But two centuries later this European devil had become really dangerous: science and revolution were in the air. When he first tempted the early Faust at the time of the Reformation in the town of Wittenberg where Luther had taught, he was still a Catholic devil, but no longer impotent. He now tempted man by offering him the forbidden knowledge of nature and the experience of earthly beauty. Faust succumbed to this devil, and was damned; like Luther, he became a protestant rebel against the authoritarian God. To Catholic Christianity, he seemed wholly evil.

A century later, when Satan personally rebelled against God in Milton's *Paradise Lost,* he became a protestant devil, although still keeping to the orthodox pattern. He became heroic, possessed of infinite courage, so that his revolt became justified emotionally; although he still remained fore-defeated. Thus the protestant Milton performed unconscious obeisance to Satan, even while consciously seeking to justify the ways of God to man. The devil grew in potentiality, if not in present power.

Finally, in Goethe's *Faust* this protestant devil achieved a more conscious justification. As in the old Faust legend, he remained the spirit of denial. As in *Paradise Lost,* he remained fore-defeated. But in Goethe's drama his defeat did not imply the defeat of man. The purely selfish striving of Faust in Part I was transmuted into the unselfish striving of Faust in Part II. The spirit of denial and rebellion

was partly justified as the necessary preliminary to the work of reformation and reconstruction. Although the devil remained evil,
Faust used him to achieve a greater good, and eventual salvation.
Thus he embodied the negative scientific spirit of criticism and
doubt, which must precede the positive scientific spirit of discovery
and reconstruction. In short, Goethe's devil came almost to embody
the protestant ideal of freedom.

But neither Goethe nor any other European writer distinguished
explicitly between the "good" protestantism of the devil and his
"bad" nihilism. Nor did any European describe clearly how negative
criticism may eventually lead to positive progress. And because
negative criticism had become inseparably associated with nihilism
in the devil's character, many European romantics began to worship
the devil blindly, instead of God. And others began to despair of all
liberal criticism, because God seemed to oppose everything negative.

Thus the romantic revolution led to confusion. The early romantic
writers celebrated Satan as the archangel of revolution. Byron and
Victor Hugo wrote impassioned poems to him. Baudelaire and Verlaine praised his "flowers of evil" in their beautiful immoralism.
Huysmans idealized the devil. But even in thus worshiping the devil
these early romantics agreed with the more conservative protestants
on two fundamental points: that Satan was primarily evil, and that
he was fore-defeated. So Havelock Ellis described Huysmans as "a
resigned and benevolent Mephistopheles who has discovered the absurdity of the Divine order but has no wish to make any improper
use of his discovery."[2] Although the early romantics worshiped evil,
they did not seek to make nihilism prevail.

But if the earlier romantics worshiped the devil—partly as the
angel of freedom, and partly as the gardener of evil—the later romantics worshiped him for his absolute evil. Where Baudelaire had
described immorality as beautiful but fore-defeated, Nietzsche now
proclaimed it all-victorious: the superman carried European diabolism to its final fruition. Where nihilism had formerly seemed attractive but impotent, it now became omnipotent. Spengler described the
decline of the West as the ultimate realization of the idea of destructive violence. The negative policy which Machiavelli had formerly
advocated as realistic, fascism now exalted as ideal. Protestant freedom might be hopeless, but unscrupulous violence could be successful. Therefore the devil who opposed God in the final Armageddon
was not to be troubled by protestant morals or liberal doubts. His
followers praised violence and denial for their own sakes, undeluded
by dreams of freedom and progress. Protestantism had worshiped the

traditional devil for his positive qualities, but fascism worshiped him for his evil alone.

In Dante and the early authors of the Faust Legend, European Catholicism had condemned both liberal criticism and revolt. In Milton and Goethe, European Protestantism praised criticism, but condemned revolt. In Nietzsche and Spengler, European romanticism condemned criticism as impotent, but exalted violent revolt. And so the devil at his most diabolic triumphed in the logic of European fascism.

II

In America the devil has had a somewhat different history. Although he has flourished, his character has altered. First, he has never been a Catholic devil. And second (partly for this reason) his protestant qualities have seldom seemed very evil, or fore-defeated. Where opposition to arbitrary authority has often been considered a virtue, men have dared to envision the victory of freedom. Therefore they have not been driven to idealize blind revolt, nor in despair to preach nihilism.

Of the four modern solutions to the problem of evil, the Catholic has found no significant expression in America. The traditional-protestant has been celebrated by those who have feared the confusions of romanticism. The romantic has usually described the victory of the devil as partial, not absolute; and has stopped short of nihilism. And the transcendental has dared to imagine the devil as part of the divine scheme, and has considered traditional evil as potentially a force for good.

This transcendental devil has become popular and even dominant in American literature. Where Europeans had usually confused the transcendental with the romantic, American writers distinguished between the two. And the ideas of Emerson and Whitman gained such currency that orthodox American moralists, like Hawthorne and Melville, took their departure from them, emphasizing them by opposition. Both logically and historically, the "good, old devil" has been prominent in American thought.

Emerson took the final theological step which Milton and Goethe had been unwilling to take. To him the courage of Satan and the critical spirit of Mephistopheles became genuinely God-like. The traditional devil, therefore, became partly "good," and, in his anti-authoritarian aspect, wholly so. True evil did not consist in courageous protest, but in craven impotence: "evil is merely privative, not absolute; it is like cold, which is the privation of heat." There-

fore American transcendentalism welcomed many un-gentle and dis-
agreeable manifestations of popular democracy, which the orthodox
moralists distrusted.

In "Self-Reliance," Emerson spoke unequivocally: "if I am the
Devil's child, I will live then from the Devil." And the conservatives
shuddered. But he had prefaced this apparent blasphemy by affirming that he believed his protestant impulses to be "from above, not
below," and that his experiments with goodness were to be genuine
experiments, not mere self-indulgence. First, Emerson affirmed his
belief in God, or objective truth; then, he affirmed that his experiments with life might discover new truths; finally, he affirmed that
even negative results would be valuable. This was very different from
denying that God existed or saying that the devil was worthy of absolute devotion. Therefore transcendentalism never fell into the confused devil-worship of romanticism. Never did it imagine final defeat,
nor preach nihilism.

What Emerson had suggested abstractly, Whitman went on to
describe in figurative language. The old devil, he declared, was part
of the divine scheme. His poem, "Chanting the Square Deific," described Satan as equal in permanence, in power, and even in value, to
the Trinity of Father, Son and Holy Ghost. Not only the protestant,
but also the revolutionary quality of the devil seemed to him part of
the divine scheme. And again the orthodox shuddered: if Emerson
had been partly moral, denouncing revolutionary violence at least,
Whitman now praised the violence of the devil as well as his protest.

Clearly Whitman's incorporation of Satan into the very nature of
God, by enlarging the "trinity" into a "quaternity," was a radical and
dangerous step. It might lead to the justification of violence, and
even to anarchy. Where Emerson had expressed a kind of protestant
transcendentalism, Whitman went beyond Christianity to a panthe-
istic transcendentalism. His acceptance of both the "good" and the
"bad" aspects of the devil led easily to later American confusions.
But Whitman did not approach the absolute confusion of the European romantics: his traditional Satan became partly god-like, but
never God. His Satan did not oppose God, but rather (like Job's ad-
versary) became an instrument or attribute of the divine power; and
therefore did not preach violence for its own sake, but in order that
men might be led to discover a larger truth beyond protest and
tragedy. This faith in the undiscovered laws of an unknown God, beyond human moralities and purposes, has distinguished American
transcendentalism from European romanticism. In America, the

traditional devil has promoted criticism, experiment, and discovery, in all forms.

But many Americans, educated in the creed of the orthodox churches, repelled by the gross practices of popular democracy, and aware of the confusions of romantic theory, reacted against transcendentalism and damned the devil once again. Fascinated as Hawthorne was by the sin of the scarlet letter, and charmed by the idealism of Brook Farm, he re-emphasized all the more intensely the destructive effects of sin and the self-delusion of the idealistic reformers. And Melville, sympathetic as he was to the Mardian quest for the unknown, and to the satanic heroism of Ahab, declared again the ambiguity of self-reliant virtue, and the eternal justice of its punishment. Reasserting the stern orthodox morality, these Americans gave much the same answer to the problem of evil which Milton had given. But in so doing, they showed a clearer consciousness of the alternative answers to the problem of evil, and took their departure from the transcendental heresy.

But the "ambiguities" of the transcendental idea of evil have led many later American writers to romantic confusion. Mark Twain, although burlesquing the consequences of extreme self-reliance, described his beloved Huck Finn as a protestant rebel to the end. In Hadleyburg, he showed how the devil's tempting might lead to a more real (in fact, to the only real) kind of moral virtue. But in the end, Mark's *Mysterious Stranger* led the damned human race into chaos and despair, much as the devil of European romance had done. And more recently Robinson Jeffers has praised violence and death so as to suggest the romantic confusion, although at other times he has continued the transcendentalism of Emerson and Whitman. Like Mark Twain (although without Mark's humor), some poems of Jeffers seem to burlesque the diabolic extremes of the idea of self-reliance, while others praise the heroic courage of protestant rebellion. In these American writers the romantic confusion of values appears, but often so that it can be separated from the liberal revaluation.

15. THE ROMANTIC TRAGEDY
OF EUGENE O'NEILL

ROBERT. (*Pointing to the horizon—dreamily*) Supposing I was to tell you that it's just Beauty that's calling me, the beauty of the far off and un-known, the mystery and spell of the East which lures me in the books I've read, the need of the freedom of the great wide spaces, the joy of wander-ing on and on—in quest of the secret which is hidden over there, beyond the horizon?

THE DREAM of an impossible beauty beyond the horizon has always fascinated Eugene O'Neill and has distinguished all his writing. Quite simply and directly it inspired the heroes of his early plays, as in *Beyond the Horizon* and *The Fountain*. Then by contrast it emphasized the ugliness of materialistic America, as in *The Great God Brown* and *Marco Millions*. Finally, the impossibility of realiz-ing the dream caused the frustration and violence of his great trage-dies, *Strange Interlude* and *Mourning Becomes Electra*. But in the center of every drama, no matter how sordid the plot or how common the characters, some scene of idyllic loveliness—some flash of un-earthly beauty—has appeared.

Although this beauty has always been the subject matter of lyric poetry, it has been rare in realistic tragedy. For instance, the Celtic imagination of W. B. Yeats has often dwelt upon "The Land of Heart's Desire":

> Where nobody gets old and crafty and wise,
> Where nobody gets old and godly and grave,
> Where beauty has no ebb, decay no flood,
> But joy is wisdom, Time an endless song.

But when the modern dramatist has imagined this land of dream, he has necessarily contrasted it with the world of here and now. And the contrast has emphasized the ugliness of modern reality. This ugliness is the reverse of the medal.

All of O'Neill's power of invention has dramatized this contrast between dream and reality. Sometimes by means of theatrical light-ing, as in the visions of *Emperor Jones* and *Marco Millions;* some-times by means of two planes or of a divided stage, as in *Desire under the Elms* and *Dynamo;* but more often by means of masks, asides, and frank unrealism, he has made objective this inner division of the human mind. In his imaginative theater, the dream has been highlighted and man's subconscious idealizations made articulate to a degree impossible in life. From this artistry a new drama infinitely rich in perspective and depth has resulted.

But if the dream of an impossible beauty has given richness to his writing, it has also caused serious distortion in it. Not that O'Neill's dramatic conception has been confused. And not that the dream has lacked universality: all men have imagined some land of heart's desire, and all Americans especially have hoped to realize it in this "new world." But here is the distortion: although O'Neill's characters have all imagined an ideal beauty, very few have even hoped to realize it. They have dreamed, that is, not of realization, but of escape. "Wandering on and on . . . beyond the horizon," they have become lost. And in their confusion their dreams have turned to nightmares.

Because the romantic dreamers of O'Neill's plays have all imagined an impossible perfection, they have necessarily despaired of realizing it. But historically the great dreamers of America have imagined a possible perfection and have sought pragmatically to realize it. Imagining only absolute freedom, O'Neill's romantics have rejected all partial freedoms. And imagining the perfect brotherhood of man, they have rejected actual democracy. In the end, because they have instinctively recognized the impossibility of their romantic absolutes, they have lost faith in the future. And their failure has led them to deny the American faith.

Eugene O'Neill himself, like the heroes of his own dramas, has followed this romantic logic to its inevitable end. First, his imagination gloried in the discovery and affirmation of the beauty of his dream. Next, he denounced in ringing words the ugliness of American reality. Then he described the tragic defeat of the romantic dream in actual life. And at last, the clear recognition of the dream's impossibility led him toward resignation and quiescence. This essay will trace the rise and fall of the romantic dream in his major works.

I

O'Neill's early plays suggest both the beauty and the impossibility of the romantic dream. From *The Long Voyage Home* to *The Fountain*, his heroes imagine the unreal. With tragic inevitability, they suffer defeat. But, nevertheless, all achieve tragic exaltation by remaining true to their dream. Denying the values of the material world, they transmute defeat into victory. Thus they seem to exemplify "the great truth that there is nothing so precious in our lives as our illusions."[1] "As is true of the great heroes of all tragedies . . . they are destroyed by their virtues."[2]

But all of these early plays describe the romantic dream in such a manner as to suggest that its very impossibility constitutes its beauty. The heroes seem to idealize it *because* it can never be realized. They not only exemplify the truth that nothing is so precious to us as our illusions, but they also imply that our illusions are really more precious than the truth: they praise the will to illusion as if it were man's major virtue. Therefore the plays, although realistic in dealing with the dream's inevitable defeat, become unrealistic in implying its immeasurable value. For a dream is truly valuable only when it leads toward the actual realization of some possible ideal.

The impossibility of the romantic dream which inspires these early heroes is sometimes explicitly stated, and always implied. In terms of the sea, the plays describe its two mutually incompatible forms. In the first the characters dream of perfect peace and security, freed from all the vicissitudes and hardships of the sea. In the second, they dream of romantic adventure and discovery, freed from all the drabness and routine of the farm. One group of dreamers possesses what the other group idealizes and each imagines the other to be perfectly happy. Both therefore seek escape from reality into an impossible ideal.

In his very first play, *Bound East for Cardiff,* O'Neill described the dream of the dying sailor Yank of: "a farm with a house of your own with cows and pigs and chickens. . . . . It must be great to have a home of your own." And O'Neill repeated this theme throughout his early "Plays of the Sea." All life symbolically became the "Long Voyage Home" toward a security and a peace which could never exist. In *Anna Christie* this impossible ideal of security found its clearest expression and its surest defeat.

But in his first successful play, *Beyond the Horizon,* O'Neill had already described the impossibility of the opposite dream of romantic adventure. And this dream of an escape into "the great wide spaces" of the world was to motivate many of his later plays. Whether seeking "ile" in the Arctic, or gold in California, silk in Cathay, or an idyllic love enisled in the South Seas, his heroes were to follow the same rainbow to the same end. Rejecting what security they already possessed, they were all to imagine the romantically impossible and to destroy themselves in their quest for it.

"The beauty of the far off and the unknown, the mystery and spell of the East which lures me in the books I've read" became the actual

protagonist of *The Fountain*. In this last and most unrealistic of
O'Neill's early plays, "the fountain of youth" (by definition an impossibility) became an actual presence. At first it was described
vaguely:

> There is some far country of the East—Cathay, Cipango, who knows—a
> spot that nature has set apart from men and blessed with peace. It is a
> sacred grove where all things live in the old harmony they knew before man
> came . . . and in the center of the grove there is a fountain—beautiful
> beyond human dreams. . . .

But at the end this fountain appeared visibly: "Oh, Luis, I begin to
know eternal youth! I have found my fountain." At the end the
"soldier of iron—and dreamer," whose two "selves" had clashed in
early life, finally became the perfect dreamer and died gloriously with
his dream: "God's will be done in death!"

This romantic philosophy is very beautiful, and O'Neill's early
dramas illustrating it described it beautifully. But it is also very unreal, and O'Neill's early dramas suffered from this unrealism. In
describing the conflict between dream and reality, the dream was
always lovely, and the reality always ugly. In response to the challenge: "There is no profit in staking life for dreams," his heroes
replied: "There is no profit in anything but that!" It was "all or nothing," and anything less than "all" was nothing.

At first, O'Neill's heroes concentrated on the dream of absolute
beauty and found salvation in dying for it. Their dreams remained
pure, and their dramas beautiful. Only in the latter plays did O'Neill
and his characters begin to question the romantic dream and to
wonder if its unreality were really as lovely as it seemed. Therefore, the later plays became more realistic, but less beautiful.

II

In his second group of plays O'Neill turned his attention from the
dream of beauty to the ugliness of reality. And by focusing upon the
immediate American scene, he achieved a greater realism. No longer
did he imagine vaguely an impossible ideal. But in describing present-
day reality, he did remember the earlier dream and contrast the
modern reality with it. Therefore, American "materialism" came to
seem excessively ugly. The modern businessman became more than
the philistine—he became the very devil's disciple. And the actual
practice of American democracy became something to be excoriated.
The remembrance of the romantic dream led to the rejection of the
actuality.

THE ROMANTIC TRAGEDY OF EUGENE O'NEILL

Like *The Fountain, The Hairy Ape* dealt with man's quest for perfection and peace. But where the first had described the pure, religious quest, the second described its social implications. Now "Yank" (the Hairy Ape) dreamed not of abstract beauty but of "belonging." Acutely aware of his social inferiority, he desired an ideal brotherhood of man. And because he could never find this absolutely ideal democracy, he rejected the partial democracy which America could offer. Therefore he could find peace at last only in death, in the arms of a gorilla. But like Juan Ponce de Leon, he did remain true to his dream, and God's will was done in death. Through his tragedy, the negative implications of the dream became more explicit.

Yank—presumably the typical American workingman—did not want a higher standard of living, freedom, or equal rights. Rather he demanded the dream-remembered harmony of the Garden of Eden. And he was very positive about it all:

. . . . Cut out an hour offen de job a day and make me happy! Tree square a day, and cauliflowers in de front yard—ekal rights—a woman and kids—a lousy vote—and I'm all fixed for Jesus, huh? Aw, hell! What does dat get yuh? Dis ting's in your inside. . . .

Our "lousy" American democracy was not for him, because he envisioned an ideal democracy. For this impossible unreality he denied both the democratic actual and also the democratic possible. Together with present American reality, he rejected future American possibility. Both were "materialistic" and ugly.

The Great God Brown magnified this American dualism of the materialistic and the romantic to universal proportions. William A. Brown—like his contemporary American, George F. Babbitt—became the "god" of our materialism. But in rejecting this false American "god," O'Neill's hero again rejected American democracy: Dion turned away from "the rabble," because "he hated to share with them fountain, flame and fruit." That is, his romantic idealism became wholly negative. Like other Americans, he even began to worship the devil, because God would not grant him his absolute ideal: "When Pan was forbidden the light and warmth of the sun he grew sensitive and self-conscious and proud and revengeful—and became Prince of Darkness." And so Dion the romantic dreamer turned against the American world in which he lived.

In *Marco Millions*, O'Neill contrasted the materialism of the workaday world more universally with the romantic "mystery and spell of the East." The modern Marco—alias George F. Babbitt, alias the Great God Brown—became the arch-enemy of all things beautiful and spiritual—truly an instrument of evil. And at the end the great Khan's voice proclaimed "with pitying scorn: 'The Word became their flesh, they say. Now all is flesh! And can their flesh become the Word again?' "

This question goes to the heart of O'Neill's thought and work. And the answer—which had lain implicit in his earlier plays—became increasingly explicit in his later ones: Man cannot achieve salvation until he renounces all worldly materialism, accepts the defeat which his dream implies, and returns to the spiritual faith of his fathers. In striving for practical goods, man denies the ideal Good. In seeking to improve the Flesh, he forgets the Word. Therefore, according to O'Neill, modern man should renounce all belief in materialistic progress and strive only for ideal perfection.

This has always been the logic of absolutism. The ideal world is good, and man instinctively worships it. The material world is bad, but man is unable to perfect it. Therefore, man should renounce the material for the absolute ideal. The early dramas had described the ideal perfection. The later ones denounced the material imperfection. It remained for the great dramas to portray the inner conflict of good and evil leading to the great renunciation.

III

Lazarus Laughed, Strange Interlude, and *Mourning Becomes Electra* form a kind of trilogy. Not only are they among O'Neill's most successful dramas, but on different levels of action they carry forward his ideal logic to its inevitable conclusion. Together they describe the human tragedy of modern man, in contrast to "The Divine Comedy" of earlier times. In the first, Lazarus realizes the paradisal beauty of an impossible ideal. In the second, Nina Leeds struggles through a purgatorial compromise between the ideal and the actual. Finally, Lavinia Mannon recognizes the impossibility of achieving the ideal and symbolically accepts damnation for man's materialism. Written in this order and moving down these steps of logic, these three dramas describe the tragedy of man, who envisions the perfect, struggles vainly to achieve it, and finally accepts inevitable defeat.

Perhaps *Lazarus Laughed* is the most perfect of all O'Neill's works. Certainly it was his own favorite.[3] It is one of the finest dramas of pure mysticism in the language. Yet it has never been produced professionally. Among the major works of America's first dramatist, it alone has never become popular. Its beauty remains strangely remote. If the reason for this lies partly in the unpopularity of all mysticism, it also lies in the peculiarly absolute quality of O'Neill's mysticism.

This modern Lazarus becomes the archetype of all O'Neill's unworldly dreamers. Like the hero of *Beyond the Horizon*, he had always been "impractical" and a "failure in life." Like the hero of *The Fountain*, he had been "born a dreamer," who can realize his ideal only in death. But now *Lazarus Laughed* actually begins where *The Fountain* ended—with the death of its hero. The plot follows the life of Lazarus *after* his resurrection from the grave. In human terms it seeks to describe the "practical effect" of "the fountain of youth" upon the divine hero and upon his human followers.

Lazarus, then, is the human being who has passed "beyond the fear of death." "His face expresses sorrow and a happiness that transcends sorrow." He moves onward from Palestine (where Jesus has just been crucified), through pagan Greece (where he is mistaken for the god Dionysus), to imperial Rome (where finally he suffers martyrdom). Meanwhile, he spreads the gospel of Christianity, not by preaching, but by living example. His mystical laughter converts men almost against their wills to the dream of human brotherhood, so that under its influence his devotees throw themselves laughing upon their adversaries' swords. But when he himself has passed on, "men forget." They leave their dream of divine love to return to acts of human hate. And at the end Lazarus himself dies gloriously at the hands of the Roman Caesar, repeating sadly: "Men forget!"

The greatness of this drama is that it translates the dream of divine perfection into human terms. Lazarus himself incarnates the perfection, and the various imperfect human beings who come under his influence illustrate various aspects of it. The psychological reactions of these people are convincing, and their physical reactions seem natural, for the most part. The conflict between Roman materialism and Christian idealism is imaginatively realized in terms both of words and of acts. Lazarus truly speaks and lives like one who has overcome the human fear of pain and death and has now learned to live affirmatively—freed from the negative dread of losing his own.

But the weakness of *Lazarus Laughed* is that this absolutely perfect hero fails to move us. His sorrows and sufferings leave us cold, because if he does not feel pain and fear, neither do we feel them for him. Only the natural reactions of other men toward him truly move us—and, paradoxically, the vestiges of human weakness which this all-too-perfect Lazarus sometimes betrays. When he stretches out his hand to prevent his wife, Miriam, from eating the poisoned peach which the Romans offer her, we feel the thrill of recognition. But when he himself dies without apparent emotion, we remain unmoved. The tragedy of absolute perfection is not tragic.

And if it be objected that Lazarus merely realizes the ideal of Jesus: "Be ye therefore perfect even as your Father which is in heaven is perfect," the answer is that no man can possibly realize this absolute perfection. Even Jesus cried out in despair on the cross: "My God, why hast Thou forsaken me?" And his human cry has echoed down the ages. But O'Neill's mystical Lazarus does dramatically realize the impossible. And O'Neill, in his other plays, either damns his human protagonists for not also realizing the impossible or praises them for rejecting the possible in favor of their dream of an impossible perfection—only the impossible is truly good.

Strange Interlude, on the other hand, describes the all-too-human compromises of Nina Leeds in her attempt to realize the ideal life which the death of her fiancé, Gordon Shaw, has denied her. Through subterfuge and deception she moves toward the fulfilment of her human desires. But in the end she rejects both these subterfuges and these desires. " 'Let's you and me forget the whole distressing episode, regard it as an interlude, of trial and preparation, say, in which our souls have been scraped clean of impure flesh and made worthy to bleach in peace.' " Only beyond the purgatorial interlude of life can one find perfection in death. Where *Lazarus Laughed* dramatized this perfection, *Strange Interlude* dramatizes the imperfection.

But unlike *Lazarus Laughed,* which was ideally perfect, *Strange Interlude* has proved widely popular and deeply moving. In spite of its irregularity and its extreme length, it has been translated more often than any of O'Neill's other plays.[4] In its characters human audiences have recognized themselves and their own failures to realize their own ideals. This dramatization of the sources of human imperfection has seemed more significant than the dramatization of superhuman perfection.

Unlike Lazarus, who had achieved happiness beyond death, Nina Leeds pursues her happiness in this life. She "dreams of Gordon," who had embodied all the ideal qualities of mankind, but who had been killed in the war. Seeking to realize the selfless love which she had felt for him, but which was never consummated, she gave herself blindly to other soldiers wounded in the war. But soon recognizing the futility of this, she marries a classmate of Gordon's named Sam Evans, who seems perfectly normal and good. With him she settles down, and by him expects a child. Apparently she is to achieve again the relative security and human happiness which the death of her ideal Gordon had denied her.

But this happiness is suddenly destroyed by the revelation that Sam Evans' father, and all his father's ancestors before him, had been insane. Therefore she cannot bear her husband's child, nor live happily with him. Instead she is forced to deception to achieve love and normal parenthood with another man, and finally to seek comfort and understanding from still another. Meanwhile Sam Evans, the normal and apparently successful husband, is relegated to the role of simple breadwinner and blind materialist. The imagined ideal proves impossible and the human actual utterly ignoble.

The plot of *Strange Interlude* is skilfully contrived to dramatize the conflicts and compromises of imperfect man. Because Nina's ideal love cannot be realized, her actual love must be divided between three different men: husband, lover, and father. And the motives underlying these imperfect types of love are made more clear by means of subconscious thoughts spoken by the characters. No other drama of O'Neill's equals this in subtlety of characterization or sharpness of conflict. Man's sinful compromises with his ideal are fully realized in terms of character and action.

Yet the plot of *Strange Interlude* is artificially contrived to make the normal achievement of true love impossible and to make this weak compromise inevitable. Not only is the ideal lover killed off before the action begins, but the substitute husband is arbitrarily declared insane. Thus the ideal, which might at least have been partially realized, is denied. And this device of insanity is truly arbitrary and romantic, resembling *Jane Eyre* and the old Gothic novels rather than modern realistic fiction. It merely declares in dramatic terms the impossibility of the realization of human dreams.

Thus *Strange Interlude* pointed to the conclusion toward which O'Neill's thought had steadily been moving. Because man's dream is impossible, and because man by nature is materialistic and sinful, his very attempt to realize his dream in this world must lead him into the evil which he seeks to escape. The very nature of his dream dooms him: " 'Romantic imagination! It has ruined more lives than all the diseases! Other diseases, I should say! It's a form of insanity!' " That same romantic dream of human perfection, which at first seemed so beautiful, has actually become the source of all evil.

Mourning Becomes Electra carried this logic to its bitter conclusion and ended O'Neill's long quest of "the secret hidden beyond the horizon." And because the logic of romantic tragedy has always been perfectly negative, this drama attained a kind of diabolical perfection. Where *Lazarus Laughed* described an impossible divine perfection, and *Strange Interlude* described a typically human imperfection, *Mourning Becomes Electra* described an almost perfect human depravity. It reached a dead end of denial.

The exact plotting of this modern Electra story and the subtle psychology by which the old myth is modernized are perhaps less important than the romantic theme of "the Blessed Isles," which motivates it. Against a somber background of Yankee "materialism," the characters describe their "dream" of peace in some ideal island of the South Seas. First Adam Brant, who has actually been there, tells Lavinia of these isles. Then Orin Mannon describes his dreams of them, suggested by reading Melville's *Typee:*

I read it and reread it until finally those Islands came to mean everything that wasn't war, everything that was peace and warmth and security. I used to dream I was there . . . —the most beautiful island in the world —as beautiful as you, Mother!

Then on board the clipper ship, in the central scene of the play, Brant and Christine Mannon plan their actual escape to "the Blessed Isles—Maybe we can still find happiness and forget!" But the avenging furies strike, and the family destroys itself until only Lavinia is left. But she raises the play to greatness by her denial of the romantic dream which has fooled all the others. Her final words seem both literal and symbolic: " 'Tell Hannah to throw out all the flowers.' " The old dream of ideal beauty has been discarded.

IV

Logically this should be the end: If perfection is impossible, and if reality is an ugly truth that must grimly be endured, then "the rest is silence." And, comparatively, O'Neill has kept silence since writing the great plays. Once, in *Dynamo,* he retold the tragedy of materialism. Twice he sought to salvage some comfort from despair: *Ah! Wilderness* reaffirmed the beauty of the romantic dream, and *Days without End* preached the value of an immaterial faith. Then for fourteen years he refused to allow the publication or production of any new play. And recently *The Iceman Cometh* proved comparatively unsuccessful.

This latter silence has, I think, been caused by his failure to find any way out of the alley into which his logic has led. If man's dream of perfection is impossible and if worldly compromise is ignoble and materialistic, then man is doomed to despair in this world. The alternatives to the American ideal of progress are the romantic dream of Beauty, the romantic reaction of despair, and the otherworldly religion of comfort. O'Neill has explored the beauty beyond the horizon, and the waste land of despair. He has genuflected before the religion of the other world. But he has not found "the secret hidden over there," nor has he fully reconciled himself to the impossibility of finding it.

16. DEATH COMES FOR
ROBINSON JEFFERS

I

To THE mind of Western man, life has always seemed the greatest good and death the greatest evil. In Homeric times the shade of Achilles exclaimed: "Nay, speak not comfortably to me of death, oh great Odysseus. Rather would I live on ground as the hireling of another, than bear sway among all the dead that be departed." And in early Christian times, Saint Paul could overcome the fear of death only by the promise of personal immortality: "O death, where is thy sting? O grave, where is thy victory?" Again in the Middle Ages the horror of "The Dance of Death" was pictured to persuade men to seek a "life eternal." And in the Renaissance, when the dying Hamlet spoke of death as "felicity," he was still imagining the joys of life after death.—In the words of Robinson Jeffers:

> . . . A few centuries,
> Gone by, was none dared not to people
> The darkness beyond the stars with harps and habitations.

Always life, here or hereafter, has seemed absolutely good; and death evil.

But now (the modern poet believes) men's minds may have changed:

> But now, dear is the truth. Life is grown sweeter and lovelier,
> And death is no evil.

Upon this reversal of values, Robinson Jeffers has sought to build a new philosophy, in which life shall no longer be the only good, nor death the ultimate evil. Instead, many of his finest poems ("Ante Mortem," "Post Mortem," *Descent to the Dead*, "Night," "Hooded Night," "Margrave," and others) have celebrated "death" and "night," and have questioned the goodness of life.

This questioning of life, and this celebration of death, have been important in causing the rejection of his poetry by many readers and critics. For the habits of thought of three millenniums are not altered so easily: even if the minds of some men have changed, death still seems the ultimate evil to the majority. And this is natural: all men instinctively love life and abhor death. From this instinctive belief, they have argued that any denial of life and any celebration of death must be nihilistic. As thinking animals they have justified their instinct by reason.

But now the question arises: is this new celebration of death merely a perversion of the old instinct? Or can it also be justified by reason? Does Jeffers' death-poetry describe the Freudian regression of a soul seeking blindly to destroy itself? Or is this modern celebration of death purposeful and positive?

There can be no single answer. Often, as in "Point Pinos and Point Lobos," Jeffers' poetry is genuinely nihilistic: "turned from creation, returned from the beauty of things to the beauty of nothing." Frequently it is regressive: remembering "deep inward/The calm mother, the quietness of the womb and the egg."[1] Sometimes it gives expression to the true Freudian death-wish: in "Self-Criticism in February" "the clay mouths go praying for destruction," not only with their own voices, but also with their author's. Philosophically, this occasional nihilism results from a confusion between the ideas of a regressive primitivism and those of a cosmic mysticism.

But more often, Jeffers' celebration of death is purposeful and positive:

> . . . make fables again,
> Tell people not to fear death, toughen
> Their bones if possible with bitter fables not to fear life.[2]

Usually his "denial" of life is conditional. "Life is good," he affirms in "The Broken Balance," qualifying only:

> . . . life is not always good . . .
> When you have ripened your berries, it is time to begin to perish,
> When you stand on the peak of time, it is time to begin to perish.

"Age in Prospect" explains his praise of death as part of a positive philosophy of life:

> . . . A creature progressively
> Thirsty for life will be for death too.

To him, death seems the culminating experience of life, rather than the denial of it.

But this new philosophy is unfamiliar. And often it becomes confused with the mere denial of life. Because of its unfamiliarity, we may explore it in detail. And because of its occasional confusion, we may compare it with orthodox thought, and seek to separate the positive elements of modern mysticism in it, from the negative elements of regressive primitivism.

II

In the past religion and philosophy have been anthropocentric. Life has seemed the absolute good because men have imagined goodness exclusively in human terms. Walking the earth in the image of man, their God has cherished humanity above all things. But now science has taught man that the earth and his humanity do not stand at the centre:

The earth was the world and man was its measure, but our minds have looked
Through the little mock-dome of heaven the telescope-slotted observatory eyeball, there space and multitude came in
And the earth is a particle of dust by a sandgrain sun, lost in a nameless cove on the shores of a continent.[3]

Now, therefore, man seeks to imagine a new God of the stellar universe. And because this cosmic God does not see creation with man's eyes, He does not cherish human life as the absolute good. The new perspectives suggest new standards of goodness.

But the cosmic remoteness and strangeness of this new God impel traditional men to say that He is no God at all. If the earth is "lost" in His eyes, then humanity becomes insignificant and the value of life seems denied. The traditionalists therefore cry out against the prophet of this new God:

Hater of men, annihilating with a sterile enormous
Splendor our lives: where are our lives?[4]

The "cosmic chill" produces the impression of annihilation.

But only the impression. To the despairing question: "Where are our lives?" the poet replies: "A little chilled perhaps, but not hurt." Human life remains real, although no longer of central or absolute importance. For every "God" has been conceived by man, and reflects the shapes of man's imagining. If the anthropomorphic God reflected man in a sort of idealized self-portrait, the modern God still reflects him as a small figure in a cosmic landscape. Human life may be dwarfed by the enormous splendors of outer space, but it remains real, and relatively good.

The difference now is that human life no longer seems the only good. Although the cosmic God values man in his proper place, He also values birds and mountains and stars in their proper places. The new standards are not absolute. Each part is good only in relation to the whole, and each within its own limitation. For man, life is still good, but for mountains and stars, life is not a good:

Only to be these things you are, as flowers for color, falcons for swiftness,
Mountains for mass and quiet.[5]

The perfection of the part can only be partial, "Life is good, but life is not always good."

It follows that life is not good when it denies its own partiality. "To people the darkness beyond the stars with harps and habitations" is to impose human values upon the super-human God. And against this sacrilege, Jeffers has consciously rebelled. His "Margrave,"[6] for instance, describes eloquently the evils of that human egotism which seeks to set itself above the laws of life. For the anthropocentric leads to the egocentric, until life itself seems evil:

. . . You would be wise, you far stars
To flee with the speed of light this infection.
For here the good sane invulnerable material
And nature of things more and more grows alive and cries.

But life is good when it recognizes its own limitations. And these limitations emphatically do not prevent the fullest realization of human potentialities: rather the opposite. Life is best when it realizes itself most abundantly, in its relation to the "nature of things." The historic fault of humanism has been only an overemphasis on the exclusively rational virtues of man. In "The Humanist's Tragedy," death results from the hero's preoccupation with "his dignity, as human being, a king, and a Greek": when King Pentheus sets himself above nature, scorning the passionate ecstasy of the mystic, he is killed. The realization of human potentialities requires a full acceptance of the unself-conscious elements of existence; and the wise man will welcome even those inhuman forces which often threaten to destroy him. "Though He slay me, yet will I trust in Him."

Life is wholly good, therefore, when it welcomes death as the evidence of its own limitations. The man who is ready to die, is ready to live. And the more he lives, the better he becomes, once he has freed himself from the old fear of death.

But even when he praises life most, Jeffers alters many of the orthodox values. Other men have praised youth and activity: Jeffers, in "Age in Prospect," praises old age and passivity.

> Praise youth's hot blood if you will, I think that happiness
> Rather consists in having lived clear through
> Youth and hot blood.

Youth is preliminary, even though it is valuable and necessary. "The steep singleness of passion" leads, in the natural course of events, to something better:

> Strength and desire possess the future,
> . . . but to die having made
> Something more equal to the centuries
> Than muscle and bone, is mostly to shed weakness.[7]

Maturity develops the power to create, which is more valuable than mere youthful desire.

But a higher value than maturity is peace. If youth has been lived to the full, and if maturity has been used to develop creative power, old age may become still more beautiful and still more valuable:

> The heads of strong old age are beautiful
> Beyond all grace of youth. They have strange quiet,
> Integrity, health, soundness, to the full
> They've dealt with life and been attempered by it.[8]

Having lived through youth and hot blood and the struggles of maturity, the heads of old age are strong, and the winter of life beautiful and peaceful; for the human potentialities have been realized to the full. Life has become progressively better.

And then death is best. For death is the ultimate experience of every living organism.—Youth, maturity, old age, and death, and if any one of these is denied, the wholeness of life is also denied. The "creature progressively / Thirsty for life will be for death too."

Thus the fulfilment of life destroys the fear of death, and makes men welcome death even while they feel most intensely the sweetness of life. In one of his finest poems, "Gale in April," Jeffers affirms at once the beauty of life and the beauty of death:

> O torture,
> Of intense joy I have lasted out my time, I have thanked God and finished,
> . . . I have passed
> From beauty to the other beauty, peace, the night splendor.

If the traditionalists believe that this death-mysticism implies a denial of life, one may point to the suggestions of this same philosophy in the poetry of that "indiscriminate" affirmer of life, Walt

Whitman. For Whitman's greatest poems were "Whispers of Heavenly Death." In the elegy to Abraham Lincoln, he apostrophized death:

> Come lovely and soothing death,
> Undulate round the world, serenely arriving, arriving . . .
> Approach strong deliveress. . .

And to Whitman also, "The Sea-Drift": "Lisp'd the low and delicious word death." Lacking the tragic emotion of Jeffers, Whitman's celebrations of death have usually been accepted as positive and beautiful. But Jeffers' are no less positive. Their appeal, in the end, is to nothing negative; but to life and death together conceived as human episodes in the divine tragedy.

But, finally, death is no more indiscriminately good than life.

> Death's like a little gay child that runs
> The world around with the keys of salvation in his foolish fingers, lends them at random where they're not wanted,
> But often withholds them where most required.[9]

When it brings fulfilment, and peace, death is good. But untimely death is bad, and remains fearful to the man who has not dared live life to the full. Therefore suicide is evil: "Death, the gay child with the gypsy eyes, to avoid you for a time I think is virtuous, to fear you is insane."

Jeffers believes that the fear of death comes, actually, from the fear of life. Therefore, he has reversed the old doctrine that life after death, in heaven or hell, will reward the just or the unjust; and substitutes a new myth:

> Happy people die whole, . . . they have had what they wanted, . . . the unhappy
> Linger a space, but pain is a thing that is glad to be forgotten; but one who has given
> His heart to a cause or a country,
> His ghost may spaniel it a while, disconsolate to watch it.[10]

Contrary to the old, orthodox belief, he imagines life after death as a punishment for potentialities not realized. Indeed, something of the old Hindu idea of transmigration is suggested: those who have not lived well must return to fulfill their predestined measures of life. But where Buddhism preached that the love of life was the fundamental evil, Jeffers describes it rather as an insufficient and exclusive love of life. To the love of life must also be added the love of death.

III

This new philosophy of death is logical and positive. When described clearly, none but a convinced fundamentalist could object to it. But it is not always described clearly. Although death as a part of life is good, and is to be desired; death for its own sake is not good, even if it is often desired. The occasional logical inconsistency and emotional confusion of Jeffers' poetry result from his praise of death for its own sake, and his desire for it. Because this "nihilism" is not central, but tangential—not instinctively simple, but emotionally complex; it may be analyzed the more objectively.

In his philosophic poems (to repeat) Jeffers has warned specifically against the death-wish:

> Yet hungering long and pitiably
> That way, you shall not reach a finger
> To pluck it unripe and before dark
> Creep to cover . . .[11]

He knows that the blind desire for death, like the blind desire for life, springs from fear, and sets the self above the nature of things. Only the man "Who falls in love with the God is washed clean/ Of death desired and of death dreaded."[12]

But Jeffers has dramatically described many characters who desire death for its own sake. And his Helen Thursos and Lance Frasers have been realized so completely that they seem a part of their creator. They pray for destruction with his sincere sympathy. When Jeffers replies to imagined criticism: "Alas, it is not uncommon in life"; he ignores this subjective sympathy.

Even his philosophic poems which warn explicitly against the blind desire for death often unconsciously praise it by their choice of words. Before condemning self-destruction, "Suicide's Stone" exclaims:

> Let trumpets roar when a man dies
> And rockets fly up, he has found his fortune.

And Jeffers' personifications of death repeat this praise implicitly. "Death, the gay child with the gypsy eyes" attracts the poet for her own sake.

> O Death
> Sweet and more sweet is your dancing.
> Like the swoon of fulfilment of love in some lonelier vale . . .[13]

Clearly, the emotion is not impersonal.

Indeed, Jeffers has praised death as pure negation on occasions. Meditating on the purpose of life, he has denied the Christian religion of love:

> Ah but look seaward
> For here where the land's charm dies love's chain falls loose . . .
> Sea-hawks wander the huge gray water, alone in a nihilist simplicity, cleaner
>   than the primal . . .[14]

And again he has exalted: "the beauty of nothing, a nihilist simplicity"; looking forward to the time when, "under the old sun's red waning/ Nothing forever remembers us." Specifically in his "Meditation on Saviors" he has rejoiced that "Light nor life sounds forever." "Quietness" becomes better than activity.

That this occasionally unqualified praise of death and quietness involves contradiction, Jeffers clearly recognizes. Some of his poems are cast in the form of interior monologues, in which his sensible and rational self debates with his nihilist self:

"Yet I am the one made pledges against the refuge contempt that easily locks the world out of doors." After writing "Margrave," he deprecated its extreme expression of anti-humanism, calling it "from that point of view just a poem." Indeed, he has suggested that his inner contradiction may even be a source of poetic strength: "I feel no impulse to disengage my own meaning from the web of my verse, and even wish not to, in order to keep an innocence of mind on my own account."[15] But this inner contradiction disturbs and confuses many readers of his poetry. Even if Nietzsche was right that "one must have chaos in one to give birth to a dancing star," it remains true that the great tragic poet must ultimately resolve the chaos within him.

The extreme nihilism and blind desire for death which troubles the poetry of Jeffers is not simple. From one point of view, it is even constructive. It expresses a personal, but typical reaction against an earlier extreme of anthropomorphic humanism. Admittedly his "Margrave" describes this reaction; and "The Humanist's Tragedy" suggests it by its title. The savage satire against that self-satisfaction which parades as human "dignity" finds voice in the anti-humanist "God" of the poem, who urges men "to break prison of yourselves and enter the nature of things." It is purposefully intended to counteract the historic humanism which has preached self-consciousness.

But the danger is that this historically justified anti-humanism may

set itself up as an absolute. The new worshiper of Nature must follow one of two courses: he may wholly reject humanism to worship
that God of external nature Who is hostile to man; or he may go
beyond humanity to worship that God of all nature Who includes
man as an integral part of the universe. Although both of these new
religions go by the name of Naturalism, they differ radically. The
first is regressive and negative; the second is progressive and positive.

Often Jeffers has expressed the ideas of a merely regressive Naturalism:

> . . . life . . . remembers deep inward
> The calm mother, the quietness of the womb and the egg,
> The primal and the latter silences: dear Night it is memory
> Prophesies, prophecy that remembers, the charm of the dark.[16]

If inanimate nature is the only good, "the primal and the latter
silences" are indeed equivalent. Memory and prophecy become
identical, and death becomes an escape from the fever of living, to
the God-like quietness of not-living. But this denies the value of life
(which Jeffers has repeatedly affirmed), and approximates Buddhism
(which he has repeatedly renounced). "Life's conqueror will not fear
Life."[17]

In praising the natural at the expense of the human, Jeffers has
fallen into the confusion characteristic of many mystics. Seeking to
advance beyond humanism, he has described the mystic ideal in
terms of inhuman nature. But the post-human is different from the
pre-human, both in time and in psychology. "The latter silence"
differs from "the primal": death is not "mother," but "deliveress."
Although the Freudian "death-wish" is regressive, the mystic love of
death as the fulfilment of life is progressive. Super-human mysticism must not be confused with pre-human naturalism or primitivism.

IV

Although Jeffers has praised inhuman nature, and the blind desire
for death, he has always suggested the super-human ideal which
transcends these. He has attacked Greek "humanism," but has added
that humanity is a means toward realizing the wholeness of nature.
In his recent poem, "Hellenistics," he has suggested the distinction:
"Nature" is beautiful, but "the natural condition of man" is not.

The Greeks sought to humanize "natural man," but in doing so they limited freedom and formalized nature. The modern mystic would go beyond formal humanism, teaching man not to return to his "natural condition," but to imitate that Nature which both includes and transcends humanity.

In "The Tower Beyond Tragedy," Jeffers early suggested this super-human ideal of mystic naturalism. Having passed beyond tragedy and the human fear of death, man may become one with nature, in a manner such as no primitive man ever dreamed. For the "natural man" struggled against nature for life, killing the beast, and fighting his fellow-man. But the super-human mystic, like Saint Francis of Assisi or Henry Thoreau of Concord, finds in nature patience and peace. This ideal, Jeffers' Orestes attempts to describe:

> I entered the life of the brown forest
> And the great life of the ancient peaks, the patience of stone,
> . . . and I was the stream
> Draining the mountain wood; and I the stag drinking,
> . . . I was mankind also, a moving lichen
> On the cheek of the round stone . . .

Imitating the patience of stone and the freedom of the stag rather than the barbarism of "natural man," the true mystic may rise to the super-human level of God.

But this super-human ideal presupposes two things. The hero must have lived clear through the experiences of life in order to climb this "tower beyond tragedy." And he must have overcome the fear of death:

> Orestes walked in the clear dawn; men say that a serpent
> Killed him in high Arcadia. But young or old, few years or many, signified
> less than nothing
> To him who had climbed the tower beyond time, consciously, and cast
> humanity, entered the earlier fountain.

Under the same conditions, Jeffers imagines the approach of death for himself:

> I chose the bed downstairs by the sea-window for a good death bed.
> . . . I often regard it
> With neither dislike nor desire; rather with both, so equalled
> That they kill each other and a crystalline interest
> Remains alone. We are safe to finish what we have to finish;

And then it will sound rather like music
When the patient daemon behind the screen of sea-rock and sky
Thumps with his staff, and calls thrice:
"Come, Jeffers."[18]

—When we have finished the work that we have to finish, we need not fear death. Only those haunted by a sense of experience denied will still desire it, or dread it.—These things remain true. But any man—even a great poet—may sometimes imagine the music of death more sweet than reality, and praise it beyond proportion.

PART VI

17. THOMAS WOLFE:
THE AUTOBIOGRAPHY OF AN IDEA

I

DURING HIS own lifetime Wolfe's novels were praised for their imaginative power, their brilliant characterization, and their ability to translate human emotion into words. But at the same time they were damned for their imaginative confusion, their obsession with autobiography and their apparent lack of all artistic form and discipline. John Chamberlain searched them in vain for any "controlling idea, or frame of reference." And Bernard DeVoto disposed of them with the phrase: "Genius is not enough."

After Wolfe's untimely death, this criticism continued. The publication of his last novel modified it a little. Clearly the author and his autobiographical hero had been striving toward some "controlling idea" greater than their individual selves. And the last three hundred pages of *You Can't Go Home Again* sought consciously to define this idea. Joseph Warren Beach suggested that the theme of Wolfe's earlier novels had been "The Search for a Father," while this last novel described "The Discovery of Brotherhood."[1] Others interpreted Wolfe's idea in other ways. But to most critics the idealism remained obscure.

It can now be proved that a single idea dominated all of Thomas Wolfe's life and writing. And even in his own time, it was possible to recognize it in his first novels.[2] His earliest play, *Mannerhouse*,[3] had already formulated the idea before he had begun to write novels at all. In the perspective of twenty years, Thomas Wolfe's idea may be defined and its development traced. Far from being the novelist of mere autobiographical emotion, Thomas Wolfe was the novelist of an idea. His whole life was dedicated to the living and describing of that idea. And when finally he had realized that idea, both in his life and in his writings, he died.

Briefly, the idea which controlled Wolfe's life and writing was the American dream of freedom and democracy. Like Walt Whitman, he sang America. And like Walt Whitman, he identified himself in imagination with the American ideal, rather than with the American actual. But like Walt Whitman also, his new democratic ideal contradicted the old aristocratic ideal, and therefore seemed to deny "idealism." "Disorderly, fleshly, sensual, eating, drinking, breeding," both he and his heroes sought to realize the equalitarian ideal in their lives and thoughts. From the orderly, genteel America of *Mannerhouse* and Main Street, they moved steadily toward the democratic America of their dream.

Walt Whitman, like Thomas Wolfe, celebrated himself in the process of celebrating his ideal. By identifying himself with his ideal democrat, each transmuted personal autobiography into impersonal idealism. But Thomas Wolfe went beyond Walt Whitman to dramatize the gradual development and realization of this ideal in actual life. Where Whitman had suddenly envisioned his American "eidolon," and thereafter had celebrated different aspects of it in different poems, Wolfe slowly groped toward it through the world of experience, and described the successive stages of its achievement in successive novels. Where Whitman had posed for the ideal portrait, Wolfe wrote the autobiography of the idea.

This autobiographical approach to the American idea gave pattern to his fiction and purpose to his life. He narrated the spiritual autobiography of the archetypal American from childhood to maturity. First, *Look Homeward, Angel* described his childhood, and his childish rebellion from Main Street. *Of Time and the River* continued with the young American's quest for new worlds, and his reluctant rejection of "Our Old Home" in cultured Europe. *The Web and the Rock* told of his gradual recognition that this democratic ideal could only be realized on the "rock" of American actuality. *You Can't Go Home Again* finally described the realization of the ideal by one American within the very framework of American materialism. And at the end, after the story of its realization, the long autobiography culminated in a declaration of faith, or definition of the idea.

This ending is obvious, and familiar. But less familiar is the fact that Wolfe had already defined the opposing ideal of slavery and privilege in his earliest serious writing, *Mannerhouse*. For as its name implies, this play had dramatized the conflict between the mannered gentility of the Southern conservative and the democratic idealism of the Northern liberal. From this starting point in the aristocratic past, Wolfe's hero (or heroes) steadily progressed toward their goal in the democratic future.

II

Thomas Wolfe's early play, *Mannerhouse,* was written in Professor Baker's "47 Workshop" at Harvard, and was subsequently rejected by commercial publishers, until 1948. But it remains more interesting and far more important than Wolfe's two one-act plays which were earlier published.[4] Not only does it point toward his later novels by introducing the character of Eugene Gant, but it shows flashes of his mature imaginative power and originality. His Harvard professors recognized its promise, and Wolfe himself praised it at length, half-humorously, in *Of Time and the River.*[5]

After a fanciful "prologue" which describes the building of "Mannerhouse" by slave labor in the early South, the play begins on the eve of the Civil War. Southern cadets are dancing with their girls before going to battle. But "Eugene Gant" is deeply troubled because he cannot accept the ideal of slavery for which he is to fight. In a stormy, romantic scene he first makes love to his heroine and then suddenly renounces her. In the climactic scene, he argues with his father, the Southern general who declares:

The General: I believe in God, in Hell and Heaven; and, in my house, in a great ladder of things on which it rests. I believe in heroes and hero worship; in men and masters; in the inequality of all things and all people. . . .
Eugene: That is your gospel. . . . founded upon the enslavement of men like us. . . . of men, who but for the grace of your own God, might own the fields we make them till; might hold the reins above us. . . .
The General: But slavery is eternal, slavery of field and house may go down to slavery of mill and wheel. And that in turn may go for slavery of another baser sort—of the slavery of a mob to itself—to Rebellion, Rebellion, Rebellion.
Eugene (his eyes afire): Yes, General! To Rebellion.[6]

As the action continues, Eugene remains unconverted to the gospel of inequality, but decides not to rebel against his own father. And at the end he declaims: "I shall go with you, my general, striking a blow for my own disbelief."

Although *Mannerhouse* failed—and justly—the reasons for its failure (as also its frequent flashes of genius) are significant. Its dramatic conflict focused sharply upon the conflicting ideals of the freedom-loving North and the slave-holding South. It defined clearly the opposing loyalties within the mind of its hero. And it described both sides fairly. Where the Southern aristocrat believed that the established order of things was based upon an eternal law of inequality, Eugene believed only in "rebellion" against the injustice of that law. And where the aristocrat prophesied truly that "slavery of field and house" would be replaced by "slavery of mill and wheel," Eugene could only proclaim his "disbelief." At this stage of his career, the traditional ideal of *Mannerhouse* seemed to Wolfe the only clear and positive ideal: therefore his Eugene felt himself impotent to oppose it. The clearness with which this anti-democratic idealism is described and realized in action gives the play its power.

But *Mannerhouse* fails precisely because of the psychological, or ideal, impotence of its hero. Eugene is unable to love the heroine because of his disbelief in the social order which she symbolizes. And he is unable to oppose his father because of his uncertainty as to his own belief. The psychological conflict within his mind, and the dramatic conflict between him and his father can only be resolved by anti-climax. Eugene gives up, and the final acts of the play lose themselves in a maze of inaction and confusion.

But the important point is that *Mannerhouse* defines the frame of reference for all of Thomas Wolfe's later thinking, writing and acting. It shows him projecting the ideal conflict in his own mind back upon the Civil War. And it shows him struggling between disbelief in the old ideal, and recognition that mere romantic rebellion against the old order is not enough. Until he could envision some positive new ideal, his writing inevitably remained confused, and his "autobiographical" hero impotent.

III

Look Homeward, Angel becomes "Book Two" in the "Autobiography of Eugene Gant: American Idealist." Or, if you prefer, it is "Book One" of the biography for which *Mannerhouse* is "Introduction." In *Look Homeward, Angel* all the characters except Eugene are new; but Eugene inherits all those civil wars of the mind which had distracted the earlier hero of *Mannerhouse*. He still seeks to resolve the conflict between the Southern tradition of inequality and the Northern dream of democracy.

In *Mannerhouse* this conflict remained subjective and confused. But in *Look Homeward, Angel* the conflict is objectified in the characters of Eugene's mother and father. Eliza Pentland is the native Southerner, born of a family which had lived for generations in the Carolina hills. But Oliver Gant is the wandering Northerner, settled at last and precariously in an alien land. Symbolically the story begins with Oliver's migration from Pennsylvania to the South. His subsequent marriage to Eliza becomes a marriage of ideal opposites.

And from this union of extremes Eugene inherits the conflicting strains of his own typically American character.

Eliza Pentland is the Mother, the Southerner, and the lover of her "house"; while Oliver Gant is the Father, the Northerner, and the eternal wanderer. But beyond this, Eliza Pentland becomes the symbol of all American materialism, and Oliver Gant the opposing symbol of the ideal of freedom. Thus, "for him the house was the picture of his soul, the garment of his will. But for Eliza it was a piece of property . . . a beginning for her hoard." The story of Eugene's youth becomes the story of conflict between his mother's materialism and his father's love of freedom.

The conflict is actual and external. But it is also subjective and internal, reproducing itself within the mind of Eugene. His "autobiography" is the story of this conflict, and (eventually) of its resolution. In his youth, he witnesses the destruction of his father's ideal by his mother's materialism, and he feels as if his father himself had been destroyed. Therefore in his young manhood he flees from his mother's "house" to his father's "North." Like Orestes, Eugene Gant takes "flight before fury," feeling as if he himself were destined to avenge the destruction of his father. From this fusion of fact with idealism, the realistic story assumes the stature and significance of universal myth.

But the peculiar significance of Thomas Wolfe's myth to America lies in his recognition of the false romanticism latent in his "father's" idealism. The "angel" which Oliver has created to compensate for the materialism of his wife Eliza is fantastically unreal: "Upon the porch, Oliver put the heavy simpering figure of an angel." Although Wolfe hated the materialism of his mother's world, he also recognized the romantic unrealism of his father's. Looking "homeward," he saw that not only his mother, but his father also had been at fault. For the ideal of romantic freedom which produced the blind escapes and drunken rages of his father, was really no better than the possessive materialism of his mother.

If Eugene's father illustrates the falsity of the romantic ideal of rebellion and escape, the young Eugene also shared this romanticism. Repeatedly the book satirizes his delusions: "Lifted by his fantasy into a high interior world," Eugene pictures himself as a great warrior, a noble lord, an irresistible lover. "Walled completely by the esymplastic power of his imagination" (the imagination loves big words), he visualizes some lovely woman "pouring the sad measure of her life into his sympathetic ears over the wineglasses of her candled, rich, but intimate table." And meanwhile, "encysted completely behind the walls of his fantasy," he lives his actual life in frenzied despair, "hurling his physical body daily to defeat." Eugene, in short, takes refuge from the actual present in a romantic world of un-reality. Compounded of egotism and fantasy, this "hero" seems most unpromising.

But the greatness of Eugene Gant and of the idea which guides his life is his infinite capacity for growth and progress. Although Eugene's mother and father embody the opposing American qualities of materialism and romanticism, and although Eugene falls heir to conflict, he eventually outgrows, and transcends it. And the story of his life becomes the story of this transcendence.

First, Eugene gradually learns to recognize the romanticism of his father's character, and also of his own. This romanticism he objecti-fies in the image of "the wounded faun." His impulses toward escape and self-pity are seen to be the evils which he must conquer; and at the end of the book he exclaims: "O sudden and impalpable faun, lost in the thickets of myself, I will hunt you down until you cease to haunt my eyes with hunger."

But this conquest of self-pity is made easier by the peculiar quality of Eugene's romanticism. Unlike his father, he has never indulged in blind rebellion or in empty escape. "It was not his quality as a romantic to escape out of life, but into it," his author emphasizes. "He wanted no land of Make-believe: his fantasies found extension in reality. . . . Eugene was no rebel. He had no greater need for rebellion than have most Americans, which is none at all." Rebellion and escape in the negative sense, that is, are rejected; but Eugene still seeks to "escape into life": "He felt sure things would be better elsewhere." Therefore he finally flees from his mother's house on Main Street, to seek a better life in a larger America.

Finally, before he leaves home the young Eugene faces frankly the ultimate defeat of the American dream of happiness:

"Fool," said Ben, "what do you want to find?"
"Myself, and an end to hunger, and the happy land," [Eugene] an-swered. "For I believe in harbors at the end."
. . . Ben said: "There is no happy land. There is no end to hunger."

But there remains "myself." The story of Eugene Gant, American idealist, is the story of his quest, not at last for "the happy land" of romanticism, but for knowledge of himself and of his own American land. This distinction between the romantic and the realistic ele-ments of Eugene Gant's American dream is fundamental, and ap-pears clearly in this first novel.

IV

Mannerhouse had described the conflict between the traditional slavery of the South and the rebellious "liberty" of the North during the Civil War. *Look Homeward, Angel* reproduced this historic conflict in the characters of Eugene's mother and father, and then described Eugene's recognition of the romantic falsity of his father's "liberty." *Of Time and the River* goes on to describe Eugene's quest for the true ideal of "liberty" in his father's North and in Europe. It tells of his "search for a father, not merely the father of his flesh, . . . but the image of a strength and wisdom external to his need and superior to his hunger, to which the belief and power of his own life could be united." Where "Book One" of the "Autobiography" had described the historic American civil war in terms of ideals, and "Book Two" described the partial falsity of both these inherited ideals: "Book Three" deals with the hero's search for a new and true "image of wisdom."

Eugene Gant, American idealist, driven by the furies of his "House," roams the world in quest of some new father-image. In the person of Francis Starwick, American aesthete and expatriate, he seems to find it. But the new is not necessarily the true: *Of Time and the River* becomes a story of progressive disillusion. But at the same time it remains a story of the gradual discovery of truth.

Like Hemingway's *The Sun Also Rises,* and like Lewis's *Dodsworth, Of Time and the River* describes the wanderings of "lost" Americans. Its hero travels through the world in quest of culture and beauty. Having rejected the materialism of the Main Streets of America, he seeks the better life in Europe. But unlike the heroes of Hemingway and of Lewis, Eugene Gant does not always remain "lost." Recognizing the romantic falsity of his friend Starwick's aestheticism, as he had earlier recognized the romantic falsity of his father's stone angels, he returns from Europe to seek his ideal within the same materialistic American life to which he had been born.

Negatively, Francis Starwick describes the cause of the failure of the American artist: he cannot cope with the materialism of American life, and he cannot understand the conflicts which cause its failure: "My God! . . . to have the spirit of the artist and to lack his hide, to feel the intolerable beauty of . . . this great America—and a skin too sensitive . . . to declare . . . the warped and twisted soul of its frustration." For the "enemy" of the American idealist is not so much the materialist, as the romanticist who seeks to escape from life.

Positively, Thomas Wolfe emphasizes that the success of the American artist will come from his courageous acceptance of his country's life, and his recognition of the causes of its failure. Not blind rebellion against materialism, nor blind escape to European aestheticism, but only active insight into the conflicts of his country can save him:

. . . Had he only known it and grasped it, there was ready to his use . . . the whole swarming web of life and error in full play and magnificently alive. As for the fancied woes and hardships of the young artist in conflict with the dull and brutal philistines,—that, he saw later, had had nothing to do with it, and was not worth a damn, any more than the plays that had been written in Professor Hatcher's class, in which a theatrical formula for living was presented in place of life. No; the conflict . . . might have been just the same had Eugene wanted to be an aviator, a deep-sea diver, a bridge-builder, a professional pall-bearer, or a locomotive engineer.

Thomas Wolfe proclaims this fundamental insight near the beginning of the book. But only from the perspective of Europe does his hero finally recognize that the very greatness of America lies in its conflicts and unrealized power: "far, far away from all this certain grace, this ease of form, this assured attaining of expression—there lay America—and all the dumb hunger of its hundred million tongues, its unfound form, its unborn art." And so, Eugene leaves Starwick, the romantic escapist, in Europe, while he himself returns to seek his ideal within American reality.

V

Thomas Wolfe's third novel, *The Web and the Rock*, is really two novels in one. The first tells of the childhood of Wolfe's new hero, "George Webber," in new terms. The second describes the adventures of George Webber after his return from Europe, in the same terms which had been used to describe "Eugene Gant's" earlier adventures in Europe. It is well known that Wolfe wrote the first part after having completed the second, in an effort to achieve greater objectivity. But although they differ in style, the two parts share the author's new insight. The first describes objectively the ideal conflicts of George Webber's early life. The second tells of his effort to apply this new knowledge actively to the guidance of his mature life.

The new novel sharply contrasts the "two worlds discrete" of the aristocratic *Mannerhouse* and of the democratic dream. But (and this is the important point) these two conflicting worlds co-exist within American experience. Reality involves the vital fusion of the two. The idealist progresses by recognizing the conflict and by choosing one world or the other. Francis Starwick, having chosen the aristocratic tradition, remained in Europe to realize it. Now George Webber seeks to realize the democratic ideal in America.

The first half of the new novel describes his slow recognition of the conflict, and his inner struggle against the old tradition: "He belonged to it, even as three hundred years of his blood and bone had belonged to it, and must unweave it from his brain, distill it from his blood, unspin it from his entrails." But this "unweaving" was hard, because the ancestral tradition seemed to be the only one which could lead to "the good life." "And he felt wretchedly that if he wanted any life at all it was assuredly 'the good life'—except that 'the good life' for him, vaguely phrased and indefinitely etched, but flaming in his vision with all the ardor, passion, aspiration of his youth . . . had so much flesh and blood in it." Therefore the first half of his career consisted in his gradual rejection of the old tradition of the merely "good" life for the democratic ideal of the full life, with its knowledge both of good and of evil.

The second half of this novel describes George Webber's search for, and achievement of "the full life." No longer fearing the world of the flesh, he wins success in it. Plunging himself into Vanity Fair, he gains love and fame. Like Faust, he bargains his soul to the traditional devil. And according to the orthodox tradition, he should lose his soul.

But George Webber was gradually "unweaving" this tradition from his brain. In the real world of the flesh, he was learning to recognize the elements both of goodness and of evil. "The flesh" was not necessarily evil, nor were "love and fame" evil; but rather the worldly compromise in which these involved him. His love, therefore, belonged to two worlds. Of Esther Jack, he wrote that: "the better part of her was loyal to the better part of life, but her loyalties, like everyone's, were mixed, and in this twin allegiance was the wrong. On the one side was the worldly society . . . and on the other side was the world of work and of creating . . ." In the actual world of reality the "two worlds discrete" of the soul's seeking co-existed; the world of "creating" was good, but the world of tradition was bad— for George Webber, American idealist.

Therefore George Webber decides to break with Esther Jack, and with her "world." The inner logic of that ideal by which he has chosen to pattern his life drives him, almost against his will. Although Esther, the artist, belonged also to his ideal world, in which "a shoddy piece of work . . . was the original sin," Esther Jack, the socialite, belonged also to "the world that Jack built"—to the traditional "Mannerhouse" of all aristocracy, whether located in Europe, in the old South, or on the Rock of Manhattan.

The Web and the Rock repeats the age-old lesson that a man must deny the world if he would save his own soul; but with this difference: The "world" of flesh and blood reality contains both the world of traditional privilege which man must renounce, and the world of creation which he must realize. Upon no unreal idealism did George Webber base his democratic dream, but upon the Rock of reality. Having faced down the materialism of his America and declared "the twisted soul of her frustration," he now could proclaim "the promise of America." To the celebration of this ideal democracy, which exists potentially within the body of the actual, Thomas Wolfe devoted his last novel.

VI

You Can't Go Home Again concludes the autobiography of Thomas Wolfe, American idealist. It first describes his final rejection of the tradition of *Mannerhouse,* with all its special privilege and worldly wisdom. Then it describes his (partial) realization of the dream of democracy through his actual life and work with the underprivileged and the unworldly. And it ends with his declaration of American faith.

The most vivid scenes of the last novel describe "The World that Jack Built." For George Webber now looks back upon the world which he has renounced, from the vantage point of his new spiritual freedom, and sees the reason for the failure of its citizens: "It was their attitude of acceptance . . . their complaisance about themselves and about their life, their loss of faith in anything better," that was wrong. As an artist, he could not belong to "this world of privilege without taking upon himself the stultifying burden of that privilege. How, then, could he sing America?" And so, having won success in this world, "in this very moment of his youthful dream come true," he finally rejects both the romantic dream and the materialistic reality. For "in America, of all places . . . privilege and truth could not lie down together."

" 'I'm looking for a way,' " he explained to Randy Shepperton. " 'Not the facts, you understand—but something truer than the facts. . . . A kind of legend, perhaps. . . . All the real things like freedom, and equal opportunity, and the integrity and worth of the individual—things that have belonged to the American dream since the beginning—they have become just words.' " And so he sets out to make real the democratic dream which is "truer than the facts."

He seeks out a cellar in South Brooklyn: "the most forlorn and isolated hiding spot that he could find." To this "wilderness" he retires, like the prophets of old, to save his soul. Only this wilderness is new—a wilderness of people: "Armenians, Italians, Spaniards, Irishmen, and Jews—in short, Americans." For these are the lost people of the new world, "the unkinged men." And he identifies himself with these, "as a man who worked and who, like other men, was a part of life." He knows and describes them in all their desolation— the pitiful neighbors in his tenement, the truck drivers, the waiters, and finally the homeless wanderers who have huddled together for warmth, in the stinking comfort stations of the city's actual underworld. And in these lost souls, he discovers "the promise of America."

This promise lies in the bitter independence of these "unkinged men." Perhaps because they have been "unkinged" from the old tradition, they—and George Webber—have been forced to rely upon themselves: "Go, seeker, throughout the land and you will find us burning in the night." "In the clay-baked piedmont of the South," a farm boy dreams of world's-series fame. "In the East-Side Ghetto of Manhattan, the Jew boy sees . . . the world distinction of an Einstein name."

So, then, to every man his chance—to every man the right to live, to work, to be himself, to become whatever thing his manhood and his vision can combine to make him—this, seeker, is the promise of America.

—But most men fail; and fame itself is false, and success turns bitter in the mouth: " 'Vanity of vanities, saith the Preacher; all is vanity.' " Replying to the fatalism of his friend, Fox Edwards, George Webber finally outlines his own "Credo." And this Credo is essentially that which American dreamers have repeated from the beginning—the belief of pioneers and of transcendentalists—the faith of the Declaration of Independence and of the Emancipation Proclamation:

There is no greater wisdom than the wisdom of Ecclesiastes [he admits], no acceptance finally so true as the stern fatalism of the rock. Man is born to live, to suffer, and to die, and what befalls him is a tragic lot. There is no denying this in the final end. *But we must, dear Fox, deny it all along the way. . . .*

You and the Preacher may be right for all eternity, but we Men-Alive, dear Fox, are right for Now. And it is for Now, and for us the living, that we must speak.

Therefore the ultimate evil—the "enemy" of Thomas Wolfe's American idealist—is not defeat, nor tragedy, nor death itself; but the denial of democracy and freedom. Eternal progress may be illusory, and the American dream of a perfect equality impossible; but the illusion is nevertheless "true" for "Man-Alive" and the dream indispensable. Emerson had celebrated "the beneficent illusions of the universe," and Whitman had sung the "Eidolon" of democracy. At the beginning of his career, Wolfe had proclaimed his disbelief in all privilege and inequality. Now at the end he affirmed triumphantly the American ideal of freedom and equality which he had gradually realized in all his life and writing.

18. JOHN STEINBECK:
THE PHILOSOPHICAL JOADS

A POPULAR heresy has it that a novelist should not discuss ideas—
especially not abstract ideas. Even the best contemporary reviewers
concern themselves with the entertainment value of a book (will it
please their readers?), and with the impression of immediate reality
which it creates. *The Grapes of Wrath,* for instance, was praised for
its swift action and for the moving sincerity of its characters. But its
mystical ideas and the moralizing interpretations intruded by the
author between the narrative chapters were condemned. Presumably
the book became a best seller in spite of these; its art was great
enough to overcome its philosophy.

But in the course of time a book is also judged by other standards.
Aristotle once argued that poetry should be more "philosophical"
than history; and all books are eventually weighed for their content
of wisdom. Novels that have become classics do more than tell a story
and describe characters; they offer insight into men's motives and
point to the springs of action. Together with the moving picture, they
offer the criticism of life.

Although this theory of art may seem classical, all important modern novels—especially American novels—have clearly suggested an
abstract idea of life. *The Scarlet Letter* symbolized "sin," *Moby Dick*
offered an allegory of evil. *Huck Finn* described the revolt of the
"natural individual" against "civilization," and *Babbitt* (like Emerson's "Self-reliance") denounced the narrow conventions of "society." Now *The Grapes of Wrath* goes beyond these to preach a positive philosophy of life and to damn that blind conservatism which
fears ideas.

I shall take for granted the narrative power of the book and the
vivid reality of its characters: critics, both professional and popular,
have borne witness to these. The novel has been a best seller. But it
also has ideas. These appear abstractly and obviously in the inter-
pretative interchapters. But more important is Steinbeck's creation
of Jim Casy, "the preacher," to interpret and to embody the philosophy of the novel. And consummate is the skill with which Jim Casy's
philosophy has been integrated with the action of the story, until it
motivates and gives significance to the lives of Tom Joad, and Ma,

and Rose of Sharon. It is not too much to say that Jim Casy's ideas determine and direct the Joads's actions.

Beside and beyond their function in the story, the ideas of John Steinbeck and Jim Casy possess a significance of their own. They continue, develop, integrate, and realize the thought of the great writers of American history. Here the mystical transcendentalism of Emerson reappears, and the earthy democracy of Whitman, and the pragmatic instrumentalism of William James and John Dewey. And these old philosophies grow and change in the book until they become new. They coalesce into an organic whole. And, finally, they find embodiment in character and action, so that they seem no longer ideas, but facts. The enduring greatness of *The Grapes of Wrath* consists in its imaginative realization of these old ideas in new and concrete forms. Jim Casy translates American philosophy into words of one syllable, and the Joads translate it into action.

I

"Ever know a guy that said big words like that?" asks the truck driver in the first narrative chapter of *The Grapes of Wrath*. "Preacher," replies Tom Joad. "Well, it makes you mad to hear a guy use big words. Course with a preacher it's all right because nobody would fool around with a preacher anyway." But soon afterward Tom meets Jim Casy and finds him changed. "I was a preacher," said the man seriously, "but not no more." Because Casy has ceased to be an orthodox minister and no longer uses big words, Tom Joad plays around with him. And the story results.

But although he is no longer a minister, Jim Casy continues to preach. His words have become simple and his ideas unorthodox. "Just Jim Casy now. Ain't got the call no more. Got a lot of sinful idears—but they seem kinda sensible." A century before, this same experience and essentially these same ideas had occurred to another preacher: Ralph Waldo Emerson had given up the ministry because of his unorthodoxy. But Emerson had kept on using big words. Now Casy translates them: "Why do we got to hang it on God or Jesus? Maybe it's all men an' all women we love; maybe that's the Holy Sperit—the human sperit—the whole shebang. Maybe all men got one big soul ever'body's a part of." And so the Emersonian oversoul comes to earth in Oklahoma.

Unorthodox Jim Casy went into the Oklahoma wilderness to save his soul. And in the wilderness he experienced the religious feeling of identity with nature which has always been the heart of transcendental mysticism: "There was the hills, an' there was me, an' we wasn't separate no more. We was one thing. An' that one thing was holy." Like Emerson, Casy came to the conviction that holiness, or goodness, results from this feeling of unity: "I got to thinkin' how we was holy when we was one thing, an' mankin' was holy when it was one thing."

Thus far Jim Casy's transcendentalism has remained vague and apparently insignificant. But the corollary of this mystical philosophy is that any man's self-seeking destroys the unity or "holiness" of nature: "An' it [this one thing] on'y got unholy when one mis'able little fella got the bit in his teeth, an' run off his own way. . . . Fella like that bust the holiness." Or, as Emerson phrased it, while discussing Nature: "The world lacks unity because man is disunited with himself. . . . Love is its demand." So Jim Casy preaches the religion of love.

He finds that this transcendental religion alters the old standards: "Here's me that used to give all my fight against the devil 'cause I figured the devil was the enemy. But they's somepin worse'n the devil got hold a the country." Now, like Emerson, he almost welcomes "the dear old devil." Now he fears not the lusts of the flesh but rather the lusts of the spirit. For the abstract lust of possession isolates a man from his fellows and destroys the unity of nature and the love of man. As Steinbeck writes: "The quality of owning freezes you forever into 'I,' and cuts you off forever from the 'we.' " Or, as the Concord farmers in Emerson's poem "Hamatreya" had exclaimed: " 'Tis mine, my children's and my name's," only to have "their avarice cooled like lust in the chill of the grave." To a preacher of the oversoul, possessive egotism may become the unpardonable sin.

If a society has adopted "the quality of owning" (as typified by absentee ownership) as its social norm, then Protestant nonconformity may become the highest virtue, and even resistance to authority may become justified. At the beginning of his novel Steinbeck had suggested this, describing how "the faces of the watching men lost their bemused perplexity and became hard and angry and resistant. Then the women knew that they were safe . . . their men were whole." For this is the paradox of Protestantism: when men resist unjust and selfish authority, they themselves become "whole" in spirit.

But this American ideal of nonconformity seems negative: how can men be sure that their Protestant rebellion does not come from the devil? To this there has always been but one answer—faith: faith in the instincts of the common man, faith in ultimate social progress, and faith in the direction in which democracy is moving. So Ma Joad counsels the discouraged Tom: "Why, Tom, we're the people that live. They ain't gonna wipe us out. Why, we're the people —we go on." And so Steinbeck himself affirms a final faith in progress: "When theories change and crash, when schools, philosophies . . . grow and disintegrate, man reaches, stumbles forward. . . . Having stepped forward, he may slip back, but only half a step, never the full step back." Whether this be democratic faith, or mere transcendental optimism, it has always been the motive force of our American life and finds reaffirmation in this novel.

II

Upon the foundation of this old American idealism Steinbeck has built. But the Emersonian oversoul had seemed very vague and very ineffective—only the individual had been real, and he had been concerned more with his private soul than with other people. *The Grapes of Wrath* develops the old idea in new ways. It traces the transformation of the Protestant individual into the member of a social group —the old "I" becomes "we." And it traces the transformation of the passive individual into the active participant—the idealist becomes pragmatist. The first development continues the poetic thought of Walt Whitman; the second continues the philosophy of William James and John Dewey.

"One's-self I sing, a simple separate person," Whitman had proclaimed. "Yet utter the word Democratic, the word En-Masse." Other American writers had emphasized the individual above the group. Even Whitman celebrated his "comrades and lovers" in an essentially personal relationship. But Steinbeck now emphasizes the group above the individual and from an impersonal point of view. Where formerly American and Protestant thought has been separatist, Steinbeck now faces the problem of social integration. In his novel the "mutually repellent particles" of individualism begin to cohere.

"This is the beginning," he writes, "from 'I' to 'we.' " This is the beginning, that is, of reconstruction. When the old society has been split and the Protestant individuals wander aimlessly about, some new nucleus must be found, or chaos and nihilism will follow. "In the night one family camps in a ditch and another family pulls in and the tents come out. The two men squat on their hams and the women and children listen. Here is the node." Here is the new nucleus. "And from this first 'we,' there grows a still more dangerous thing: 'I have a little food' plus 'I have none.' If from this problem the sum is 'We have a little food,' the thing is on its way, the movement has direction." A new social group is forming, based on the word "en masse." But here is no socialism imposed from above; here is a natural grouping of simple separate persons.

By virtue of his wholehearted participation in this new group the individual may become greater than himself. Some men, of course, will remain mere individuals, but in every group there must be leaders, or "representative men." A poet gives expression to the group idea, or a preacher organizes it. After Jim Casy's death, Tom is chosen to lead. Ma explains: "They's some folks that's just theirself, an' nothin' more. There's Al [for instance] he's jus' a young fella after a girl. You wasn't like that, Tom." Because he has been an individualist, but through the influence of Casy and of his group idea has become more than himself, Tom becomes "a leader of the people." But his strength derives from his increased sense of participation in the group.

From Jim Casy, and eventually from the thought of Americans like Whitman, Tom Joad has inherited this idea. At the end of the book he sums it up, recalling how Casy "went out in the wilderness to find his own soul, and he found he didn't have no soul that was his'n. Says he foun' he jus' got a little piece of a great big soul. Says a wilderness ain't no good 'cause his little piece of a soul wasn't no good 'less it was with the rest, an' was whole." Unlike Emerson, who had said goodbye to the proud world, these latter-day Americans must live in the midst of it. "I know now," concludes Tom, "a fella ain't no good alone."

To repeat: this group idea is American, not Russian; and stems from Walt Whitman, not Karl Marx. But it does include some elements that have usually seemed sinful to orthodox Anglo-Saxons. "Of physiology from top to toe I sing," Whitman had declared, and added a good many details that his friend Emerson thought unnecessary. Now the Joads frankly discuss anatomical details and joke about them. Like most common people, they do not abscond or conceal. Sometimes they seem to go beyond the bounds of literary decency: the unbuttoned antics of Grandpa Joad touch a new low in folk-comedy. The movies (which reproduced most of the realism of the book) could not quite stomach this. But for the most part they preserved the spirit of the book, because it was whole and healthy.

In Whitman's time almost everyone deprecated this physiological realism, and in our own many readers and critics still deprecate it.

Nevertheless, it is absolutely necessary—both artistically and logically. In the first place, characters like the Joads do act and talk that way—to describe them as genteel would be to distort the picture. And, in the second place, Whitman himself had suggested the necessity of it: just as the literature of democracy must describe all sorts of people, "en masse," so it must describe all of the life of the people. To exclude the common or "low" elements of individual life would be as false as to exclude the common or low elements of society. Either would destroy the wholeness of life and nature. Therefore, along with the dust-driven Joads, we must have Grandpa's dirty drawers.

But beyond this physiological realism lies the problem of sex. And this problem is not one of realism at all. Throughout this turbulent novel an almost traditional reticence concerning the details of sex is observed. The problem here is rather one of fundamental morality, for sex had always been a symbol of sin. *The Scarlet Letter* reasserted the authority of an orthodox morality. Now Jim Casy questions that orthodoxy. On this first meeting with Tom he describes how, after sessions of preaching, he had often lain with a girl and then felt sinful afterward. This time the movies repeated his confession, because it is central to the motivation of the story. Disbelief in the sinfulness of sex converts Jim Casy from a preacher of the old morality to a practitioner of the new.

But in questioning the old morality Jim Casy does not deny morality. He doubts the strict justice of Hawthorne's code: "Maybe it ain't a sin. Maybe it's just the way folks is. Maybe we been whippin' the hell out of ourselves for nothin'." But he recognizes that love must always remain responsible and purposeful. Al Joad remains just "a boy after a girl." In place of the old, Casy preaches the new morality of Whitman, which uses sex to symbolize the love of man for his fellows. Jim Casy and Tom Joad have become more responsible and more purposeful than Pa Joad and Uncle John ever were: they love people so much that they are ready to die for them. Formerly the only unit of human love was the family, and the family remains the fundamental unit. The tragedy of *The Grapes of Wrath* consists in the breakup of the family. But the new moral of this novel is that the love of all people—if it be unselfish—may even supersede the love of family. So Casy dies for his people, and Tom is ready to, and Rose of Sharon symbolically transmutes her maternal love to a love of all people. Here is a new realization of "the word democratic, the word en-masse."

III

"An' I got to thinkin', Ma—most of the preachin' is about the poor we shall have always with us, an' if you got nothin', why, jus' fol' your hands an' to hell with it, you gonna git ice cream on gol' plates when you're dead. An' then this here Preacher says two get a better reward for their work."

Catholic Christianity had always preached humility and passive obedience. Protestantism preached spiritual nonconformity, but kept its disobedience passive. Transcendentalism sought to save the individual but not the group. ("Are they *my* poor?" asked Emerson.) Whitman sympathized more deeply with the common people and loved them abstractly, but trusted that God and democracy would save them. The pragmatic philosophers first sought to implement American idealism by making thought itself instrumental. And now Steinbeck quotes scripture to urge popular action for the realization of the old ideals.

In the course of the book Steinbeck develops and translates the thought of the earlier pragmatists. "Thinking," wrote John Dewey, "is a kind of activity which we perform at specific need." And Steinbeck repeats: "Need is the stimulus to concept, concept to action." The cause of the Okies' migration is their need, and their migration itself becomes a kind of thinking—an unconscious groping for the solution to a half-formulated problem. Their need becomes the stimulus to concept.

In this novel a kind of pragmatic thinking takes place before our eyes: the idea develops from the predicament of the characters, and the resulting action becomes integral with the thought. The evils of absentee ownership produce the mass migration, and the mass migration results in the idea of group action: "A half-million people moving over the country. . . . And tractors turning the multiple furrows in the vacant land."

But what good is generalized thought? And how is future action to be planned? Americans in general, and pragmatists in particular, have always disagreed in answering these questions. William James argued that thought was good only in so far as it satisfied a particular need and that plans, like actions, were "plural"—and should be conceived and executed individually. But Charles Sanders Peirce, and the transcendentalists before him, had argued that the most generalized thought was best, provided it eventually resulted in effective action. The problems of mankind should be considered as a unified whole, monistically.

Now Tom Joad is a pluralist—a pragmatist after William James. Tom said, "I'm still layin' my dogs down one at a time." Casy replied: "Yeah, but when a fence comes up at ya, ya gonna climb that fence." "I climb fences when I got fences to climb," said Tom. But Jim Casy believes in looking far ahead and seeing the thing as a whole: "But they's different kinda fences. They's folks like me that climbs fences that ain't even strang up yet." Which is to say that Casy is a kind of transcendental pragmatist. His thought seeks to generalize the problems of the Okies and to integrate them with the larger problem of industrial America. His solution is the principle of group action guided by conceptual thought and functioning within the framework of democratic society and law.

And at the end of the story Tom Joad becomes converted to Jim Casy's pragmatism. It is not important that the particular strike should be won, or that the particular need should be satisfied; but it is important that men should think in terms of action, and that they should think and act in terms of the whole rather than the particular individual. "For every little beaten strike is proof that the step is being taken." The value of an idea lies not in its immediate but in its eventual success. That idea is good which works—in the long run.

But the point of the whole novel is that action is an absolute essential of human life. If need and failure produce only fear, disintegration follows. But if they produce anger, then reconstruction may follow. The grapes of wrath must be trampled to make manifest the glory of the Lord. At the beginning of the story Steinbeck described the incipient wrath of the defeated farmers. At the end he repeats the scene. "And where a number of men gathered together, the fear went from their faces, and anger took its place. And the women sighed with relief . . . the break would never come as long as fear could turn to wrath." Then wrath could turn to action.

IV

To sum up: the fundamental idea of *The Grapes of Wrath* is that of American transcendentalism: "Maybe all men got one big soul ever'body's a part of." From this idea it follows that every individual will trust those instincts which he shares with all men, even when these conflict with the teachings of orthodox religion and of existing society. But his self-reliance will not merely seek individual freedom, as did Emerson. It will rather seek social freedom or mass democracy, as did Whitman. If this mass democracy leads to the abandonment of genteel taboos and to the modification of some traditional ideas of morality, that is inevitable. But whatever happens, the American will act to realize his ideals. He will seek to make himself whole—i.e., to join himself to other men by means of purposeful actions for some goal beyond himself.

But at this point the crucial question arises—and it is "crucial" in every sense of the word. What if this self-reliance leads to death? What if the individual is killed before the social group is saved? Does the failure of the individual action invalidate the whole idea? "How'm I gonna know about you?" Ma asks. "They might kill ya an' I wouldn't know."

The answer has already been suggested by the terms in which the story has been told. If the individual has identified himself with the oversoul, so that his life has become one with the life of all men, his individual death and failure will not matter. From the old transcendental philosophy of identity to Tom Joad and the moving pictures may seem a long way, but even the movies faithfully reproduce Tom's final declaration of transcendental faith: "They might kill ya," Ma had objected.

"Tom laughed uneasily, 'Well, maybe like Casy says, a fella ain't got a soul of his own, but on'y a piece of a big one—an' then—'

" 'Then what, Tom?'

" 'Then it don' matter. Then I'll be aroun' in the dark. I'll be ever'where—wherever you look. Wherever they's a fight so hungry people can eat, I'll be there. Wherever they's a cop beating up a guy, I'll be there. If Casy knowed, why, I'll be in the way guys yell when they're mad, an'—I'll be in the way kids laugh when they're hungry an' they know supper's ready. An' when our folks eat the stuff they raise an' live in the houses they build—why, I'll be there. See?' "

For the first time in history, *The Grapes of Wrath* brings together and makes real three great skeins of American thought. It begins with the transcendental oversoul, Emerson's faith in the common man, and his Protestant self-reliance. To this it joins Whitman's religion of the love of all men and his mass democracy. And it combines these mystical and poetic ideas with the realistic philosophy of pragmatism and its emphasis on effective action. From this it develops a new kind of Christianity—not otherworldly and passive, but earthly and active. And Oklahoma Jim Casy and the Joads think and do all these philosophical things.

19. THE TIME OF
WILLIAM SAROYAN'S LIFE

OF ALL American authors who have achieved fame since 1930, William Saroyan is perhaps the most original, the most versatile, and closest to the mood of the common people. His stories, his plays, and his novels have not only achieved popularity with the reading public, but have appealed vividly to that public which does not usually read. Some professional book reviewers also have acclaimed him. But at the same time, other professional reviewers have expressed a hearty disapproval. And, strikingly, every serious literary critic who has discussed his writing in book or in essay form has enthusiastically damned William Saroyan. The abyss in America between popular opinion on the one hand, and critical judgment on the other, has never been illustrated more graphically.

Of course there are good reasons for the critics' disapproval. Even Saroyan's best work is faulty, and very little of his work is "best." The bulk of his writing, although vivid, is careless and formless. His many volumes of stories contain few masterpieces, and much third-rate material. His plays are amorphous; and many of his prefaces are bumptious. He has produced, I think, only two really first-rate things: *The Human Comedy,* and a one-page preface to *The Time of Your Life.* Judged by purely literary and artistic standards, the formal critics are often right in condemning him.

But Saroyan's obvious artistic faults do not explain the hostility of the formal critics. All of them have specifically attacked his "morality" or his "philosophy." Grouping him with "The Boys in the Back Room," Edmund Wilson deprecated his "barroom philosophy." Philip Rahv used his writing to illustrate the "decay of values and taste,"[1] in modern literature. Edwin Berry Burgum—certainly no reactionary—described him as evidencing a "flight from maturity and responsibility."[2] And Joseph Remenyi characterized Saroyan as "a sentimental romanticist."[3] If these critics grudgingly admitted the vitality of his work, they had little good to say of its intellectual or moral qualities.

Yet it is just these intellectual and moral qualities which make Saroyan's work most interesting and most important. If he were merely a romantic and sensationalist, we might dismiss him as a second- or third-rater. But the fact that he arouses such enthusiasm combined with such hostility suggests that he has something important to say.

In his artistic and moral faults and virtues alike, Saroyan suggests comparison with Walt Whitman. Like Whitman, he is an American "natural." Like Whitman, he celebrates himself and his America, but above all the America of his dreams. Not only his personality and his method suggest the good gray poet, but most of all his philosophy and his moral values are those of Whitman, Emerson, and the American transcendental tradition.

But obviously Saroyan is no traditionalist. Rather he is a product of the California of the twentieth century. If he seems to repeat the pattern of transcendental individualism, it is because that pattern has again become natural to the time and place in which he lives. Certainly he is as closely akin to the other California writers of his time —to Steinbeck, Sinclair, and Jeffers—as he is to Emerson and Whitman. For contemporary California has produced a school of writing which may well be called "the new transcendentalism." Seen in relation to the transcendental past and to the California present, William Saroyan takes on new stature.

I

If the most striking thing about Saroyan's writing is its originality, the most striking thing about Saroyan himself is his egotism. He shows a whole-hearted contempt for other people's rules, for society's customs, and for traditional values. In his prefaces he appears almost insolent. But this same egotism makes his creative writing fresh, vivid, and exciting. In the realm of morals, or philosophy, it creates an emphasis on the "transcendental" values of individual freedom and integrity. Perhaps Saroyan's combination of egotism, originality, and integrity may best be described by the old phrase: "self-reliance."

Saroyan's self-reliance produces much the same impression that Emerson's and Whitman's did a century ago. Indeed his first and most famous story repeated the theme of Emerson's early poem, "Good-bye, proud world! I'm going home." The daring young writer of the 1930's ventured forth to an employment agency, learned that the work-a-day world considered "writing" a mechanical and somewhat anomalous occupation, and returned home to live on the flying trapeze of the imagination. But his story made dramatic the contrast between the worldly values, and the esthetic or spiritual values of "writing." And this conflict of values has motivated all his subsequent work.

Indeed, another early story ironically entitled, *Love, Death, Sacrifice and So Forth,* developed this moral conflict in more general terms and commented on it explicitly. The traditional ethics of a Hollywood movie which the "writer" had witnessed, not only seemed utterly conventional to him but contrasted with the reality which he had observed. Therefore, he generalized, "A long while back we made the rules, and now, after all these years, we wonder if they are the genuine ones, or if, maybe, we didn't make a mistake at the outset." Following this idea, Saroyan devoted most of his early writing to satirizing the conventional "rules," or values, of worldly society. If his later writing has been devoted more to the imagining and illustrating of new "rules" better fitted to a modern, democratic society, the negative struggle against all convention and all "society" came first.

Opposing himself to "the world," Saroyan exaggerated his ego, just as Emerson and Whitman did a century before him. "Vastest of all is the ego, the germ of humanity, from which is born God and the universe, heaven and hell . . . " he declaimed. And speaking personally, in preface after preface, he repeated, "I discovered that the rules were wrong. The trouble was, they had been leaving me out . . . so I made some new rules." And he repeated Emerson's old idea in different words: "The greater your faith [in yourself], the greater your talent." If Saroyan were not primarily a writer of fiction, able to clothe his transcendental ideas in the imaginative reality of human character and action, one might easily dismiss him as a mere disciple of Emerson and Whitman. But where Emerson had dealt with abstract ideas, and Whitman had applied them poetically and personally, Saroyan has written authentic fiction. Only in prefaces and in occasional short stories has he stopped at mere personal self-assertion.

And even in his earlier stories Saroyan often illustrated the positive values of integrity and self-knowledge, without which "self-reliance" remains mere egotism. *The Man With the French Post Cards,* for instance, described a down-and-out gambler who preserved his "integrity" at last by *not* selling pornographic pictures. A later story, *War and Peace,* told of a pitiful young misfit who finally won peace of mind by facing down his own problems and by understanding himself. All the characters of Saroyan's best play, *The Time of Your Life,* achieved happiness by doing what they wished most to do. So a stage direction described them: "The atmosphere is now one of warm, natural, American ease; every man . . . doing what he believes he should do, or what he must do. There is a deep American naïveté and faith in the behavior of each person." That Saroyan's characters are usually failures makes little difference; they realize the "inalienable" (but often alienated) American rights of "life, liberty, and the pursuit of happiness."

As he has developed, Saroyan seems to have become increasingly conscious of this peculiarly "American" quality of the "rules," or values, which his fiction has illustrated. After producing *My Heart's in the Highlands,* he observed with rare humility, "I am now five years an American writer. Several weeks an American playwright. Yet all I know is that I have not so much as made a real beginning." And he stated clearly the task ahead of him: "The imperative requirement of our time is to restore faith to the mass and integrity to the individual."

II

If Saroyan's early writings were mostly devoted to the assertion and fictional realization of the "integrity of the individual," his later writings have emphasized the value of "faith to the mass," or of belief in social democracy to all Americans. Not only have his values become more clearly defined, but they have become more social. The most successful realization of them occurs in *The Human Comedy.* The best statement of them appears in the prologue to *The Time of Your Life.* Since this prologue sums up his whole democratic philosophy, it may be read in full:

In the time of your life, live—so that in that good time there shall be no ugliness or death for yourself or for any life your life touches. Seek goodness everywhere, and when it is found, bring it out of its hiding-place and let it be free and unashamed. Place in matter and in flesh the least of the values, for these are the things that hold death and must pass away. Discover in all things that which shines and is beyond corruption. Encourage virtue in whatever heart it may have been driven into secrecy and sorrow by the shame and terror of the world. Ignore the obvious, for it is unworthy of the clear eye and the kindly heart. Be the inferior of no man, nor of any man be the superior. Remember that every man is a variation of yourself. No man's guilt is not yours, nor is any man's innocence a thing apart. Despise evil and ungodliness, but not men of ungodliness or evil. These, understand. Have no shame in being kindly and gentle, but if the time comes in the time of your life to kill, kill and have no regret. In the time of your life, live—so that in that wondrous time you shall not add to the misery and sorrow of the world, but shall smile to the infinite delight and mystery of it.

Where Saroyan's earlier writing was often rebellious and negative, his later writing has become wholly positive: "In the time of your life, *live!*" Indeed he may have tended to "accentuate the positive" too much. But he has also tended increasingly to face the problem of evil, and has made clear—both in his prefaces and in his fiction— that he belongs to the *interbellum* generation, when "the time comes to kill." Living in this time he has sought to reaffirm the old American faith, and even in war to treat all men as brothers and equals. In this also he recalls the faith of Walt Whitman during the Civil War.

But this transcendental optimism which Saroyan reaffirms is more than a faith; it is also an American philosophy of equality. All men are equal; under the skin "every man is a variation of yourself." Like Whitman, Saroyan has sought to convert this idea into reality through the chemistry of the creative imagination, not only embracing all men with a vague, cosmic sympathy, but imagining individual characters who realize the ideal values stated in the prologue. Thus the actors in *The Human Comedy* observe and suffer the misery of the world, but also live fully and smile at the infinite delight of it. In so doing they realize the old American democratic faith in new ways.

The Human Comedy is more than a miscellaneous collection of short stories about the Macauley family, or a whimsical exercise in autobiography. It is a carefully constructed book, describing the growth to emotional maturity of a typical American boy, through four clearly-defined stages. If the chapters resemble short stories in construction, they are all focused on a single purpose. And if intrusions of the old irresponsible whimsy appear (as in the "Speech on the Human Nose") they follow a definite design. Moreover, interwoven suggestions of myth and symbolism tend to raise the particular and personal to the realm of the universal.

Perhaps the most interesting and original character of this *Comedy* is not the boy, Homer, but the manager of the telegraph office, Spangler, whose ultimate function seems to be "to restore faith to the mass." A breezy, utterly American young man, who dislikes to wear neckties, both his name and his actions nevertheless constitute him a living refutation of Spengler's philosophy of pessimism, and an interpreter of what Emerson called "the beneficent illusions of the universe." Yet this Spangler never loses his personal identity as the official employer and human companion of young Homer.

If Homer Macauley of Ithaca, California, is a typical young American boy, he is also heir to all the world's civilization. As the book opens he has just left home to work for the local telegraph office. Because his father is dead, and his older brother is in the army, he feels a vague emptiness. But in Spangler he finds a substitute

father and older brother, all in one. And from his mother he learns
faith in life: "It doesn't make any difference, because I *believe*."

But when Homer later returns to school, he confronts social evil
and injustice. His track coach is a snob who treats him unfairly, and
tries to give his protégé, Hubert Ackley III, special privileges. Opposing this injustice, Homer's history teacher explains to him the
American principle of equality: "Every man in the world *is* better
than someone else, and not as good as someone *else*. . . . In a
democratic state every man is the equal of every other man up to the
point of exertion, and after that every man is free to exert himself
to do good or not . . . " Inspired by her advice, Homer is vaguely
moved to try to change the world: "The ideas I get," he said. "A
different world, a better world, a better people, a better way of
doing things." And then he realizes: "Yeah, I guess I've changed
all right. I guess I've grown up."

But this is only the half of it. In the second part of *The Human
Comedy*, Homer Macauley confronts natural evil, and learns that
there are evils inherent in human nature which personal effort and
social progress cannot change. "Death, Don't Go to Ithaca," introduces a series of illustrations of natural and human perversity: boys
stealing green apricots and a child unreasonably demanding "cookies
—raisins in"; grown-ups indulging in travel as an escape from life,
women selling themselves for money, and men making themselves
"half-human, half-dead," like the fantastic Mr. Mechano. All this
causes Homer to exclaim, "I thought a fellow would never cry when
he got to be grown up, but it seems that's when a fellow starts, because that's when a fellow starts finding out about things." But a
letter from his brother, Marcus, warns him that he must face the
facts of death and evil by learning to "live, in the years of your life,
forever."

Because Homer Macauley has learned to fight against social evil,
but to meet the inevitable fact of natural evil in the only way it can
be met—by living as fully as possible; and because he has learned
faith from his mother and brother and from Spangler, he is finally
ready to accept the news of his brother's death as an adult, and to
comfort his mother and older sister, rather than the reverse. And he
is able consciously to adopt his brother's friend, Tobey, into the
family, just as he had unconsciously adopted Spangler as a substitute
for his dead father.

Thus *The Human Comedy* describes how a typical American boy
goes out from his home, experiences the injustices of the world and

fights against them, experiences the evils of human nature and learns to accept them, and finally achieves a mature faith not founded on childish optimism. Unlike the adolescent "young man on the flying trapeze," he does not retreat from the world to indulge in romantic self-pity; nor, on the other hand, does he abandon his self-reliant independence or his faith in human nature. Rather, he carries his self-reliance over into the world of society, and tempers his faith by the facts of experience. Saroyan's hero achieves maturity, not through rebellious self-reliance, nor through any desperate conformity to convention, but through a gradual realization of the old American faith in one's self and one's fellow men.

III

But William Saroyan remains the least bookish and the least traditional of contemporary American writers. His material is drawn from living experience with his California environment and from the living traditions of his immigrant family. His style, for better or for worse, is utterly colloquial, instinctive and unliterary; if he has ever read Emerson, he gives no hint of it, and he sounds his democratic yawp without benefit of Whitman. He remains an American natural, whose similarities to writers living or dead are entirely coincidental. Here is no question of literary influence. And yet the similarities remain.

The time and the place of William Saroyan's life (let us repeat) is twentieth-century California. His fiction is peopled with vineyard workers, suburban householders, wandering laborers, barflies, insurance salesmen, newsboys, evangelists, and back-porch philosophers—with all the colorful kaleidoscope of human beings who make up a California community. These live with the optimistic insecurity of a people on the make, a people struggling and starving, falling and bouncing up again and never despairing. In this California a failure is only an opportunity for a fresh start, and all things are always possible. ". . . the world," says Mrs. Macauley, "waits to be made over by each man who inhabits it, and is made over every morning like a bed."

William Saroyan's actual California, that is, resembles very closely Emerson's actual New England and Whitman's actual Manhattan of a century ago. Therefore, it has inspired the same feelings, in its people and the same ideas in its writers. "Nature is not fixed, but fluid" in Los Angeles and Fresno today, just as it was in Boston and Concord a century ago. For both societies are young, recently past their pioneering days, and both are imbued with the progressive spirit of adolescence, groping toward the articulation of new and exciting ideas. Both believe that "all things are possible," because in a new, unsettled society almost all things really are possible. Therefore the literatures of both exhibit a bold self-reliance combined with a bumptious self-assertion. At best, both suggest the feeling that there *is* something new under the sun. At worst, they produce the painfully self-conscious posturing of a Saroyan or a Whitman boasting of his own greatness.

At worst, both Saroyan and Whitman belong to "the lunatic fringe" of this "transcendental" ferment. For modern California has produced the same medley of "Muggletonians, come-outers . . . men with beards and philosophers," that Emerson once observed in New England. Upton Sinclair and his "Utopians," seeking to reform the world, are related to Saroyan's heroes. The Oriental mysticism of Gerald Heard and Aldous Huxley, and the "saturnalia of faith" proclaimed by the California revivalists have further confirmed the religious faith which Saroyan inherited from his Armenian family. And the air of "unreality" (observed by so many people in southern California) which made credible the feats of *The Flying Yorkshireman* (who needed only faith in order to soar at will through space) has also made credible the feats of *The Daring Young Man on the Flying Trapeze*. But with this distinction: Saroyan's "flying trapeze" is firmly anchored to the rafters of this unfinished California society, whereas the utopians, the theosophists, and the fantasists belong to that homeless, floating population which is half Hollywood and half imported European intelligentsia.

At best Saroyan's fiction gives expression to a philosophy of life which is typically Californian, and also is central to the American transcendental tradition. Unlike the muckraking and socialistic writing of Upton Sinclair, Saroyan has no axe to grind, no gospel to preach. Unlike the naturalistic and sociological fiction of John Steinbeck, Saroyan treats human nature and social injustice without violence and anger. But because he rejects the utopian socialism of Sinclair and the revolutionary violence of Steinbeck, Saroyan does not adopt the pessimistic nihilism of Robinson Jeffers. Rather he reaffirms the old American faith of Emerson and Whitman, who, skeptical both of social reformers and of prophets of doom, proclaimed that the world could be reformed only by reforming the individual, and that this could not be accomplished by social compulsion and physical violence but only by personal freedom and loving tolerance. "Build therefore your own world."

William Saroyan has not yet realized the full potentialities of his talent. His work has often been shoddy and his idealism fuzzy. But he has shown a capacity for steady growth, both in art and in thought. He is firmly rooted in the rich soil of his California reality. And he has absorbed—no matter by what mysterious processes of photosynthesis—the ideal truths of the American tradition. Far from being a decadent sensationalist or immature romantic, he has progressively realized a consistent American philosophy and has steadily advanced toward individual maturity and toward social responsibility.

20. HEMINGWAY ACHIEVES
THE FIFTH DIMENSION

IN *Green Hills of Africa,* Ernest Hemingway prophesied: "The kind of writing that can be done. How far prose can be carried if anyone is serious enough and has luck. There is a fourth and fifth dimension that can be gotten." Since then many critics have analyzed the symbols and mythical meanings of Hemingway's prose.[1] A few have tried to imagine what he meant by "a fourth and fifth dimension."[2] But most have agreed that the phrase is pretty vague.

"The fourth dimension" clearly has something to do with the concept of time, and with fictional techniques of describing it. Harry Levin has pointed out that Hemingway's style is lacking in the complexity of structure that normally describes "the third dimension," but that it offers a series of images (much like the moving pictures) to convey the impression of time-sequence and immediacy. Joseph Warren Beach has suggested that "the fourth dimension" is related to an "aesthetic factor" achieved by the hero's recurrent participation in some traditional "ritual or strategy"; while "the fifth dimension" may be an "ethical factor" achieved by his "participation in the moral order of the world." And Malcolm Cowley has also related "the fourth dimension" of time to "the almost continual performance of rites and ceremonies" suggesting the recurrent patterns of human experience, but has called "the fifth dimension" a "mystical or meaningless figure of speech."

But is the prophecy of a fifth dimensional prose "a meaningless figure of speech"? Certainly Hemingway has often attacked the critics for indulging in grandiose abstractions. Perhaps in *Green Hills of Africa,* one of his poorer books, he may have lowered his guard and relaxed his muscles. "The fifth dimension," moreover, has no accepted meaning to modern physicists. But Hemingway's art has always been self-conscious, and in the years of his apprenticeship in Paris he often discussed this art with Gertrude Stein—a trained philosopher, and an admirer of Henri Bergson's theories of the two kinds of "time."[3] Finally, I think, "the fifth dimension" is too strikingly specific a figure of speech to be "meaningless," although it may be "mystical."[4]

Actually, the specific phrase "the fifth dimension" was used in 1931 (*Green Hills of Africa* was published in 1935), by P. D. Ouspensky, who defined it to mean "the perpetual now." Ouspensky, a mystic, was an admirer of Bergson and of William James. Bergson (also an admirer of James) had emphasized the difference between psychological time and physical time. And both these ideas go back to William James's philosophy of "Radical Empiricism" (that is, of "immediate" or "pure" experience), which Gertrude Stein (a former pupil of James) had adapted for literary purposes. There is strong internal evidence that Hemingway's philosophy and practice both of style and of structure have followed this pattern of philosophic ideas. His literary ideal has been that of "immediate empiricism." And his "fifth dimensional prose" has attempted to communicate the immediate experience of "the perpetual now."

This mystical idea of a "fifth-dimensional" experience of "the perpetual now" might seem fantastic except that Hemingway first suggested it explicitly, and then practiced it consciously in his best fiction. *For Whom the Bell Tolls* embodies the idea both implicitly in structure, and explicitly in the speeches and thoughts of its characters. If this major novel is analyzed with this philosophic idea in mind, the structure and the purpose become unmistakable. The same structure (although less explicitly) informs the two great short stories which preceded this novel: "The Short Happy Life of Francis Macomber" and "The Snows of Kilimanjaro." And the writing of these three major works immediately followed Hemingway's prophecy of a "fifth dimension" to be achieved by prose.

Finally, this idea of "the perpetual now," and the philosophy of immediate empiricism which underlies it, suggest an explanation for the sharp alternation of brilliant success and painful failure in Hemingway's fictional career. In its sentimental or isolated form, this idea degenerates into "the cult of sensation,"[5] or of violent experience divorced from the routine of living. In this form it explains the frequent spectacular badness of *To Have and Have Not* and of *Across the River and Into the Trees*. But when related to the routine experiences of life, which give the more "sensational" experiences both a frame of reference and a meaning, this philosophy suggests the heights to which human nature can rise in moments of extreme stress. No longer the cult of "sensation," it becomes the ideal of "intensity" or "ecstasy," and produces that telescoping of experience and those flashes of illumination which make the "short" life of Francis Macomber supremely "happy," and the snows of Kilimanjaro blindingly brilliant.

In the 1920's, Albert Einstein's scientific theory of relativity—with its interpretation of "time" as a fourth dimension necessary to the

measurement of the space between the stars and within the atoms—
spawned a generation of pseudo-scientific speculators who attempted
to interpret the meaning of these physical theories for philosophic
and literary purposes. The most spectacular (and the least scientific)
of these was the Russian-born mystic, P. D. Ouspensky, who published his *Tertium Organum* in 1921, and *A New Model of the Universe* in 1931. Specifically, Ouspensky defined the "fifth dimension"
as "a line of perpetual now. . . . The fifth dimension forms a surface in relation to the line of time. . . . Though we are not aware of
it, sensations of the existence of other 'times' continually enter our
consciousness. . . . The fifth dimension is movement in the circle,
repetition, recurrence."[6] And at considerable length he analyzed and
illustrated these pseudo-scientific ideas with reference to James's
"moments of consciousness," Bergson's theory of time, and "the
Eternal Now of Brahma." I do not mean to imply that Hemingway
necessarily read Ouspensky's books, but his conversations with
Gertrude Stein and her friends in the twenties might well have included discussion of them. Moreover, his specific reference to "a
fifth dimension" finds partial explanation here, and Ouspensky's
description of "the perpetual now" closely parallels passages in *For
Whom the Bell Tolls* (as we shall see later).

With Bergson's theory of the "fourth dimension" of time, we approach firmer ground. Closer to the main stream of philosophic
thought, Bergson tried to interpret Einstein's scientific theory of the
relativity of time for literary purposes. In 1922 he used recent experiments measuring the speed of light, and proving that light rays
are "bent" by the force of gravitation, to illustrate his own already-
published theories of time. If physical "time" may be distorted by
motion in space and by gravitation, the measurement of psychological time may be distorted even more. Bergson had always emphasized
that mechanic time could never measure the intensities of the *élan
vital* in human experience, and that the human organism distorted
"time" through the devices of memory and intuitional thought. Now
Einstein's theory of relativity suggested that time was not a final
measurement in physics, either. In human consciousness time might
be telescoped, and sensation intensified, just as a passenger on a train
approaching a warning signal at a road-crossing hears the ringing
intensified in pitch as he approaches. Again, these ideas find echoes in
Hemingway's prose.

But all these ideas are speculative. The matrix from which they
spring, and in which their "mysticism" finds relation to reality, is
the philosophy of William James—acknowledged as "master" by

Ouspensky, Bergson, and Gertrude Stein equally. Approaching philosophy by way of psychology, James had interpreted all religious and artistic experiences as empirical phenomena: he had sought to observe, report, and analyze those intense "moments of consciousness," which men of religion and of art alike have described as the most "real" and important. With James, therefore, "realism" had become psychological, and "empiricism" had expanded to include all "immediate" or subjective as well as "mediate" or objective experience. Studying under James, Gertrude Stein had developed artistic techniques for communicating this "immediate" experience in prose style. Hemingway now carried these techniques further, and incorporated their psychological and philosophic patterns (outlined by James, Bergson, and perhaps Ouspensky) in the structural forms of his fiction.

To trace the development of these philosophic ideas, and to illustrate their application to literature, a book would hardly suffice. But to summarize: A brief, immediate experience, observed realistically, is described first as it occurred "in our time"; the protagonist is intensely moved, but remains confused, so that the meaning of it all seems nothing, or "nada." But this immediate experience recalls individual memories of other, similar experiences, or historic memories of parallel experiences in the history of other nations, or mystical, "racial" memories. And these "mediate" experiences are suggested by "flashbacks," or by conversations, or by the suggestion of recurrent myth or ritual patterns. And these fragmentary remembrances of similar experiences, by relating the individual to other people, places and times, suggest new meanings and forms. Finally this new awareness of the patterns and meanings implicit in the immediate, individual experience intensifies it, and gives it a new "dimension" not apparent at the time it actually happened.

For Whom the Bell Tolls is Hemingway's first full-length novel to describe, and partially to achieve, this radical intensification of experience. Both explicitly and implicitly, it seeks to realize the "fifth dimension" of an "eternal now," beyond the usual "fourth dimension" of time. It consciously describes—as well as subconsciously suggests—the telescoping of time involved in this realization of immediate experience. Indeed the very explicit self-consciousness with which it describes this idea constitutes its chief fault. But, although the idea has been suggested before, its formal pattern has never been clarified.

On the surface, the novel describes the tragedy of an American volunteer, fighting for the loyalists in the Spanish Civil War, who is sent to dynamite a bridge and does so, but is killed as a result. The action takes place in three days and involves a love affair with a Spanish girl named Maria, who has been rescued by the band of communist guerillas, after having been raped by the Fascists. This love affair has been criticized as irrelevant and obtrusive, but it actually forms the core of the book. And paradoxically it seems obtrusive *because* it struggles under so heavy a weight of conscious meaning.

The love affair begins immediately (and sensationally) when Maria crawls into the hero's sleeping bag the first night out. She hopes thus to exorcise the memory of the evil that has been done to her. But, even while loving her, the hero remains conscious of the passage of time, asking " 'what time is it now?' . . . It was one o'clock. The dial showed bright in the darkness that the robe made."[7] Later when he declares his love for Maria to Pilar, the gypsy mother-confessor, she warns him that "There is not much time." Because the ending is destined to be tragic, the love affair must be brief. But it will be meaningful, later.

After the second experience of love on the second day, this new meaning is suggested: ". . . and time absolutely still and they were both there, time having stopped and he felt the earth move out and away from under them." Later, thinking of this experience, the hero generalizes:

. . . Maybe that is my life and instead of it being threescore years and ten it is . . . just threescore hours and ten or twelve rather. . . .

I suppose it is possible to live as full a life in seventy hours as in seventy years; granted that your life has been full up to the time that the seventy hours start and that you have reached a certain age.

. . . So if your life trades its seventy years for seventy hours I have that value now and I am lucky enough to know it. . . . If there is only now, why then now is the thing to praise. . . . Now, *ahora, maintenant, heute.*

This telescoping of time becomes the new "value," and a universal one. Meanwhile, the hero continues to speculate about this tragic and enigmatic wisdom suggested by Pilar, the gypsy:

. . . She is a damned sight more civilized than you and she knows what time is all about. Yes, he said to himself, I think that we can admit that she has certain notions about the value of time. . . .

Not time, not happiness, not fun, not children, not a house, not a bathroom, not a clean pair of pyjamas, not the morning paper. . . . No, none of that. . . .

So if you love this girl as much as you say you do, you had better love her very hard and make up in intensity what the relation will lack in duration and in continuity.

As explicitly as possible the hero develops these new "notions about the value of time," speculating that the intense experience of a perpetual "now" may equal in value a lifetime of "duration and continuity." "It was a good system of belief," he concluded. "There is nothing else than now. . . . A good life is not measured by any biblical span."

In the ecstatic experience of perfect union with his beloved, time has stood still, and the value of intensity has been substituted for that of duration. From this experience has emerged the philosophy of the eternal now. Meanwhile, as the larger action of the novel approaches its climax, the hero seeks to understand the strange combination of violence and idealism which characterizes the Spanish people.

On the last night, Maria pours out to him the story of her violation. And again he generalizes:

Those are the flowers of Spanish chivalry. What a people they have been. . . . Spain has always had its own special idol worship within the Church. *Otra Virgen más.* I suppose that was why they had to destroy the virgins of their enemies. . . . This was the only country the reformation never reached. They were paying for the Inquisition now, all right. . . .

Maybe I have had all my life in three days, he thought.

In the hero's mind, "Maria" thus becomes a symbol of the traditional mariolatry of the Spanish Catholic Church, which "the reformation never reached"; and the violence of the Spanish Civil War becomes an intensified version of all modern history since the Reformation, compressed in symbolic time. His love for this modern Maria becomes both a symbolic fulfilment of history, and a transcendence of the old "time." In a flash, the immediate experience of the eternal now becomes not only a personal "system of belief," but a philosophy of history illuminating the action of the whole novel.

Shortly after, the third and final experience of love obliterates time ("the hand on the watch moved, unseen now"), the ecstasy is complete ("not why not ever why, only this now"), and this individual experience becomes one with the experience of all mystics: "It is in Greco and in San Juan da la Cruz, of course, and in the others. I am no mystic, but to deny it is as ignorant as though you denied the telephone." And this mystic transcendence of time and of self informs the final chapters of the book, as, after being fatally wounded, the hero comforts Maria: "Thou art me too now. Thou art all there will be of me" (p. 464), and accepts his own death: "He began to accept it and let the hate go out. . . . Once you saw it again as it was to others, once you got rid of your own self, the always ridding of self that you had to do in war. Where there could be no self." Thus finally the experience of "the perpetual now" leads to the mystical experience.

This intensification of experience under the emotional stress of love or war, resulting in an ecstasy transcending the traditional limitations of time and of self, and producing a "system of belief" verging on the mystical, is the subject of *For Whom the Bell Tolls*, both implicitly and explicitly. In a sense it has always been the subject of all Hemingway's fiction. But of course the emphasis has changed over the different periods of his writing, and he has developed this "system of belief" progressively.

Hemingway's early fiction, in general, described the immediate experience, of love or war, with a minimal awareness of meaning, and a minimal experience of ecstasy; therefore the experience seemed largely "sensational," and the meaning "nada." But beginning with "The Short Happy Life of Francis Macomber" and "The Snows of Kilimanjaro," his stories began to achieve ecstasy and to imagine a transcendence of the futility of the past. The sudden illumination of the vision of snow-capped Kilimanjaro prophesied the ecstasies and the transcendence of time in *For Whom the Bell Tolls*. But this novel exaggerated perhaps the author's new consciousness of meaning, and his concern with the "system" of his belief. In *The Old Man and the Sea* the idea became at last incarnated and the mysticism completely naturalized.

But the idea of the intensified experience of the immediate "now" is not simple, nor is its mysticism traditional. Hemingway himself has suggested some of the necessary qualifications: his Robert Jordan "supposed" that the final fulfilment of life in seventy hours was possible, "granted that your life has been full up to the time that the seventy hours start, and that you have reached a certain age." That is, the intensity of experience which transcends time, and achieves a new "value" or "dimension," depends upon an earlier fulness of experience of time and the appreciation of its value. The mysticism of this fifth dimensional experience implies no denial of the old "values" or "dimensions," but rather a fulfilment beyond them. These heroes do not seek escape from time (as do the hero and heroine of Robert Penn Warren's *World Enough and Time*), nor do they build a "tower beyond tragedy" (like the heroes of Robinson Jeffers), but rather they seek the intensified fulfilment of life within tragedy.

Further, this achievement of a new dimension of experience requires maturity—the hero must have reached "a certain age." Besides having lived a full life in the past, he must have reached a turning point, or crisis of life. So Francis Macomber—a natural aristocrat who has excelled at sports in the past—confronts the final test of courage, fails, but suddenly overcomes his fear and achieves a brief ecstasy of happiness. And the autobiographical hero of Kilimanjaro—who has prospered well enough in love and in literature—sees suddenly the ecstatic vision of supreme success, as he dies.

Finally, the achievement of this new dimension of experience, whether in "prose" or in life, is exceptional—"one must have luck." So Robert Jordan "had learned that he himself, with another person, could be everything. But inside himself he knew that this was the exception." The new experience requires a fulness of past life, a certain age, and an ecstasy which is mystical in every sense.

A fourth dimensional sense of time (Cowley and Beach have suggested) is often achieved by a detailed description of the patterns of experience which have crystallized in rituals, ceremonies, traditions, habits of action, codes of behavior. On the level of pure realism, this may be suggested by that loving description of the techniques of any work or sport which is characteristic of all Hemingway's stories.[8] The absence of this work-a-day realism contributes to the failure of *Across the River,* while the exact techniques of fishing make real the occasional mysticism of *The Old Man and the Sea.* On the level of art, the patterned ritual of the bull-fight and the sporting code of the big-game hunter also suggest this sense of repetition in time. While on the level of religion, mythical or symbolic actions, which sometimes seem unreal or irrational, may provide the pattern. The aesthetic sense of the perfect fulfilment of some pattern of action in time is the necessary pre-condition for achievement of the final "magic."

The "fifth dimensional" intensity of experience beyond time may come, finally, from a profound sense of participation in these traditional patterns of life experience. Beach's description of the fifth dimension as a "sense of participation in the moral order of the world" is suggestive. "You felt an absolute brotherhood with the others who were engaged in it," observed Robert Jordan of his Spanish Civil War. Paradoxically, love and war become supremely "moral," and the intensity of the experience they offer may communicate a mystical ecstasy. If only the sensational and the violent aspects are described, with only a traditional, third-dimensional realism, "nada" results. But these violent sensations have always been the elemental stuff, both of human tragedy and of mystical transcendence. If the red slayer think only of slaying, and if the slain think only of being slain, no fourth or fifth dimension is achieved. But Santiago in *The Old Man and the Sea,* performing realistically the ritual techniques of his trade, goes on to identify the intensity of his own suffering with that of the great fish that he is slaying. And telling his story, Hemingway has achieved that synthesis of immediate experience and mysticism which, perhaps, is "the fifth dimension."

PART VII

21. THE GOOD AND THE BAD

IN CONTEMPORARY American literature, the dream has continued to suggest the new patterns of our thinking. In O'Neill, the search for an impossible beauty has led to an inevitable tragedy. In Jeffers, the desire for absolute freedom has often resulted in moral anarchy. In Wolfe, the quest for a perfect democracy inspired the hero's odyssey through the western world. In Steinbeck, the hope of economic opportunity motivated the Okies' migrations, although the later novels have implied the failure of that hope. And in Saroyan, the contemporary West has suggested a new partial realization of the old dream.

Even those contemporary authors who have seemed most realistic have often dealt indirectly with the dream. Sinclair Lewis, after satirizing its corruption in *Main Street* and *Babbitt,* turned crusader in later novels to preach the reform of American abuses. And Faulkner, even while damning all Northern attempts to reform the South, has always described slavery as the ancient curse upon the land. Hemingway, whose favorite subjects have been war and sudden death, has still created heroes who continue to fight for freedom and human decency. Dos Passos, after the earlier novels describing a corrupt capitalism, has returned to the founding fathers for inspiration. And novelists like Conrad Richter and Walter Van Tilburg Clark have fashioned modern myths out of the old dreams of the pioneers.

In the twentieth century as in the nineteenth, the American dream has sometimes seemed admirable and desirable, sometimes deluded and impossible. But more often than not, the modern temper has distrusted it. Even those contemporaries who have celebrated it most enthusiastically have suggested its weaknesses: O'Neill and Jeffers have carried it to romantic extremes, Steinbeck and Saroyan have confused it with sentimentality, and Thomas Wolfe, who realized it most completely, described it with too intense an egotism. In the course of the centuries of its imaginative treatment in fiction and drama and poetry, the dangers—as well as the values—of the dream have become increasingly apparent. Perhaps it is time to cast up the balance.

First and most obviously, the dream has led to delusion when it has been merely romantic. Increasingly in modern times American writers have satirized the old folk tales of "pie in the sky" and *The Big Rock Candy Mountain*. The quest for "el dorado" or the pot of gold at the end of the rainbow was historically real, but—of course—psychologically false. On the philosophic level, this romantic confusion substituted the "expectation of happiness" for the ideal "pursuit of happiness." Therefore, modern reactionaries have even attacked the Declaration of Independence for being deluded. Meanwhile many novelists who have imagined the pursuit of happiness in fictional terms—as Steinbeck did in *The Grapes of Wrath*—have reacted to cynical disillusion when the pursuit has failed. Even in the nineteenth century the Transcendental Dream often ended in tragedy—as with Margaret Fuller. Whenever American dreamers have expected happiness and success as their "inalienable right," they have suffered disillusion. Modern literature has often been confused by this romantic expectation.

On the other hand, modern American literature at its best has accepted tragedy as a condition of modern life, and has imagined a happiness "beyond tragedy." Most realistically, the novels and stories of Hemingway have repeatedly described happiness as something to be realized in the face of death: "The Short Happy Life of Francis Macomber" suggests the simple answer to the romantic confusion. More mystically the poetry of Jeffers has imagined *The Tower Beyond Tragedy*, from whose height man can observe even his own defeat and death with equanimity. And most explicitly Thomas Wolfe celebrated the final "Credo" of the democratic dream in the last chapter of his fictional autobiography, in contrast to the disbelief of *Ecclesiastes*, and to the romantic illusions of his own youth.

Second, the dream has also led to delusion when it has been messianic, or self-righteous. Historically, the most common fault of many transcendental dreamers was that they sought to reform the world at once. Hawthorne effectively satirized this delusion in his story, "The Celestial Railroad," and in his novel, *The Blithedale Romance*. But no critic of the dream ever satirized it so effectively as the over-enthusiastic transcendentalist, Sylvester Judd, in his "epic" poem, *Philo: An Evangeliad*. In 1850, his hero announced the advent of the millennium, and in so doing reduced the dream to its ultimate absurdity:

Their swords
To ploughshares, spears to pruning-hooks, they beat;
Nor ever blacksmiths gave such lusty blows.
They rend the forts and whoop down citadels.
The slaves are frolicking; to-morrow they
With freeman's will a freeman's work will do.
A mob of Adventers the gallows touze;
See bands of exiles singing to their homes;
Scrimp jails to airy hospitals arise;
Cities exude their poisons, as a fog;
The mephitism is banished by the winds.
The Cumberland road, with many wagon loads
Of reparations for the Indians,
A mirthful rabble crowd. There is a town
In Phalansteric change; the houses move,
As trees of old, to sweet synergic pipes.
See gardens multiply, and bulbs increase,
See tasteful cottages adorn the plains.
Our senators eventful progress feel,
And meet to Christianize the constitution.
The epoch deepens, wide our God hath rule;
Beyond the seas prophetic crises thrill.
Love balances their power, and soothes their fears;
Their ships of war convoy Millennial rapture
Around the earth; the serf to burgher mounts;
The lazzaroni weave in factories;
The Moslem is agape, and opes his mosque
To Gospel preachers. The glad news spins on
To Ispahan, and shakes the Chinese wall.
Enough for one day; let us homeward wend,
And in our hearts the solemn lessons tend.

Poor Sylvester Judd seriously imagined the immediate and universal reform of the world by the power of the American dream. And a century later something of the same messianic delusion transformed the later novels of Sinclair Lewis into pamphleteering tracts, and his heroes into fanatic puppets.

It is one of the "ironies of American history" that many Americans who have most effectively imagined the dream of liberty have also fallen prey to the delusion that this dream can be legislated, and imposed on others. So Emerson, whose essay on "New England Reformers" effectively demolished the idea that evil can be "reformed" from without, nevertheless enthusiastically supported emancipation and the Civil War, and later imagined that the defeat of the slaveholders implied the final reform of American evil. Only Thoreau—

in this respect the most clear-eyed of all American dreamers—spent his life in "reforming" himself, and achieving his own independence of the social evils which he criticized, before formulating his program of "Civil disobedience." Few Americans have entirely escaped the messianic delusion.

Third, the dream has led to delusion when it has been identified with the fact of material progress. In the nineteenth century the supposition was common that progress was a law of nature, whose working was both universal and inevitable. In general terms, the theory of evolution implied it; more specifically, the westward progress of the pioneer suggested it; and the steady, scientific progress of commerce and industry reinforced it. Whether evolution always produced higher forms of life, and whether Western settlement always resulted in a better society, and whether the greater production of machines and gadgets guaranteed greater individual happiness and social progress, were questions seldom seriously considered in the great, expansive nineteenth century. Only in our twentieth century has the idea of progress become suspect, and the evils accompanying Western settlement—and even civilization itself—been emphasized. Reversing the anti-fundamentalist trend of the last hundred years, modern philosophers have described the idea of progress as an ancient Christian heresy.

But most of the earlier dreamers did not accept the idea of progress whole. So Whitman, in celebrating a "Passage to India," and citing the transcontinental railroad and the Atlantic cable as instruments of progress, emphasized primarily their potential role in improving world understanding and achieving a "passage to more than India." The westward "progress" of "O, Pioneers" became rather the symbol of the spirit of discovery. And science, as the word implies, was celebrated not so much for its material gifts, as for its imaginative value. Sinclair Lewis's one genuine hero, Martin Arrowsmith, incarnated for modern Americans the best of this spirit of science: independence of mind, objectivity, and the ideal of intellectual discovery. Just as Thoreau escaped the messianic delusion by reforming himself, subjectively, before attempting to reform the world, so Arrowsmith escaped the delusion of materialistic progress by seeking, objectively, to advance the frontiers of knowledge.

The last delusion to which American dreamers have been subject is that of nationalism, or "Americanism" in its narrowest sense. From the "manifest destiny" of the nineteenth century to the crusades of our "American century" to make the world safe for democracy, this delusion has persisted. Now "Americanism" has come sometimes to imply a denial of the old dream, and the "un-American activities committee" implies suspicion of those who fight for civil liberties and the rights of the individual. In this confusion of values modern men have come to distrust the American dream of the past, believing its Americanism also to have been isolationist and illiberal.

Of course the word "American" does imply a difference from "European" or "Asiatic." But the American dream was different from the European, or the Christian, chiefly in that the new American world offered an opportunity for a new realization of the old religious ideals. America has seemed the new Atlantis where the old Platonic Republic, and the old Christian City of God might be realized. So when the Puritans emigrated to America, they dreamed of a commonwealth purified of European faults; and when the Transcendentalists rejected the feudalism of Europe, they did so in the name of the freedom which European idealists had preached. The "Americanism" of the dream has not been narrowly national.

Therefore the dream persists, in spite of the delusions of its supporters, and the misinterpretations of its critics. It imagines a way of life which the disillusion of modern times has not discredited. It praises—not nationalism, but freedom for all men; not materialism, but the progress of science; not the compulsory reform of society, but the education of the individual; and not mere success, but self-realization through struggle and even tragedy. Although it is "American" in a sense, it existed before America was discovered—indeed, it helped to discover America. And because it is not merely national, it is likely to persist even though American civilization, as we know it, should pass away.

22. THE LOGIC OF
AMERICAN LITERATURE

THIS BOOK has interpreted American literature as a kind of imaginative and experimental projection of the questions which the American dream has raised:—Is the ideal of perfect freedom and democracy realizable? And is it desirable?—That is, how true is the dream? And how good is it? The answers have depended a good deal on definition: the dream has been realistic and good when it has avoided romantic extremes and messianic delusions, when it has understood "progress" in terms of science and art rather than materialism, and "democracy" in terms of individual freedom and equality rather than politics. But although it has never been defined clearly, the answers of the great American writers to its questions have followed a logical pattern.

The transcendental idealists have believed that the dream can be realized, and that it is good. The traditionalists have believed that it can never be realized, and that it is bad. The pragmatists have believed that parts of it can be realized, but that any "dream" is bad. But the romanticists have believed that any dream is good, although the dream of democracy can never be realized. Thus Emerson celebrated the dream wholeheartedly, while Melville rejected it; and William James rejected all dreams but sought to realize many particular ideals, while Eugene O'Neill praised it but described it as unrealizable. In different forms and from different points of view, American writers have imagined these or similar attitudes toward the dream.

But if the dream has been so undefinable and vague, what difference has it made? And why write a book about it? How does it affect our understanding or interpretation of American literature? And how may this understanding affect our actual living in the present, and our thinking about the future?

The foregoing critiques of American writers in terms of the dream have implied (but not made fully explicit) a re-interpretation of American literature. For, although the dream has been vague, it has suggested clearly alternative ways of thinking about American problems. Traditionally, our literature has been interpreted either historically ("the colonial period") or technically ("the rise of literary realism"). But this book suggests the re-interpretation

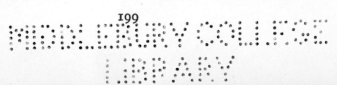

of American literature and thought primarily in terms of the logic of the dream.

Traditionally, the years 1820–1860 have been labeled "the romantic period of American literature."—Emerson and Thoreau, Melville and Hawthorne, and Poe have been called the chief "romantic" writers. And from the point of view of literary history, all these developed the techniques and forms of the European romantic movement. Hawthorne even defined his novels as "romances" to distinguish them from novels of manners. But from the point of view of logic, these writers described three sharply contrasting attitudes toward history, and toward the American dream. And this book has emphasized these contrasting attitudes which found simultaneous expression within the historic romantic movement, rather than the similar literary forms.

Within the historic "romantic movement" of American literature, Emerson and Thoreau gave expression to the belief that the dream of perfect freedom could be realized in the new world; Melville and Hawthorne rejected this belief; while Poe celebrated his private dream. The contrast of Emerson's acceptance and Melville's rejection is clear. But the contrast between the "transcendental" dream of freedom in the new world, and the purely "romantic" dream of escape to a world of imagination, is less clear. But this contrast is fundamental to any definition of "the American dream." Let us take Thoreau and Poe as examples.

Thoreau carried the transcendental dream of individual independence to its logical conclusion, and sought perfect freedom from American economic and social traditions. But Thoreau did not idealize escape from American actuality, from economic necessity, or from human society. His dream was localized at Walden Pond, his first chapter described his "Economy" of individual independence there, and many of his later chapters described the farmers whom he visited and the friends who visited him. Nothing in his "transcendental" idealism implied a romantic escape to fantasy. Nor did he ever describe the dream of sudden perfection: his "Civil Disobedience" detailed the means of achieving a "better government," not "at once" but gradually. He sought reform not by means of government intervention, but of individual education. Unlike romantic voyagers to far places, he had "traveled a good deal in Concord." He dreamed not of past times, but of reforming the American present; not of freedom in a world of fantasy, but in actuality; and not of immediate perfection, but of gradual improvement through individual effort.

And he had faith in his dream, because he himself had practiced it in his own experience.

By contrast, Poe described the traditionally romantic dream of beautiful past times and far places, set in a world of fantasy. In the "misty mid-region of Weir," he imagined the beauty which he could not find in American actuality—in a "kingdom beside the sea," he and his ideal love would live a life of impossible perfection. His poetry described life as "A Dream within a Dream," for dreams were his only truth and his only beauty. Like all Americans he imagined and sought for "Eldorado"—

> But he grew old—
> This knight so bold—
> And o'er his heart a shadow
> Fell as he found
> No spot of ground
> That looked like Eldorado.

He believed in the world of dream, and in its truth and beauty, more passionately than did either Emerson or Thoreau, but he wholly disbelieved in any possibility of its realization. In the intellect he conceived the absolute ideal, and even cried out a philosophical "Eureka." But his dream was unreal and his cry without conviction. Poe echoed the poetic despair of Byron, and prophesied the beautiful evil of Baudelaire, but his romantic nihilism found few counterparts in the American literature of his nineteenth century. Only later would the haunted heroes of O'Neill and Jeffers repeat his denial of hope and his celebration of violence.

In the nineteenth century the transcendental dream of liberty described concretely by Thoreau, contrasted with the romantic dream of escape described fancifully by Poe. The one was progressive and responsible, the other regressive and irresponsible. But because both dreams found expression in the historic "romantic movement," they were often confused: Hawthorne and Melville, writing novels to discredit the dreamers whom they distrusted, sometimes confused them. At best they described the dream of freedom clearly: *The Scarlet Letter* told the transcendental tragedy of Hester Prynne without distortion; and *Moby Dick* embodied both the heroism and the fanaticism of dream-led Ahab. But at worst, these same traditionalists often confused transcendental idealism with romantically irresponsible emotion: Hawthorne created the passionately irresponsible Zenobia to discredit the Utopian idealism of Blithedale, but failed to make his fiction live; and Melville created the impossibly romantic *Pierre* to demonstrate (unconvincingly) the hopeless dilemma of the American dreamer. The conflict within the romantic movement of the transcendental dream of liberty with the merely romantic dream of escape suggests the first re-interpretation of American literature.

Historically, "the romantic period" gave expression to three attitudes toward the dream; but its transcendental celebration of liberty has often been confused with its romantic celebration of escape, although the rejection of all dreams by the traditionalists has been clear. Then, as "the romantic period" gave way to "the age of realism" following the Civil War, a fourth attitude emerged. Like the traditionalists the pragmatic realists distrusted dreams, as such. Therefore it has seemed that "the age of realism" represented a complete reaction from "the romantic period," and that the realists and the traditionalists on the one hand contrasted with the romanticists and the transcendentalists on the other. But the historic realists contrasted as sharply with the traditionalists as they did with transcendentalists—indeed, "the age of realism" continued many of the earlier ideals, although it rejected all abstract "idealism" and all vague "dreams." Just as the transcendental dream contrasted with the romantic, so the pragmatic realism contrasted with the old traditionalism. This contrast implies a second major re-interpretation of American literature.

That the philosophic realism of William James continued and developed many of the transcendental ideals of Emerson, we have observed in detail. But that the parallel literary realism of such novelists as Howells and Dreiser continued and developed similar ideals is equally true. Howells, for instance, first narrated how Silas Lapham "rose" in moral stature by renouncing the dishonest business practices of "society"; then, in *A Hazard of New Fortunes*, suggested an idealism which dared defy social injustice; and finally, in *The Traveler from Altruria*, imagined a socialism like that of the earlier transcendental "communities." Similarly, Dreiser's "realism" first described *Sister Carrie* as the victim of society, then described the crime of Clyde Griffiths as *An American Tragedy* caused by the false standards of society; until finally Dreiser, the extreme "realist," preached a social idealism more extreme than that of the transcendentalists themselves. Although "the age of realism" developed literary techniques and fictional forms contrasting with those of "the romantic period," it often used those forms to embody and to make real particular ideals of the transcendentalists. Although it rejected dreams in general, paradoxically it sought to re-alize much of the American dream.

Considered as an experimental projection of the logic of the dream, historic American literature thus falls into new patterns. "The ro-mantic movement" expressed both the transcendental dream of lib-erty and democracy, and the romantic fantasy of license and escape. Similarly, historic "realism" criticized vague dreams, but also sought to realize many democratic ideals. Historically, these re-in-terpretations are significant.

But beyond history, the logic of the dream suggests new ways of reading American literature, and of thinking about the problems of American life. Often the best American writing has been ambiguous, and even ambivalent, suggesting the alternative attitudes toward the problems described, and the conflicting values involved, without choosing. We have observed the three clearly contrasting "morals" which different readers have found in *The Scarlet Letter*. Similarly Melville's fictions suggested alternative solutions to the problem of liberty and authority. And these alternative solutions (or ambigui-ties) have continued to enrich, (and to confuse) modern American fiction.

The alternative answers to the problem of liberty and authority have appeared most clearly when embodied in the stories of ships at sea—particularly in time of war. The alternatives may be de-fined briefly in reference to Melville's *Billy Budd*. In more detail, the recent *Caine Mutiny* by Herman Wouk has raised (and suggested answers to) the same problem: Is the American dream of liberty and democracy realizable—or even desirable—in a world at war?

The clear answer which Melville consciously declared in *Billy Budd* is that individual liberty must be denied in time of war. This is the traditional solution. But the plotting of *Billy Budd* suggests an opposite answer (which Lincoln actually affirmed in the Civil War), that a maximum of liberty should be preserved even in time of battle, and mercy should temper authority. This is the "transcen-dental" solution. The pragmatic answer was later defined historically by Justice Oliver Wendell Holmes, Jr., in his judgment that liberty should prevail over authority, except in time of "clear and present danger." Finally, the romantic answer glorifies the ideal of inde-pendence, but denies that it can be realized.

Recently *The Caine Mutiny* has explored essentially the same problem as *Billy Budd*, but in more complex and more modern terms: one of the characters in *The Caine Mutiny* specifically compares his problem to that of *Billy Budd*. Meanwhile, Melville's tale was rewritten into a successful Broadway drama. Against the background of Melville's man-of-war, let us consider the alternative answers to the old problem suggested by the modern fiction.

The Caine Mutiny explores once again the alternative attitudes toward the dream of liberty in time of war. It embodies the different alternatives both in its different characters, and also in the progressive changes in the character of its hero, Willie Keith. Since the reader experiences the action through Willie's eyes, his own attitudes change with those of the hero, whose frequent confusion he shares. Thus the ambivalence which the problem of unjust authority always causes is described from the partial and changing point of view of the individual, and is clarified only toward the end—first in the court martial, and finally in the rise to authority of the hero himself. Beginning with the dream of perfect liberty and justice common to most Americans, the novel (and its hero) gradually changes to an acceptance of the traditional authority which partly denies the dream. But unlike *Billy Budd*, the modern novel compromises the problem in terms of action, although defining it sharply in terms of words: the book ends with the "mutinous" liberals acquitted, but (in various degrees) discredited.

The Caine Mutiny begins with the romantic attitude toward authority, emphasized by the hero's youthful romance with May Wynn. The irresponsibility of this affair almost causes him to be expelled from officers' training school. On board the Caine, however, this attitude of romantic irresponsibility is embodied in the character of Keefer, the true villain of the story. For it is Keefer—always complaining and always shirking—who gradually seduces both the idealistic Willie and the pragmatic first-mate, Maryk, to mutiny. Not only does the romantic Keefer write fiction, but he creates the fiction of the psychotic incompetence of Captain Queeg in the minds of his associates. But only in the end does Willie grow to recognize his friend's irresponsibility for what it is, and his own earlier irresponsible romanticism as well.

The contrasting, traditional attitude toward authority is complicated by its embodiment in the unjust and incompetent Captain Queeg. Unlike the just and noble Captain Vere in *Billy Budd*, Queeg seems the villain through most of the story. And because Queeg is the worst type of captain, the partial acquittal of the mutineers by the court-martial is justified. But the "liberal" defense lawyer, Greenwald, actually praises the Queegs of the world as a necessary evil, and the hero finally accepts his verdict: "The idea is, once you get an incompetent ass of a skipper—and it's a chance of war—

there's nothing to do but serve him as though he were the wisest and the best." Although the book begins with the dream of individual liberty, it ends with the affirmation of traditional authority.

Between the two extremes of irresponsible romanticism and unjust authority stand the hero, Willie Keith, and the first-mate, Steve Maryk. These two embody the old American idealism of independent judgment and equal justice, although often inarticulately. Maryk is led to depose Captain Queeg because he believes that he will sink the ship. And Willie supports the first-mate both for this pragmatic reason, and because he hates Queeg's tyrannical injustice to his men. Through the bulk of the novel, the old American idealism dominates. But in the end it is rejected, because of the exigencies of war, although it is reaffirmed for times of peace.

The importance and immense popularity of *The Caine Mutiny* results from its clear and concrete embodiment of the old problems of the dream in terms of contemporary fiction. Unlike *Billy Budd*, these problems are not simply stated; nor are they finally judged; and the novel ends with the return of peace, and the return of the hero to the responsibility of a marriage which will cut across the traditional social patterns. The old American ideals have been tested in both war and peace: in war authority prevails, in peace responsible liberty will prevail; but at all times the alternative attitudes and the conflicting values are present.

This is the American dilemma: the ship of state is sailing stormy seas.—Shall the captain's orders be obeyed, even though they sink the ship?—Shall they be obeyed even though they deny the principles of "life, liberty, and the pursuit of happiness," upon which America was founded? Is liberty impossible in time of war? And in the ambiguities of our "cold" war, does a clear and present danger invalidate the principles of the past? Seen in perspective, all American literature has explored the alternative answers to this contemporary dilemma.

The answers to this dilemma which American literature has suggested are not abstract and academic, but vital and immediate. And as the cold war and the threat of war intensifies, the traditional answer looms always larger: "Though an army be all volunteers, martial law must prevail." Unpopular a century ago, Melville's warning has become accepted as universal truth.—The American dream briefly imagined the impossible; the Bill of Rights assumed the protection of the Atlantic Ocean, which the progress of science has shrunk to the size of a pond. The dream of individual liberty and universal democracy ignored the bitter lessons of history, and now weakens our defenses against a dictatorship which understands only the arguments of power. Not only is the dream unrealistic, but it is dangerous, for if "the world's peaces are but truces," martial law must prevail for the very preservation of American democracy.— This is the traditional answer.

But the answer which the transcendental idealists proclaimed a century ago contradicts or qualifies this argument now, as it did then. The ideals of individual liberty and equal rights which the Declaration of Independence first proclaimed have become the universal American goal, and to deny this is to deny America itself. Moreover, this dream was not suggested by the passing facts of nineteenth century history, but by the accumulated idealism of three millennia: to reject this dream is to reject much of the classical and Christian heritage of Western man. The fact of war and the threat of war do not warrant the denial of liberty in the name of security: to preserve American democracy by abrogating the laws of democracy is self-contradictory: freedom can only be preserved by means of freedom. Although the world's peaces have always been truces, the enlightened experience of Western man suggests that when martial law prevails over liberty in time of truce, the people perish. The security of the sword is the death of soul, and of the body also.— This is the transcendental answer.

But in modern times the answer of the pragmatic realists has loomed larger than that of the idealists, and has suggested a more popular alternative to the traditional. In time of war martial law must prevail, but not blindly: in every case circumstances should modify the application of law. Men are responsible for all human laws: in this sense, the hanging of the good Billy Budd constituted a denial of man's humanity, and the acquittal of the Caine Mutineers constituted an affirmation both of human justice and mercy. In time of peace on the other hand, the due processes of constitutional democracy should prevail, modified only by considerations of clear and immediate danger. In time of peace it is the burden of authority to demonstrate this danger, just as in time of war it is the burden of democracy to prove circumstances mitigating the application of martial law. If the world's peaces are but truces, "cold" wars have always existed: the danger of alien attack cannot justify the denial of civil rights, except in particular and extreme cases—and for brief periods of time.—This is the pragmatic answer.

Finally, the romantic extremists have found more support for their prophecies today than ever in the nineteenth century. Why quibble about pragmatic means and circumstances when final destruction is probable? Why argue the politics of democracy and dictatorship when one bomb will destroy both? The old ideals of progress and democracy are only a bunch of carrots to tempt the ass onwards. Eat, drink and be merry—speed, violence, and sensation—and forget both traditions and ideals. Shine, Perishing Republic, for The Iceman Cometh. From Here to Eternity, the Naked will soon be the Dead. Only the free imagination of the individual—only the unfettered exercise of the human spirit—only the escape of the soul into intensity and beauty beyond time and circumstance is important; for the old dream of gradual progress and democracy is dead.—This is the romantic answer.

All American writers have explored one or another of these answers to the question of the dream. But some of the answers have been contradictory, and there has been little agreement. It is not even possible to say whether the dream—taken in the broadest sense —has been good or bad for America. But the omnipresence of the dream throughout our history has made it all-important to American writers and philosophers. Whether it has been good or bad, it has deeply influenced all out thinking and feeling. Freedom and democracy have always been the most "American" of our activities.

In a world at war, any insistence on the old ideals of individual freedom and democracy may be "bad" for the military efficiency of America. It is even possible that the total effect of the American dream may always have been to complicate our thinking and to delay our acting. Certainly it is important to define what aspects of the dream have been good, and what bad,—as the preceding chapter has attempted to do. But whether the dream has been good or bad in the past, and whether it may prove valuable or dangerous in the future, it has become an essential part of our history and psychology. The love of freedom has always been the essential quality of American man.

NOTES

CHAPTER 2

1. Captain Edward Johnson, *A History of New England, or Wonder-working Providence of Sions Saviour* (London, 1654).
2. J. T. Adams, *The Epic of America* (Boston, 1931), viii.
3. See Ernest Tuveson, *Millennium and Utopia* (Berkeley, California, 1953).
4. See John Baillie, *The Belief in Progress* (London, 1950).
5. See Perry Miller, *The New England Mind* (New York, 1939).

CHAPTER 3

1. Emerson's *Journals,* October 6, 1836.
2. V. L. Parrington, *Main Currents,* II, 379.
3. O. B. Frothingham, *Transcendentalism in New England,* 108.
4. Perry Miller, *The New England Mind,* 194, 214; and "Jonathan Edwards to Emerson," in *The New England Quarterly* (December, 1940), XIII, 589.
5. Theodore Parker, "Transcendentalism," in *The World of Matter and the Spirit of Man.*
6. The conflict between "piety" and "moralism" has often been described. See chapter on "The Genteel Tradition"; and J. Haroutunian, *Piety and Moralism in Puritan New England;* and P. Miller, *The New England Mind.*
7. See, for instance, H. B. Parkes, *The Pragmatic Test;* and Yvor Winters, *Primitivism and Decadence.*

CHAPTER 4

1. Rewritten from "Introduction" to *Emerson,* American Writers Series.
2. See Lowell's essay on "Democracy."
3. *The Epic of America,* 198.
4. See D. G. Haskins, *Emerson's Maternal Ancestors.*
5. He is so described in the only surviving document; see *The Emersons of Ipswich,* by B. K. Emerson.
6. See Ernest Marchand, "Emerson and the Frontier."
7. *Journals,* I, 247–8.
8. *Uncollected Writings,* 31–32.
9. *Works,* VII, 121.
10. The complete letter is of great interest. See J. E. Cabot, *A Memoir,* I, 34–36.
11. *Works,* II, 89; "Self-Reliance."
12. See *Works,* XI, 1–25.
13. See H. H. Clark, "Emerson and Science," 234.
14. *Journals,* III, 163.
15. O. W. Firkins, *Emerson,* 297; G. E. Woodberry, *Emerson,* 109; R. M. Gay, *Emerson,* 8; *et al.*
16. *Works,* I, 60; "Nature."
17. "Transcendental," in the sense of mystical, and not yet tested by sensuous experience. See H. S. Commager, "Theodore Parker," *New England Quarterly,* VI, 275–6 (June, 1933).
18. J. T. Adams, *The Epic of America,* 198.

CHAPTER 5

1. Odell Shepard, *The Journals of Bronson Alcott* (Boston, 1938), 186 ff.
2. *Journals*, 197.
3. *Journals*, 197.
4. *Journals*, 81.
5. *Journals, xvii;* and Austin Warren, in *American Literature*, III (1931), 3.
6. H. S. Canby, in *The Saturday Review of Literature* (September 24, 1938), paraphrasing Odell Shepard, *Pedlar's Progress* (Boston, 1937), 221 and 478.
7. *Pedlar's Progress*, 290.
8. Emerson's *Works* (Centenary edition), I, 340.
9. *Journals*, 73.
10. H. C. Goddard, "Transcendentalism," in *Cambridge History of American Literature*, I, 326.
11. O. B. Frothingham, *Transcendentalism in New England* (Boston, 1876), 105.
12. See J. T. Adams, *The Epic of America* (Boston, 1931), 194–198.
13. See George Santayana, "The Genteel Tradition in American Philosophy," in *Winds of Doctrine* (New York, 1926); and *The Genteel Tradition at Bay* (New York, 1931). The writer accepts Santayana's identification of "the genteel tradition" with "the new humanism."
14. *Journals*, 7 and 11. Professor Shepard suggests that Alcott's occasional gentility was inspired by Miss May, his future wife. Like Mrs. Hawthorne and Mrs. Clemens, she may have influenced him against "coarseness" and "arrogant" independence. But, for whatever reason, Alcott never realized the ideal of self-reliance as consistently as Emerson and Thoreau.
15. See "Emerson and the Frontier," by Ernest Marchand, *American Literature*, III, 149–174 (May, 1931).
16. *Journals*, 313.
17. *Journals*, 313.
18. *Winds of Doctrine*, 187–188. See also *The Genteel Tradition at Bay*, 3–7.
19. Sanborn and Harris, in their *Life of Alcott* (Boston, 1893), 622–627, described this opposition as a chronological matter. Of course some aspects of it were. But others were not (*Cf.* the footnotes to this paper). And the gentility of Alcott's early style gradually lessened, even while his genteel dislike of utilitarian labor and of reform increased.
20. Because Emerson's philosophical *ideas* were sometimes as confused as Alcott's, he also has been accused of inconsistency. But Emerson preached the moral *ideal* of self-reliance with remarkable consistency. From the group of opposites (see above), Emerson consistently chose the first, and rejected the second. And Thoreau did so even more consistently.
21. *Journals*, 94.
22. *Journals*, 11.
23. *Journals*, 21.
24. *Journals*, 455.
25. *Journals*, 80.
26. *Journals*, 445. In *Pedlar's Progress* (452), Professor Shepard traces Alcott's belief in heredity to the Englishman, James Pierrepont Greaves, and points out its logical opposition to the American faith in education. But Professor Shepard will not "blame" Alcott for holding two opposite faiths at once, or believe that this contradiction harmed him. It is the thesis of this essay that this fundamental contradiction largely caused Alcott's failure as a thinker and writer.
27. *Pedlar's Progress*, 430.
28. Quoted in *Pedlar's Progress*, 427.
29. "Satanic" in its effect upon Alcott—not upon others.

30. Again his wife probably influenced his thinking. It was she who vetoed his proposal to return to peddling. But see her remarks, *Journals,* 152.
31. *Journals,* 152.
32. *Journals,* 178.
33. *Journals,* 199.
34. *Journals,* 185.
35. *Journals,* 345.
36. Emerson's *Works,* I, 37.
37. *Pedlar's Progress,* 514. Here, as always, Professor Shepard suggests clearly the contradictions of Alcott's career, but does not follow them to their logical conclusions.
38. *Pedlar's Progress,* 493.
39. Cf. F. I. Carpenter, "William James and Emerson," in *American Literature,* II, 39 ff. (March, 1939).
40. *Journals,* 485.
41. *Journals,* 195.
42. Emerson's *Works,* I, 181.

CHAPTER 6

1. Harvey O'Higgins, *Alias Walt Whitman* (Newark, N.J., 1930), first published in *Harper's Monthly,* May, 1929; and Esther Shepherd, *Walt Whitman's Pose* (New York, 1938).
2. Article in the *Dictionary of American Biography* (1936).
3. T. F. Wolfe, *Literary Shrines* (Philadelphia, 1895).
4. F. P. Hier, Jr., "End of a Literary Mystery," *American Mercury,* I (1924), 471–78.
5. Shepherd, *op. cit.* It is a paradoxical fact that Miss Shepherd, in summarizing the case against Whitman, never mentioned the article by O'Higgins which had clearly outlined this general argument before her.
6. Mr. O'Higgins did not relish this.
7. Shepherd, *op. cit.,* 141.
8. Quoted in S. P. Sherman, *Americans* (New York, 1924), 156.
9. See Floyd Stovall, "Main Drifts in Whitman's Poetry," *American Literature,* IV (1932), 3–21; and Henry A. Myers, "Whitman's Conception of Spiritual Democracy," *American Literature,* VI (1934), 239–53, and "Whitman's Consistency," *ibid.,* VIII (1936), 243–57.
10. Quoted in G. L. Sixbey, "Chanting the Square Deific," *American Literature,* IX (1937), 171–95.

CHAPTER 7

1. George Santayana, "The Genteel Tradition in American Philosophy," in *Winds of Doctrine* (New York, 1912; hereinafter, "The Genteel Tradition"), 186–215.
2. "The Genteel Tradition," 187–188.
3. Puritanism, the historical, religious, and political movement, is distinguished by capitalization from puritanism, a temperament prevalent throughout Anglo-Saxon history.
4. "The Genteel Tradition," 188.
5. In *Interpretations in Poetry and Religion* (New York, 1900), 180. See also H. A. Myers, "Whitman's Conception of the Spiritual Democracy," *American Literature,* VI (November, 1934), 241.
6. In *Character and Opinion in the United States* (New York, 1920), 64–97.
7. If this essay emphasizes the Puritanism of New England to the partial exclusion of the culture of the Central and Southern States, it is partly because the Puritanism of New England was more articulate than the religious culture of other regions, and partly because Santayana so emphasized it.

8. See Joseph Haroutunian, *Piety versus Moralism* (New York, 1932); and Perry Miller, *The New England Mind* (New York, 1939; hereinafter, "Miller").
9. John Dewey, "Emerson: the Philosopher of Democracy," in *Characters and Events* (New York, 1929), 69–77.
10. See Miller, 20.
11. Miller, 21.
12. Miller, 97.
13. Miller, 161.
14. Miller, 166.
15. Quoted in Herbert Schneider, *The Puritan Mind* (New York, 1930), 90.
16. See Schneider, *The Puritan Mind*, 97.
17. *The Autobiography* in *The Complete Works of Benjamin Franklin*, edited by John Bigelow (New York, 1887–1888), I, 139.
18. S. P. Sherman, "Tradition," in *Americans* (New York, 1924), 13–27.
19. "The Genteel Tradition," 196.
20. "The Genteel Tradition," 201.
21. See Yvor Winters, *Maule's Curse* (Norfolk, Connecticut, 1938).
22. From "New England Two Centuries Ago," *Among My Books* (Boston, 1871), 244.
23. *Literature and the American College* (Boston, 1908), 20.
24. *The Genteel Tradition at Bay* (New York, 1931), 28.
25. Wylie Sypher, "Irving Babbitt," in the *New England Quarterly* (March, 1941), XIV, 64.
26. Bernard Smith, *Forces in American Criticism* (New York, 1939), 384.
27. *Forces in American Criticism*, 40.
28. John P. Marquand, *H. M. Pulham, Esquire* (Boston, 1941), 131.

CHAPTER 8

1. Cf. Austin Warren, *Hawthorne* (New York, 1934), xxxv.
2. H. W. Schneider, *The Puritan Mind* (New York, 1930), 259.
3. Yvor Winters, *Maule's Curse* (Norfolk, Conn., 1938), 16.
4. Régis Michaud, *The American Novel Today* (Boston, 1928), 36.
5. *Ibid.*, 44.
6. L. E. Chrétien, quoted in A. Warren, *Hawthorne*, lxxviii.
7. Michaud, *op. cit.*, 37.
8. Critics suggesting this "transcendental" point of view include the following: Moncure D. Conway, *Life of Nathaniel Hawthorne* (London, 1870); John Erskine, "Hawthorne," in *CHAL*, II, 16–31; and Stuart P. Sherman, "Hawthorne," in *Americans*, 122–52.
9. Cf. Conway, *op. cit.*

CHAPTER 9

1. See Ralph H. Gabriel, *The Course of American Democratic Thought* (New York, 1940), 67 ff.
2. Italics added.
3. Yvor Winters, *Maule's Curse*, 87; cf. also F. O. Matthiessen, *American Renaissance*, 513.
4. I use the words "catholic" and "protestant" in the etymological sense, without capitals.

CHAPTER 10

1. *Webster's New International Dictionary* (1930 edition).
2. *The Collected Papers of C. S. Peirce*, V, 7.
3. John Dewey, *Characters and Events*, I, 76.

4. In a personal letter to the writer.
5. Cf. R. B. Perry, "The Ego-Centric Predicament," *The Journal of Philosophy, Psychology and Scientific Methods,* VII (1910), 5–14. Reprinted in Muelder and Sears, *The Development of Modern Philosophy,* 304–310.
6. *A Pluralistic Universe* (New York, 1909), chapter I.
7. *Pragmatism,* (New York, 1907), 19.
8. *A Pluralistic Universe.*
9. The first definition in *Webster's International Dictionary.*
10. *Essays in Radical Empiricism,* 10.
11. C. G. Boring: *The Physical Dimensions of Consciousness,* (New York, 1933), 8.
12. *Ibid.,* v.
13. C. I. Lewis, *Mind and the World Order.*
14. See C. Hartshorne, "C. S. Peirce" in *The New England Quarterly* (March, 1941), XIV, 58–60.
15. G. Santayana, *Winds of Doctrine,* 209, 211.
16. G. Santayana, *Winds of Doctrine,* 209, 211.
17. *The Letters of William James,* II, 346–8.
18. John Dewey, *Character and Events* (New York, 1929). See especially Book III. entitled "America."
19. "Pragmatic America," in *Characters and Events,* 546.
20. "Philosophy and Democracy," in *Characters and Events,* 843.
21. "Pragmatic America," in *Characters and Events,* 547.

CHAPTER II

1. See the *Dictionary of American Biography,* article on Peirce by Paul Weiss; Morris Cohen, introductory essay to Peirce's *Chance, Love and Logic* (New York, 1923); H. G. Townsend, *Philosophical Ideas in the United States* (New York, 1934); and P. R. Anderson and H. M. Fisch, *Philosophy in America* (New York, 1939).
2. *Collected Papers of Charles Sanders Peirce,* edited by Charles Hartshorne and Paul Weiss (Cambridge, 1931–1935), V, page 274. (In this chapter, all footnote numbers refer to pages and not, as in many articles on Peirce, to paragraphs.)
3. *Collected Papers,* VI, 86–87.
4. R. B. Perry, *Thought and Character of William James* (Boston, 1935), II, 424–425.
5. *Collected Papers,* V, 272 ff.
6. *Collected Papers,* V, 286.
7. R. W. Emerson, *Complete Works,* Centenary Edition (Boston, 1903–1904), I, 94–95. (James also read and marked this passage.)
8. *Collected Papers,* I, 361.
9. *Collected Papers,* VI, 189.
10. "Philosophical Conceptions and Practical Results," *Collected Essays and Reviews* (New York, 1920), 412.
11. "What Pragmatism Is," *Collected Papers,* V, 284.
12. "Charles Sanders Peirce," in *The New Republic* (February 3, 1937), Volume 89 (lxxxix), page 416.
13. *Collected Papers,* VI, 111.
14. *Collected Papers,* VI, 20.
15. *Collected Papers,* I, 337–338.
16. *Collected Papers,* VI, 106.
17. *Collected Papers,* VI, 106.
18. *Collected Papers,* V, 92.
19. *Collected Papers,* V, 90, 106.
20. *Collected Papers,* V, 121.
21. Emerson, *Works,* I, 338.
22. *Collected Papers,* V, 107.

23. *Collected Papers*, VI, 356.
24. *Collected Papers*, V, 130.
25. *Cf. Collected Papers*, I, 25, 75.
26. Emerson, *Works*, III, 83; essay on "Experience."
27. See H. G. Townsend, *Philosophical Ideas in the United States*, 210.
28. *Collected Papers*, VI, 190.
29. *Collected Papers*, VI, 191; see also Perry, *Thought and Character of William James*, II, 426.
30. This comparison of Edwards and Peirce is suggested by Townsend, 222–224. See also F. I. Carpenter, "The Radicalism of Jonathan Edwards," *New England Quarterly*, IV, 629 (1931).
31. *Collected Papers*, VI, 191.
32. *Collected Papers*, I, 21.
33. *Collected Papers*, I, 25.
34. Jonathan Edwards, "The Nature of True Virtue" (1775).

CHAPTER 12

1. Woodbridge Riley, *American Thought*.
2. *Letters of William James*, I, 9.
3. See R. B. Perry, *The Thought and Character of William James*, chapters 3 and 4.
4. *Notes of a Son and Brother*, 204.
5. R. B. Perry, *op. cit.*, I, 100.
6. For a more complete study of James's reading of Emerson, see "William James and Emerson," in *American Literature*, XI (March, 1939), 39–57.
7. These volumes are: *Miscellanies: Nature and Addresses* (1868); *Essays: First Series* (1869); *Essays: Second Series* (new ed., 1889); *Essays: Second Series* (Centenary ed. 1904); *Representative Men* (1895); *The Conduct of Life* (1889); *Letters and Social Aims* (1883); *Lectures and Biographical Sketches* (1884); *Natural History of Intellect* (1893); and *Emerson in Concord*, by E. W. Emerson (1889).
8. *Works* (Centenary ed.), I, 99. All page references have been corrected to refer to this standard edition. James cross-referenced this to the chapter on "Language," in *Nature*.
9. I, 178–179.
10. *The Collected Papers of Charles Sanders Peirce* (Cambridge, Mass., 1931–1935), V, 248–271.
11. *Ibid.*, V, 131. Since Peirce, "the grandfather of pragmatism," occupies a position midway between Emerson and James, both in history and, to some extent, in logic, occasional reference to his writings may help to clarify this discussion. The "gate of purposive action" is more peculiar to pragmatism.
12. *Works*, I, 180–181.
13. O. W. Firkins, *Emerson* (Boston and New York, 1915), 297.
14. *Winds of Doctrine* (New York, 1926), 197.
15. *The Varieties of Religious Experience* (New York, 1925), 31 ff.
16. *Ibid.*, 33.
17. II, 68.
18. Cf. *The Varieties of Religious Experience*, 387–393.
19. *Varieties of Religious Experience*, 510.
20. *Ibid.*, 499.
21. *Works*, III, 50.
22. *Letters of William James*, II, 190, ff.
23. *Ibid.*, II, 194.
24. *Ibid.*, II, 196–7.
25. See R. B. Perry, *Thought and Character* . . . , I, 144.

CHAPTER 13

1. Warren Beck, "How Good Is Sinclair Lewis?", *College English*, IX, 173 (January, 1948).
2. Bernard De Voto, *The Literary Fallacy* (Boston, 1944), 98.
3. Sinclair Lewis, *The Man from Main Street* (New York, 1953), 10.
4. See Lionel Trilling, "Reality in America," in *The Liberal Imagination* (New York, 1950).
5. Sinclair Lewis, *The Man from Main Street*, 254–268.
6. See *From Main Street to Stockholm*.
7. These notebooks were summarized by Henry Seidel Canby in "Sinclair Lewis's Art of Work," in *The Saturday Review of Literature*, Feb. 10, 1934.

CHAPTER 14

1. Books about the devil are legion. One of the best is by Paul Carus, *The History of the Devil and the Idea of Evil* (Chicago, 1900).
2. Havelock Ellis, *The New Spirit* (The Modern Library edition), 222.

CHAPTER 15

1. A. H. Quinn, *Representative American Plays* (4th ed.; New York, 1928), 966.
2. S. K. Winther, *Eugene O'Neill* (New York, 1934), 8.
3. See Bennett Clark, *Eugene O'Neill* (New York, 1929), 181: "The most successful thing I ever did. I think I've got it just right. It *is*, from my viewpoint."
4. See H. Frenz, "Eugene O'Neill's Plays Printed Abroad," *College English*, V (March, 1944), 341.

CHAPTER 16

1. "Night."
2. "Crumbs or the Loaf."
3. "Margrave."
4. "Crumbs or the Loaf."
5. "Woodrow Wilson."
6. See Jeffers' remarks on "Margrave," in a letter to the author quoted in: F. I. Carpenter, "The Values of Robinson Jeffers," *American Literature*, XI (Jan., 1940), 356.
7. "Wise Men in Their Bad Hours."
8. "Promise of Peace."
9. "Margrave."
10. "Post Mortem."
11. "Suicide's Stone."
12. "Birth-Dues."
13. "The Songs of the Dead Men to the Three Dancers," in *Tamar and Other Poems*.
14. "Point Pinos and Point Lobos."
15. Letter to the writer, November, 1933.
16. "Night."
17. "Point Pinos and Point Lobos."
18. "The Bed by the Window."

CHAPTER 17

1. See *American Fiction, 1920–1940* (New York, 1941).
2. See letter by the present writer in *The Saturday Review of Literature* (January 25, 1936), outlining this "idea."

3. Published: New York, 1948.
4. *The Return of Buck Gavin,* in *Carolina Folk Plays (Second Series),* ed. F. A. Koch (New York, 1924); and *The Third Night,* in *Carolina Folk Plays* (New York, 1941).
5. Pp. 544–553.
6. Pp. 61–63 (N.Y., 1948).

CHAPTER 19

1. In *The American Mercury,* LVII (Sept. 1943).
2. In *The Virginia Quarterly Review,* XX (Summer 1944).
3. In *College English,* VI (Nov. 1944).

CHAPTER 20

1. See esp. Carlos Baker, *Hemingway: The Writer as Artist* (Princeton, 1952), and Philip Young, *Ernest Hemingway* (New York, 1952).
2. Joseph Warren Beach, "How Do You Like It Now, Gentlemen?" *Sewanee Rev.,* LIX (Spring 1951), 311–328; Harry Levin, "Observations on the Style of Hemingway," *Kenyon Rev.,* XIII (Autumn 1951), 581–609; Malcolm Cowley, *The Portable Hemingway* (New York, 1944), "Introd."
3. See Bergson, *Durée et Simultanéité: à propos de la théorie d'Einstein* (Paris, 1922).
4. I use the term "mystical" in its most general sense, to describe any intense experience or "ecstasy" which results in insight or "illumination." I have defined this kind of mysticism at length in my *Emerson Handbook* (New York, 1953), 113–116.
5. See R. P. Warren, "Hemingway," *Kenyon Rev.,* IX (Winter 1947), 1–28.
6. *A New Model of the Universe* (1st publ. 1931, rev. ed., New York, 1950), 375.
7. *For Whom the Bell Tolls* (New York, 1940), 72.
8. See Joseph Beaver, " 'Technique' in Hemingway," *College English* (March 1953), 325.

INDEX

Across the River ..., 186, 192
Adams, Henry, 92, 128
Adams, J. T., 19, 29, 208, 209
Ah, Wilderness!, 142
Alcott, Bronson, 28, 30–39, 107
Aldrich, T. B., 58
"The American Scholar," 5, 19, 21, 22, 25, 27, 46, 109
An American Tragedy, 202
Americanism, 22, 48, 97, 197, 198
Among My Books, 58
Ann Vickers, 123
Anna Christie, 135
Anna Karenina, 63
Aristotle, 59
Arrowsmith, 116, 118, 121–123
Augustine, 12, 13

Babbitt, 116, 119–123, 137, 167, 194
Babbitt, I., 38, 58, 59, 60, 61
Bacon, F., 92
Baillie, J., 208
Baker, C., 215
Baker, G. P., 157
Baudelaire, 129, 201
Beach, J. W., 155, 185, 192, 215
Beaver, J., 215
Beck, W., 116, 214
Bergson, 185, 186, 187, 188
Berkeley, 89, 90
Beyond the Horizon, 133, 135, 139
Billy Budd, 56, 73–77, 79, 80, 81, 82, 203, 204, 205
Blithedale Romance, 56, 72, 195
Boring, E. G., 90, 212
Bound East for Cardiff, 135
Brahma, 187
Brook Farm, 56, 132
Brownell, W. C., 115
Buddhism, 149, 152
Burgum, E. B., 176
Burroughs, J., 41
Byron, 129, 201

Cabell, J. B., 119
Caine Mutiny, 203, 204, 205
Calvinism, 51, 53, 55
Canby, H. S., 209, 214
Carlyle, 25

Carpenter, F. I., 210, 213, 214
Carus, P., 214
Chamberlain, J., 155
Clarel, 56, 74
Clark, B., 214
Clark, H. H., 208
Clark, W. V. T., 194
Clarke, J. F., 22
Clemens (see Twain)
Cohen, M., 212
Coleridge, 101
Commager, H. S., 208
Conversations on the Gospels, 35, 37
Conway, M. D., 214
Cowley, M., 185, 192, 215

Dante, 64, 128, 130
The Daring Young Man ..., 183
Days Without End, 142
Death of a Salesman, 120, 121
Desire Under the Elms, 133
DeVoto, B., 116, 121, 122, 155, 214
Dewey, J., 9, 17, 34, 38, 83, 84, 85, 86, 87, 90, 92, 93, 94, 98, 105, 168, 170, 173
diabolism, 16, 47, 48, 49, 76, 78, 126–132, 142
The Dial, 22
Dodsworth, 123, 125, 161
Dos Passos, J., 194
Dreiser, 83, 202
Dynamo, 133, 142

Edwards, 7, 11, 14, 55, 103, 104
Einstein, 186
Eliot, T. S., 56, 61
Ellis, H., 129, 214
Elmer Gantry, 122, 123
Emerson, 5, *passim*, 19–29, 105–115
Emperor Jones, 133
Epic of America, 6, 10
Erskine, J., 211
Euclid, 100
Experience and Nature, 85

Faulkner, 194
Faust, 128, 130
Firkins, O. W., 208, 213
Fiske, J., 86
Fitzgerald, 10

For Whom the Bell Tolls, 186–188, 191
The Fountain, 133, 134, 136, 137, 139
St. Francis, 153
Franklin, 10, 24, 54, 61
Franklin Evans, 42
Frenz, H., 214
Freud, 40, 145, 152
Frothingham, O. B., 208, 209
Fuller, M., 107, 195

Gabriel, R. H., 211
Garrison, 37
Gay, R. M., 208
Goddard, H. C., 209
The God-Seeker, 117, 119, 122
Goethe, 128, 129, 130
Grapes of Wrath, 17, 167–175, 195
Great Gatsby, 10
Great God Brown, 133, 137
Green Hills of Africa, 185

Hairy Ape, 137
Hamlet, 144
Haroutunian, J., 208, 211
Harte, 20
Hartshorne, C., 212
Hawthorne, 8, 9, 10, 52, 56, 57, 60, 63–72,
    74, 78, 130, 132, 172, 195, 200, 201
Hazard of New Fortunes, 202
Heard, G., 183
Hedge, F. H., 87, 94, 95
Hegel, 55, 85, 94, 97, 100
Helicon Hall, 117
Hemingway, 161, 185–193, 194
Hergesheimer, 119
Holmes, O. W. Jr., 82, 86, 87, 107, 203
Holmes, O. W. Sr., 19, 21, 87, 107
Homer, 144
Hook, S., 98
House of the Seven Gables, 56
Howells, 83, 202
Huckleberry Finn, 121, 167
Hugo, 129
Human Comedy, 17, 176, 179, 180, 181
Huxley, A., 183
Huysmans, 129

Iceman Cometh, 142
Inferno, 64, 128

Jackson, A., 21
James, H. Jr., 63, 106, 115
James, H. Sr., 87, 95, 102, 106, 107

James, Wm., 9, 17, 28, 29, 34, 38, 51, 56,
    83–93, 94, 95, 96, 98, 102, 105–115, 168,
    170, 173, 186, 187, 188, 199, 202
Jane Eyre, 141
Jeffers, R., 10, 83, 128, 132, 144–154, 177,
    183, 192, 194, 195, 201
Jefferson, 8, 83, 85
St. John of the Cross, 190
Johnson, E., 208
Judd, S., 195, 196

Kant, 12, 25, 31, 32, 55, 85, 89, 94, 97, 100,
    101
Kingsblood Royal, 125

Lawrence, D. H., 66
Lazarus Laughed, 138, 139, 140, 142
Leaves of Grass, 5, 40–50
Levin, H., 185, 215
Lewis, C. I., 90, 98, 212
Lewis, S., 116–125, 161, 194, 196, 197
Lincoln, 5, 19, 82, 149
Lindbergh, 119
Literature and the American College, 59
Locke, 12, 89
Long Voyage Home, 134, 135
Longfellow, 23, 57, 58
Look Homeward Angel, 17, 156, 158, 161
Lowell, J. R., 19, 21, 23, 57, 58, 60
Luther, 128

Machiavelli, 129
Main Street, 116, 119, 120, 122, 123, 194
Mann, H., 39
Mannerhouse, 155–158, 161, 162, 164
Marble Faun, 56, 72
Marco Millions, 133, 137
Marchand, E., 208, 209
Mardi, 56, 73, 74, 75, 76, 79
Marquand, 62
Marsh, J., 87
Marx, 61, 171
Mazeppa, 15
Melville, 8, 9, 10, 52, 56, 57, 58, 60, 73–82,
    130, 132, 142, 199, 200, 201, 203
Metaphysical Club, 86, 107
Michaud, R., 211
Michelangelo, 30
Millennium, 7, 92
Miller, A., 120
Miller, P., 208, 211
Milton, 126, 128, 130, 132
Moby Dick, 52, 56, 60, 73–82, 121, 167,
    201
Moody, W. V., 49, 127

More, P. E., 38, 60
Mourning Becomes Electra, 133, 138, 141, 142
My Study Windows, 58
Myers, H. A., 210
Mysterious Stranger, 49, 127, 132
Mysticism, 28, 138, 139, 146, 152, 183, 190, 191, 192

Napoleon, 23, 126
Nature, 26, 109
The New England Mind, 7, 11
New Model of the Universe, 187
Nietzsche, 65, 129, 130, 151
Nobel Prize, 116, 123
Norton, C. E., 58, 59

Of Time and the River, 156, 157, 161
O'Higgins, H., 41, 210
Old Man and the Sea, 191, 192, 193
O'Neill, 9, 10, 128, 133–143, 194, 199, 201
Our Mr. Wrenn, 118
Ouspensky, 185, 186, 187, 188

Paradise Lost, 126, 128
Parker, T., 208
Parkes, H. B., 208
Parrington, 11, 117, 208
Peirce, C. S., 9, 17, 83, 84, 85, 86, 87, 90, 91, 92, 93, 94–104, 105, 107, 110, 112, 173
Perry, R. B., 212, 213
Philo, 195
Pierre, 56, 74, 75, 77, 202
Plato, 6, 31, 115
Pluralistic Universe, 88
Poe, 10, 28, 200, 201

Quinn, A. H., 214

Rabelais, 59
Rahv, P., 176
Rankin, H. W., 115
Remenyi, 176
Representative Men, 115
Richter, C., 194
Riley, W., 213
Robinson, E. A., 36
Rousseau, 11, 58, 63, 65
Royce, 94, 102

Sanborn, F. B., 209
Sand, G., 41, 43
Santayana, 11, 34, 46, 51, 52, 55, 59, 91, 111, 209, 210, 212

Saroyan, 17, 176–184, 194
Satan (see diabolism)
Saturday Club, 107
Saturday Review of Lit., 116
Scarlet Letter, 47, 52, 56, 63–72, 78, 167, 172, 201, 203
Schiller, F. C. S., 102
Schneider, H., 211
Shepard, O., 36, 38, 208, 210
Shephard, E., 210
Sherman, S. P., 54, 210, 211
Sinclair, U., 117, 177, 183
Sister Carrie, 202
Sixbey, G. L., 210
Smith, B., 211
Society and Solitude, 107
Socrates, 23
Spengler, 129, 130, 180
Spirit of St. Louis, 119
Stedman, E. C., 58
Stein, G., 185, 187, 188
Steinbeck, 10, 12, 17, 47, 167–175, 177, 194, 195
Stovall, F., 210
Strange Interlude, 133, 138, 140, 141, 142
The Sun Also Rises, 161
Swinburne, 40
Symonds, J. A., 44
Sypher, W., 211

Temple School, 35, 37, 39
Terence, 59
Tertium Organum, 187
Thoreau, 9, 15, 16, 17, 21, 30, 31, 33, 34, 35, 36, 38, 58, 70, 87, 97, 98, 103, 107, 118, 122, 153, 196, 197, 200, 201
Timbuktu, 15
Time of Your Life, 176, 178, 179
To Have and Have Not, 186
Townsend, H. G., 212, 213
Trail of the Hawk, 119
Transcendental Club, 86, 87
Traveler from Altruria, 202
Trilling, L., 214
Tuveson, E., 208
Twain, Mark, 49, 83, 127, 132
Typee, 142

Utopia, 6, 25, 118, 183

Van Doren, M., 40
Varieties of Religious Experience, 97, 108, 111
Verlaine, 129

Walden, 97, 122
Walt Whitman's Pose, 41
Warren, A., 209, 211
Warren, R. P., 191, 215
Washington, 127
Web and the Rock, 156, 162, 164
Weiss, P., 212
Western Messenger, 22
Whipple, E. P., 58
White Jacket, 74, 75
Whitman, 5, 8, 9, 12, 16, 17, 35, 40–50, 51, 52, 56, 74, 83, 107, 126, 127, 128, 130, 131, 132, 149, 155, 156, 166, 168, 170, 171, 172, 173, 175, 177, 178, 180, 182, 183, 197
Wilson, E., 176
Wilson, W., 5

Winters, Y., 60, 208, 211
Winther, S. K., 214
Wolfe, T., 10, 12, 17, 47, 155–166, 194, 195
Woodberry, G. E., 208
Work of Art, 118, 123, 124
World Enough and Time, 191
World So Wide, 123, 125
Wouk, H., 203
Wright, C., 86

Xanadu, 15

Yeats, 133
You Can't Go Home Again, 17, 155, 156, 164
Young, P., 215